Killing
Albert
Berch

Alan Berch Hollingsworth

Killing Albert Berch

Alan Berch Hollingsworth

Foreword by Yvonne Kauger

PELICAN PUBLISHING COMPANY
GRETNA 2017

The word "Pelican" and the depiction of a pelican are trademarks of Pelican Publishing Company, Inc., and are registered in the U.S. Patent and Trademark Office.

ISBN: 9781455623556
Ebook ISBN: 9781455623563

All photographs from the Hollingsworth family collection unless otherwise noted

Printed in the United States of America

Published by Pelican Publishing Company, Inc.
1000 Burmaster Street, Gretna, Louisiana 70053

To
Albert Berch, Lula Berch,
and their daughter, Almarian Berch Hollingsworth

The only thing new in the world is the history you don't know.
—Harry S. Truman

Only a dream, only a dream,
And glory beyond the dark stream;
How peaceful the slumber,
How happy the waking;
For death is only a dream.

Refrain from "Death Is Only a Dream"
lyrics by C. W. Ray, music by A. J. Buchanan, 1892
(favorite hymn of Albert Weldon Berch, sung at his funeral December
19, 1923, shortly before his widow stormed out of the church)

Contents

Foreword

The obsession of three generations to uncover the unvarnished truth about a double murder integrates a family into events that shaped Oklahoma, the United States, and, by butterfly effect, the entire world. Several religions teach that everything is interrelated. This book, a potpourri of history and mystery, certainly illustrates that tenet.

We are given a close-up look at early aviation, the oil business, the suffragette movement, religious intolerance, conspiracy, politics, education, the Underground Railroad, racism, the Civil War and civil rights, the formal recognition of osteopathy, burlesque, the Ku Klux Klan, the impeachment of a governor, a precedent-setting opinion by the Oklahoma Supreme Court, and two miraculous cures of breast cancer. And that is just for starters.

I first met Dr. Alan Hollingsworth when my mother, Alice Bottom Kauger, consulted with him about her surgery. I was honored to be asked to write the foreword to his book and to be able to read his work after hearing updated snippets from time to time—usually during my annual examination. It is a page turner that I couldn't wait to finish, and it cries out to be a television series.

I am so pleased that our serendipitous friendship prompted the appearance of the trial transcript in *Lincoln Health & Accident Ins. Co. v. Johnigan,* 1926 OK 356, 245 P. 837. It exhibits the theory of six degrees of separation, first espoused in 1929 by the Hungarian author Frigyes Karinthy. The concept is that anyone can be connected to any other person through the chain of a "friend of a friend" with no more than six intermediaries. I certainly experienced it when I introduced Dr. Hollingsworth to Oklahoma Supreme Court Chief Justice Douglas Combs—only to discover that they were fraternity brothers, as well as distant cousins, who could trace their ancestry back to the Earl of Combes and Stratford-upon-Avon. One of the Combs relatives sold land to William Shakespeare, and another was left Shakespeare's sword in his will. In 1923, at the time of the murders described in this book, Hall of Famer Earle Combs, another cousin, was waiting to be called up to the New York Yankees to become the best lead-off man in the American League. He played on what was considered the best team the Yankees ever had, with teammates Babe Ruth, Lou Gehrig, Waite Hoyte, Tony Lazzeri, and Herb Pennock. And Doug has the autographed baseball to prove it. See what I mean? If only the widow of Albert Berch, Lula Combs, had known.

While the rest of the nation was fascinated with gangster and mob stories of Al Capone in Chicago in the mid- to late 1920s, Oklahoma apparently had its own little gangster/mob paradise in Marlow. It took the form of organized KKK membership, coupled with prominent citizens who fought ruthlessly for its success. Thankfully, other town leaders fought back, eventually putting the Klan to rest.

For those fortunate enough to have taken Oklahoma history in high school, one doesn't recall any mention of Marlow, Oklahoma nor its colorful past that included outlaws and mob rule. I suspect if textbooks were written as this story has been, history would be one of the most popular subjects at school! With facts that are quintessentially "stranger than fiction," with remarkable coincidences, Dr. Hollingsworth has woven a tale that engages readers from beginning to end and teaches them a little fascinating history along the way.

Yvonne Kauger
Oklahoma Supreme Court Justice (1984-present),
Chief Justice 1997-98

Killing Albert Berch

Albert Weldon Berch

Lula Combs Garvin Berch

Almarian Berch

1

The Cascade

The social experiment failed after a mere ten days, the peril too great. Hotel owner Albert Weldon Berch settled onto the edge of his bed and said with a sigh, "I'm indeed sorry to lose you." He wrote a severance check for the departing porter, a man eager to catch the next train out of town.

Berch was disappointed, if not drained. His heartfelt, or foolhardy, undertaking to challenge bigotry had been thwarted. His wife, Lula, who stood nearby in the owner's suite, holding their young daughter in her arms, harbored more pragmatic thoughts, such as how to replace the dedicated porter when no whites in town, boys or men, were willing to stoop to shine another man's shoes. With their hotel business flourishing in the midst of an oil boom, the demand for quality help was greater than the labor pool could satisfy.

Turning back our clocks to this precise moment on the evening of December 17, 1923, Albert Berch has three minutes left to live, while the departing porter, a "crippled negro" named Robert Johnigan, will yearn for a death so swift.

With a morbid nod to destiny, it was fortunate for my two sisters and me that our maternal grandfather was shot and killed at age thirty in the lobby of Johnson's Hotel in Marlow, Oklahoma. Had Albert Berch lived to continue as proprietor of the hotel, we three siblings would not have appeared on this planet. The unusual cascade of events that followed the murder led to our existence, and the murder profoundly altered our family's history.

Johnson's Hotel was owned and operated by Albert and Lula Berch when our mother was born in one of its rooms, located only steps away from where her father would be murdered. Our grandmother and mother barely avoided the spray of bullets that killed Albert Berch and Robert Johnigan, the latter being the primary target. Or so we were told.

13

Almarian, named for her father, Al, was a couple of months shy of her second birthday when the murder occurred. She was in the arms of her mother, and according to Lula, the mother-daughter duo entered the lobby at the exact moment that gunfire erupted, whereupon a bullet intended for Lula pierced Almarian's baby gown without causing harm. So, to take the conjectural folly of "what if" one step further, the trajectory of this bullet charted the course of our existence, my sisters and me, even more than the one that killed Albert Berch.

Our mother spent much of her life embroiled in the "why" of it all until she was finally laid to rest in a Marlow grave eighty-eight years after the murders. Oddly, prior to her death, Almarian orchestrated a family burial plot for her father, her mother, and herself, the only child of the Berch couple.

This was "odd" for several reasons. First, Marlow had not offered consoling arms after the murders. In fact, when our grandmother left town with her life in jeopardy and her daughter in tow, Albert was resting eternally in a poorly marked grave, with Lula vowing never to return during her lifetime. She came close to fulfilling that promise. It was odd, too, that our mother had such a strong need for the three of them to be together, even though they had been a family for a mere twenty-two months. She had no memory of her father or of being a Marlow resident. My sisters and I marvel at this bond, so powerful for our mother that our father's remains went along for the ride. We are bewildered that the ashes of Francis W. Hollingsworth, MD, are now part of the landscape in a town that he had barely visited. Meanwhile, the cemetery in our hometown of El Reno, Oklahoma doesn't host a single blood relative.

I am the fourth-generation Al Berch. Indeed, the Berch saga should begin with Albert's father, "Doctor" Albert W. Berch, Sr., the quotation marks as apt today as when they enclosed his title in a 1924 anonymous letter to my widowed grandmother, claiming shady maneuverings on the part of her father-in-law. Yet, newspapers after the murder refer to Albert Sr. as a "prominent physician," a peculiar description in light of the fact that he was new to Marlow and arrived there apparently free of the nagging need for credentials.

Let me interject a comment about the personal pronouns that will be scattered throughout this narrative. When I say "my grandmother" or "my mother," it is really "our grandmother" or "our mother." For Susan Hollingsworth Aggarwal and Dawn Hollingsworth, my two sisters, this is their family story, too.

As for source material, I will offer references as the story requires, while letting the reader judge reliability. Nothing has ever been formally assembled and published to chronicle this notorious double murder other than newspaper accounts, in spite of the fact that the crime extended beyond the "crippled negro" and into the heart of white America, a particularly egregious act in 1923 that drew nationwide attention.

My grandmother was a prolific scribbler. In fact, both my mother and grandmother were afflicted by hypergraphia, faithfully recording minutiae into their diaries throughout both of their long lives. But it didn't stop at the diaries. Their free-floating anxieties found a place to land on any available scrap of paper. My grandmother was particularly resourceful here, often mimicking the ancient palimpsest where parchment was scraped clean and reused. Lula wrote her notes between the lines on Procter & Gamble invoice forms, the flip sides of personal letters, and the backs of many envelopes. On one occasion, during a tense mother-daughter imbroglio, they became dueling banjos thirty miles apart, each feverishly writing about the other.

Still, many blanks remain in the story of this double murder. While reconstructing the crime and its aftermath, then by sleuthing through the evidence for long-lost answers, I will leave the blanks alone and simply tell the tale, as true to the facts as I can be. And when I drift toward speculation, I will paint it as such. Furthermore, I pledge not to pad the story with the intent to impart fabled nobility, a common theme in genealogic pursuits. Whether or not my grandfather died as part of an honorable act is a central issue in the differing versions of the murder. I do not seek blue blood. Hasn't history already taught us that blue blood tends to run downhill? If my research indicates an ancestor to be a scalawag, then so be it.

Grandmother Lula was, of course, the first to become obsessed with this story. Then, in midlife and with an empty nest, my mother and her lifelong fixation hit full stride, so my narrative addresses that angle as well, including her search for her father's grave followed by her novelization of the saga.

And finally I turn to my obsession, which began with the death of my mother, the moment when this ripening tale slipped from her fingers to mine. Up until that time it had been *her* story, *her* entrée as an author, *her* obsession, *her* unknown father. For me, it had been unconfirmed rumor. Did Albert Berch even exist? Even as his namesake, I had only seen one photographic portrait, and we were led to believe that this was all that remained. For me, Albert Berch was mythical, providing a colorful conversation starter, from playground days ("my grandfather was killed by the Ku Klux Klan") extending to the present, where the refined version draws in complexities and nuances, kicking and screaming all the way toward a disquieting truth.

My name is Alan Berch Hollingsworth, and this is my take on the murder of my grandfather, Albert Berch. But it's Lula's story, too, and my mother's. Indeed, it is a family plot.

2

Marlow, Oklahoma

Marlow was probably like most small towns of the era, in that the "good" and the "bad" shook hands every day to keep the machinery well oiled. So, let me begin a portrait through signage. Today, a notice with fading print leans askew at the northern outskirts of Marlow:

MARLOW
Home of Joe Dial
U.S. Pole Vault Champion
19'2 1/2"   May 19, 1985
NCAA Indoor Champion 1984-1985
NCAA Outdoor Champion 1984-1985

Marlow H.S. Cheerleaders
85-86 National Champions

Like the "good" in any small town, citizens bask in the accomplishments that come from its anointed few whose feats reach beyond city limits, beyond state lines, all the way to national headlines.

But in 1923, a very different sign stood in the place that today lauds pole vaulting and cheerleading:

Negro, Do Not Let the Sun Go Down on You in This Town

Before jumping to conclusions about this placard and Marlow, understand that there were hundreds, if not thousands, of nearly identical signs scattered around the country, in nearly every state. In his book, *Sundown Towns: A Hidden Dimension of American Racism* (New York: The New Press, 2005), sociologist Dr. James W. Loewen suggests the practice was as prevalent in the Northern states as in the South. Since few community boosters today care to admit that their city limits were ever demarcated by such a sign, much of the evidence for being a "sundown town" is hearsay. However, Loewen allows for varying degrees of evidence rather than labeling all suspects as guilty.

Dr. Loewen's website is one of the few online locations where the murders of Albert Berch and Robert Johnigan are recorded. Both names are misspelled, but this is because the site is quoting a 1923 article in the *Pittsburgh Courier*, and nearly all journalists of the day misspelled both men's names, even the *Marlow Review*.

The sundown mentality, be it staked out by a sign or not, was pervasive. Nevertheless, growing up, I somehow adopted the belief that Marlow was unique with regard to being a sundown town. It was not.

For the current citizens of Marlow, there should be no indictment and no retrograde guilt. Descendants of the principals in this account should neither feel offended nor honored by the actions of their grandparents and great-grandparents. No one who was an adult at the time of the murders is alive today. All cities have skeletons. I'm simply telling a story, and if there be a moral, it will be of the reader's own choosing.

In painting the history of Marlow prior to its sundown era, a few strokes of primer are applied to cover first what is *not* true, given the stereotypes assigned to Oklahoma. The city was not born from an Oklahoma Land Run. And even though it was once Indian Territory, Marlow was never a tent city of teepees. Finally, Marlow did not blossom overnight during one of the oil booms, though oil does spill into the story.

In Stephens County, south-central Oklahoma, the Rock Island Railroad laid its tracks upon the cattle-stomped template of the Chisholm Trail, where Marlow grew as one of the many buds on the stem. The Rock Island Line was later traced by U.S. Highway 81 through Duncan, Marlow, and El Reno, three of the principal towns in this story. A fourth town, Fargo, North Dakota, a distant dot on the map, will play a key role as well, also on U.S. 81.

Originally called Marlow Grove, the founding is steeped in legend, but with more confirmed facts than, say, Romulus and Remus. The five Marlow brothers were considered outlaws by most early historians. Indeed, the town has no qualms about this moniker that appears on its water tower, while many businesses today use the "outlaw" name and cowboy logo. And when the Friday Night Lights brighten the football field, it's the Marlow Outlaws versus the enemy high school.

One historical source paints a malevolent portrait of the Marlow family without controversy—*Oklahoma: A Guide to the Sooner State*

(Norman: University of Oklahoma Press, 1941), written by "Workers of the Writers' Program of the Work Projects Administration in the State of Oklahoma." From page 374:

> Although MARLOW, 176.9 *m*. (1,308 alt., 2,899 pop.), is now a peaceful law-abiding center for a prosperous farming community . . . it was named for a family of outlaws.
>
> In the early 1880s five Marlow brothers lived in a dugout in the brush on Wildhorse Creek in what is now the town site, near the Chisholm Trail. It was the nocturnal custom of the Marlow boys to raid the herds being driven up from Texas and drive off longhorns to the timber twelve or fifteen miles east of the trail, then in a day or two drive the cattle back to the herd pretending to have found them straying or in possession of cattle thieves. For a long time they were successful in collecting rewards, but the cattlemen, victimized too often, became suspicious, set a trap for them, and wiped out the band.

Well, this is not exactly accurate. When this version was published in 1941, one of the Marlow boys was still alive, living comfortably in California. In fact, two Marlow brothers had escaped their planned extermination—George and Charlie. They were not at all fond of the legacy that had been built for them, writing their self-defense into a book of their own. This led to a swarm of historians buzzing about the Marlow brothers and eventually—no kidding—a popular 1965 John Wayne movie, costarring Dean Martin, *The Sons of Katie Elder.*

While the Marlow brothers' adventures took place more than thirty years prior to the story at hand, the chronicle serves as allegory for limited historical perspective when trying to distinguish the white hats from the black ones, especially when vigilantes overpower due process. The complex saga of the Marlow brothers spans many years and includes a cavalcade of characters. Interested readers who want to learn more can start with William Rathmell's 1932 account, which includes interviews with the two surviving brothers and became the source for the film.

That said, I must mention the singular event that, even by today's standard of gory news, can still raise an eyebrow. Four of the five Marlow brothers were shackled at the ankles, hands free, en route to Dallas to stand trial on trumped-up charges. However, their prison wagon was ambushed by thirty vigilantes hoping to streamline justice. Two Marlows were killed on the spot, leaving the two surviving brothers each shackled to a dead brother. In a macabre twist, George Marlow freed both himself

Charlie (left) and George Marlow (Courtesy of Marlow Chamber of Commerce)

and brother Charlie from the shackles by amputating the feet of their dead brothers at the ankles. Then, against nearly impossible odds (thirty to two), they overpowered the mob. These two surviving Marlow brothers were later vindicated and spent the rest of their lives in law enforcement. I'll let the blood dry now on that drama and return to the upcoming hemorrhage.

The railroad tracks in Marlow that covered the Chisholm Trail are still in place, running between Railroad and First streets. And where First intersects Main Street, Johnson's Hotel stood proudly, the nearest of the old Marlow hotels to the Rock Island line—and the murder site of Albert Berch and Robert Johnigan in 1923. But our story here begins in 1918, near the end of the Great War, when my grandmother made the decision to purchase the hotel, shortly after the death of her first husband.

Charlie and George Marlow in Colorado after a lifetime of law enforcement, many years after some historians had reported them deceased (Courtesy of Marlow Chamber of Commerce)

At the end of World War I, the population of Marlow was 2,300 whites, 0 blacks. Today, there are roughly 4,600 residents, with Google demographics indicating 1 percent African American, a lonely percentage point that seems to wane more than wax. But these rather static numbers don't tell the story of Marlow at its peak, when the aroma of nearby oil overpowered the cattle pens that had fragranced the town since its founding. It was a time of transition, when good citizens sought to bury the image of the Wild West in this brand-new state. On the horizon, strangers were packing their bags and coming to town.

Oil and gas drilling had already begun in Stephens County, and true boomtowns had overnight populations that rivaled the size of Marlow. Marlow was close enough to the action to feel the fever, however. "New gusher" and "big strike" were the headlines used repeatedly in the

Marlow Review. Then on March 10, 1918, the O Nah Dy Well, drilled by Magnolia Petroleum at nearby Duncan, hit a pool that became the first to produce oil with commercial value. "Pick and shovel" industries swarmed in to assist. A new species proliferated, called "lease hounds." And a new genus emerged—"oil men"—having no experience with oil or how to find it. But they filled the hotels of Marlow.

A revealing picture of Marlow during this era was penned by an eyewitness, Cecil A. Darnall, valedictorian of the 1928 class of Marlow High School, writing in 1982 for the Stephens County Historical Society:

Marlow 1920s—Do You Remember???

We did not think of it as the Roaring Twenties nor of the Good Old Days, but, if you are of a certain age, you will remember Marlow for:

Carnivals on Main Street, Saturday Night Band Concerts, Airplanes landing at Carter Park, all the trees along Broadway whitewashed at the same level, Medicine Shows, Tent Shows, First Monday Tradesday, Ku Klux Klan Parades, Christmas trees at the Churches, going to the depot to watch the trains, searching along Whitehorse Creek for the Marlow Boys' Caves, the Littrell-Garvin Fueds [sic], the Dr. Mullins mystery, the shootout at the Johnson Hotel. . . .

While "Ku Klux Klan Parades" or "shootout at the Johnson Hotel" might have jumped out most prominently, let me redirect to "Airplanes landing at Carter Park" as an introduction to the prominent Marlow family that will play a role in this story—patriarch George Carter, a blind businessman, and his aviatrix daughter, Pearl Carter Scott. At age fourteen, Pearl became the youngest person in the U.S. to earn a pilot's license. The father-daughter entrée into the newfangled world of aviation occurred when a young Wiley Post, on his *maiden* solo flight, landed his plane in a pasture belonging to George Carter, who lived across the street from the pilot's brother, Joe Post. A friendship was born when the blind George became Wiley's first passenger.

The next day, George's young daughter Pearl became Wiley's second passenger, and her fearless enthusiasm for flying was so evident that Wiley gave Pearl flying lessons. After she was licensed, George bought Pearl an airplane, both for surveying his real-estate holdings and for her barnstorming pleasure. Pearl's remarkable life was chronicled in *Never Give Up! The Life of Pearl Carter Scott,* by Paul Lambert (The Chickasaw Press, 2007), and in the 2009 feature film *Pearl,* produced by the Chickasaw Nation.

George Carter had achieved his wealth through a variety of enterprises, primarily real estate, an intriguing story of success when considering his unnecessary and tragic blinding as a sixteen-year-old. From Pearl's biography, we learn that George and his teenage brothers were working the broomcorn harvest when their eyes became irritated by the chaff. A doctor administered caustic drops of some sort to two of the brothers, and both were blinded ("blood began to pour from the boys' eyes"), while the third brother, who hid from the doctor, was spared and his "pink eye" resolved without treatment. With remarkable tenacity, George overcame his disability, walked tall, and never used a cane. We will meet up with the Carters several times throughout this story.

Lula Combs was four years old when the Marlow brothers began their misadventures. She was fourteen years old, living in Montague (pronounced "*Mon*-tayg") County, Texas, when Marlow was incorporated as a town. And she was thirty-four years old, newly widowed, having lived a lifetime of woe already, when she purchased Johnson's Hotel.

But as for Albert Berch, he was one of the strangers who came to town. Albert's story would not invoke the raw courage that the surviving Marlow brothers might have possessed, nor songs of adulation, nor fireside tales, nor movies starring the Duke. Nor would there be historical revisions in search of a truth that eventually lies "somewhere in between." No, the chapter that Lula and Albert were about to write would be nearly exorcised from history.

Let me make one other point about Marlow. Even though the Hollingsworth hometown of El Reno is located sixty-five miles due north on the old Rock Island line (and U.S. 81), during the time I was growing up, Marlow could well have been on another planet. I didn't travel there until I was nearly thirty, my grandfather's age when he died. I went there to scout Johnson's Hotel during the mid-1970s, out of a curiosity spawned by my mother's new obsession with her father's murder and the search for his grave. After three more visits for interments in the Marlow cemetery, spread out over the years, I began regular trips to the town in 2011 as part of my fact-finding mission and to put a cork in the bottle of this story.

Finally, as we begin this time-traveling chronicle, I should mention another sign that greets you as you enter Marlow from the north on U.S. 81, before you reach the pole-vaulting, cheerleading notice. On the right, the signpost up ahead reads: "Welcome to Outlaw Country."

3

Johnson's Hotel—the Cradle That Rocks

Every Christmas morning, in chaotic ritual turned imperative tradition, I make pancakes for the family, from scratch. It's my only culinary exercise for the year. On the back of the ancient recipe card for "HOT CAKES," my mother wrote the following: *This recipe was originally used at the Hotel Johnson coffee shop, where I was born. Mother got the recipe and passed it on to me.* "Mother" refers to Lula, and in support of precise pancake history, Lula once enumerated several thousand pieces of flatware and kitchen utensils in a lease of the hotel's café, now in my collection of memorabilia. Among the many items is: "Hot Cake Turner—1."

One question that shouts at me now, but was a mere whisper when I received the recipe card as a young man about to leave home, is this: why the name "Hotel Johnson"? Why not "The Berch Hotel," if Albert and Lula were the owners?

The hotel's official name, according to early signage, is "Johnson's Hotel," though "Johnson Hotel" appears on its stationery. In its heyday, these titles were used interchangeably. Scribbled on the back of one old photo of the hotel, in Lula's distinctive handwriting, is "The Berch Hotel," as if my grandparents never got around to changing the name.

Years later, it would be known as "The Myers Hotel," with some old-timers in Marlow still referring to it accordingly. More recently, it seems, as the building grew old and sad, perhaps as a death knell, locals resumed calling it "The Johnson Hotel," honoring its roots. Its lobby was partitioned by drywall and used for A.A. meetings by the time of Almarian's funeral in 2011.

Marlow hosted a bustling downtown and busy railroad in the 1920s, and there were three hotels in addition to Johnson's. Earlier, in 1914, a Parks Hotel had burned to the ground, killing one, and providing the town with its first newsworthy disaster. Sensing an opportunity after the blaze, Mr. W. A. Johnson decided the town needed a new hotel in a most ideal location, directly across the street from the railroad station.

The original deed to the land was held by the Choctaw and Chickasaw nations, who signed it over to Marlow pioneer George Siever on February 11, 1916. Very likely, this strip of land was transferred as "railway rights," given that Siever was the agent of the Chicago, Rock Island & Pacific Railway Company at Marlow. His brother Lloyd plays a minor role in this story. More precisely, it will be Lloyd's drugstore, "Siever's," where a mob decides to rock the cradle.

Opening day for Johnson's Hotel was May 25, 1916. Newspaper accounts described it as "the largest and most up to date hotel in Stephens County and is furnished with appropriate furniture and electrical fixtures." The paved sidewalks in front of the hotel were new in 1915, but this stretch of Main Street would not be paved until 1921.

George Siever deeded the land to William A. Johnson more than two years *after* the hotel doors had been opened. The next transfer of the real-estate deed was directly from Johnson to my grandmother, Lula Combs Garvin. Her unique, angular signature is easily recognizable in the abstract log at the Stephens County office, the ink drying on January 2, 1919, three months after the death of her first husband.

In a front-page story on November 28, 1918, the *Marlow Review* announced Lula's purchase:

> "Important Real Estate Deal"
> One of the most important real estate deals of the year was made last Friday when W. A. Johnson sold his hotel property to Mrs. Lula Garvin, consideration being $10,000. . . .
> Mrs. Garvin has assumed the management of the hotel with Will Steel and wife, experienced hotel people assisting her. . . .

The grand opening of Johnson's Hotel in 1916 had sounded the gun for a building boom in downtown Marlow, and the hotel would serve as the eastern anchor on Main Street. While drilling reports and gushers were becoming part of the daily news, at this point it was mostly a distant drumroll generating the economic optimism. The hard dollars were coming from abundant harvests on the farms, most notably the thriving broomcorn business. Cotton may have been king, but the boll weevil was heir apparent, with harvests under siege and cash rewards being paid to citizens willing to pluck weevils by hand, by the bushel.

The key player in this downtown boom was George Carter, father of Pearl. One month before the opening of Johnson's Hotel, a short blurb in the *Marlow Review* noted that "contracts are at work this week on the new Carter building to be erected just west of the Johnson hotel."

Five months after the opening of Johnson's Hotel, the *Marlow Review* (October 26, 1916) offers this headline: "Eight New Buildings To Be Erected Soon." Four men—J. A. Hadnott, George Carter, C. A. Tally, and Charles Briscoe—would be behind these efforts. Subsequent reports in the *Marlow Review* refer to the east-end construction collectively as the "New Carter Buildings." George Carter's fingers, perhaps supersensitive given his blindness, touched nearly every brick downtown, with the exception of Johnson's Hotel.

Two years later, Lula Combs Garvin, the only single woman mentioned in the many commercial real-estate transactions researched for this book, would waltz into this downtown development boom and acquire Johnson's Hotel.

In the early photographs of the hotel, one sees a two-story brick structure with a porte-cochère that reaches over the sidewalk on Marlow's Main Street. To the left of the porte-cochère, facing Main Street, is a plate-glass window with *Café* painted in the center. This window would be the site for several family photos, including our only photograph of Albert Berch, Sr., Lula's father-in-law.

Although the porte-cochère marked the original main entrance, by the time Lula took over, the front door had been moved to the southeast end, Main and First, opening to the street corner where a tall electric streetlight stood as sentry. A sign denoting *Johnson's Hotel,* bejeweled with new and trendy neon, reached out at right angles from its second-story mount near this entrance. One of my copies of this photograph has a circled exterior window, indicating the birthing room of Almarian in 1922. However, by the time of the murders, the family lived in an interior suite near the lobby.

In our only interior photograph, taken in 1920, we see Lula standing at the front desk with her night clerk. Above them looms a photograph of Pres. Woodrow Wilson, ready to witness the action unless his likeness was later replaced by one of Calvin Coolidge, who had become president by the time of the bloodbath in the hotel's lobby. Had the photographer rotated just forty-five degrees to the right, he or she would be aiming directly at the murder scene.

In the Marlow town museum, a large composite photograph is

Johnson's Hotel in its prime. A faint X *marks the room where Lula notes that Almarian was "borned."*

displayed where fifty-four male faces are identified as "1912 Business Men of Marlow, Oklahoma." Lula Combs Garvin must have been quite the oddity when she purchased Johnson's Hotel, very likely the only businesswoman in town. We can only imagine the whispers, mutterings, or open harassment that she might have encountered. Yet, never once in her exhaustive writings did she complain about gender discrimination. Perhaps she was oblivious, focused entirely on forging a new life for herself and her thirteen-year-old son, Guy, from her first marriage. The only emotion that bubbles up from her diaries is the pride she felt in becoming a hotelier.

In one logbook, we have a short passage written by Lula about Johnson's Hotel in its prime:

> Bought 1918. Sold 1925. 40 rooms and large dining room . . . 20 rooms down, large Lobby with adjoining writing room for traveling salesmen to make out their day's orders, all rooms fully carpeted, inner spring mattresses (Simmons), steel beds. The Hotel was red brick, tile lobby with telephone booth and shoe shine chair in writing room adjoining lobby. Our Dining Room seated 100 people. There was a large town trade for the Dining Room. Marble top counters, mahogany tables and chairs . . . After the tragedy there I could not pay expenses and no one would buy it so it broke me completely. I had it hard after that, a 2 year old baby, no money, and no income.

In a separate document, Lula added this:

> Our price for rooms was three dollars a day, but six months from the time we bought it, an oil well was brought in 10 miles south of our town, it was a gusher it was. . . . We of course didn't realize it would affect us, our hotel being 10 miles away. But after being gone a half day (to watch the gusher) when we returned, every room was full and a waiting list enough to fill it again . . . we began to get telephone calls and telegrams out of the state wanting reservations and telling us that they would pay 10 dollars a day for a room as soon as one was empty. We realized that we had something big, we talked with geologists and they said it would last a long time. People came by train, car and buggies. . . . The wild wild oil well had as guests wild wild men . . . we filled our halls with cots and charged three dollars a day to live in the halls.
>
> We leased our Café to a couple who was from Ft. Worth, Texas who had managed a large café for three years and they really knew how to run one. . . . We bought a six by ten foot map of the state of Oklahoma with the help of a geologist we pasted it to the wall. . . . Colored pins were placed to denote dry holes (red), producing wells (blue), planned wells (black). Not just the area but the entire state . . . Many oil people said it was the most remarkable piece of work they had ever seen worked out so they didn't have to ask or guess all they had to do was look at the map.

Lula recreated lists of people and places, years after her association with them. In one logbook, she recorded the addresses of properties (nearly one hundred) she had flipped from the 1920s through the 1970s in central Oklahoma. In another diary, she listed names of people and events that took place twenty-five years earlier, such as "Marlow town regulars at the Café." She also documented 110 patrons of Johnson's Hotel and their hometowns, most of these being "regulars" (see "Lists" on accompanying website).

Lula's list of employees at Johnson's Hotel is where this story is launched. Remarkably, two porters were not enough once the oil began to flow. Albert Berch had teamed with Lula in hotel management after their marriage in 1920, and the couple came to believe that they needed *one more porter*. And frankly, even though porters were already at the lower end of the hotel hierarchy, there were some jobs, such as cleaning spittoons and shining shoes, where the current help balked.

So, Albert Berch and his right-hand man, J. L. Clark, traveled to Duncan, some ten miles south, where they recruited a black man, Robert

Johnigan, who had past experience as a porter at Duncan's Wade Hotel. Johnigan's work there was described as "impeccable," and his track record showed that he had "never been any trouble there."

In his forties at the time, Robert Johnigan had been shot in his left ankle accidentally during his youth, with the ankle permanently frozen. With no movement in that critical joint, he was forced to drag his leg as he walked. It must have been quite noticeable, as there are almost no references to the man apart from his disability, always "crippled."

Albert Berch was fully aware that Marlow was a "whites only" town and that their sponsoring of Robert Johnigan to work and stay in Johnson's Hotel was a marginal call. Johnigan's employment in the hotel was one thing, but staying there overnight—living there—was quite another, a direct violation of the signs posted at the outskirts of town.

Not oblivious to this violation of the "unwritten law," Albert Berch sought the blessing of the town leaders before officially hiring Robert Johnigan. Lula reported that he was given the go-ahead. Although Albert

Lula Berch, Albert Berch (center), and J. L. Clark, who served as "right-hand man" to the Berch couple in the management of the hotel.

was considered a newcomer in town, having lived in Marlow just shy of three years, Lula had been in Marlow for over twenty years. So it seems that she would have served as a guide to her husband when it came to local politics.

Furthermore, Albert Berch appears to have been in good standing with many of the town's leading citizens. The local newspaper, the *Marlow Review*, would refer to him as "one of Marlow's substantial and respected citizens," so it begs the question: from whom did Albert Berch get the okay to hire Robert Johnigan? In contrast to her bountiful lists of names, Lula never tells us, nor will other sources give us the answer. After the murders, some will deny permission was ever sought or granted.

A different set of "town leaders," or perhaps the same leaders wearing different faces, began to circulate rumors that Albert Berch was Catholic, anathema at the time, especially to the Ku Klux Klan. The idea that someone might start such a rumor is easily explained. Perhaps Albert mentioned, even to just one person, that he had once lived in a Catholic orphanage, or that he had a rich aunt who was thought to be Catholic. Lula would deny the "accusation" of Catholicism the rest of her life, though we will buzz about that flower several times before landing.

Another point of antipathy toward Berch, once again from family lore, was that he had refused to sell Johnson's Hotel to a powerful suitor who was attracted by its lucrative profits during the oil boom, not to mention the lease agreement on the popular café. While any offers to buy the hotel would have been rejected well before Robert Johnigan came to town, such snubs have a way of being shelved in brine by potential enemies, allowed to pickle over time, then pulled from the shelf later on to satisfy a hankering. Lula alleged that the suitor for the hotel was very likely the mastermind behind the "massacre," but I am cautious here, as the value of Johnson's Hotel plummeted after the murders.

Clearly, it was the hiring of Robert Johnigan as a live-in porter at Johnson's Hotel that became the focal point of hostility, with collective eyebrows raised as the news swarmed over the city. Warnings and intimidations were launched on cue with Mr. Johnigan's first day at work, spilling over to Albert Berch, who shrugged off the threats.

For Robert Johnigan, life turned ruinous in a hurry. Persecution was unrelenting. Within a mere ten days, the threats of lynching made directly to Johnigan were so convincing that he was ready to call it quits. In nearby Duncan, he had enjoyed a quiet life and the respect of his employers, but now it appeared he was going to be killed for nothing more than the color of his skin. After a particularly virulent threat from a mob gathered in the heart of busy downtown Marlow on the evening of December 17, 1923, he walked a few blocks east to Johnson's Hotel and resigned. He told his employer, Albert Berch, that he couldn't take it anymore. He was quitting his job and going back to Duncan on the next train out of town.

Perhaps the employer had been threatened enough as well. He did not argue. According to Lula's account, Al Berch said, "I'm indeed sorry to lose you." Then, my grandfather sat down on the edge of his bed in the Berch family suite in Johnson's Hotel, wife Lula and toddler Almarian nearby, and wrote out a check to Robert Johnigan for severance pay covering ten days of labor. Yes, the experiment had failed, though perhaps both men were relieved.

In the lobby, just steps away, a voice called out asking if anyone was available to shine the shoes of a hotel guest, an important "traveling man." Although Robert Johnigan was no longer an official employee of the hotel, he did not hesitate to stoop at the feet of J. L. Campbell from Norman, Oklahoma and begin the shine. The "crippled negro" would not get beyond the initial buff.

4

The Facts of the Case Will Reveal . . .

Newspaper accounts relate how Albert Berch and Robert Johnigan had been given "fair warning" of their violation of the "unwritten law." Al Berch had "pushed Marvin Kincannon," who then shot the hotel owner; the "negro did not obey the earlier command to leave town"; and the melee in the lobby began after "the negro started an argument."

Yet, there were many witnesses to the "massacre" (the widow's descriptor), given that it happened in the lobby, in full view of hotel guests and employees. In addition, a street crowd had gathered outside like moths at the windows to view the carnage inside. Not surprisingly, the accounts vary. According to testimony delivered at the preliminary hearing and two homicide trials, here's how it went down, more or less.

One week before Christmas, with the evening temperature a cool but tolerable forty degrees, a group of young men gathered on Main Street, as they often did, in front of Siever's drugstore. Had this been a typical night, the main attraction would have been a silent movie playing at the Whiteway theater, so named not for racial implications, nor for Broadway's new moniker as the Great White Way, but for its owner, J. S. White. A local contest had been held in the summer of 1921 to christen the new theater. One of the five winning entries had been submitted by J. L. Clark, who is about to have a very busy night this December 17, 1923.

For the past nine evenings, ever since the arrival of Robert Johnigan in Marlow, the gatherings at Siever's drugstore had increasingly acquired a bloodlust, with several spokesmen rallying the young men to a greater pitch night after night. Most vocal, the alpha on the soapbox, was Elza Roy Gandy, son of one of the town's policemen, H. R. Gandy, the sole officer assigned to night watch. Each evening, the voices grew louder and louder, and the ultimatums, sometimes delivered to Johnigan face to face, grew stronger and stronger.

On this evening, the tenth night of the sundown violation, the "crippled

32

Interior of Johnson's Hotel (1920). Lula is at the front desk with an unidentified clerk. The photographer is standing near the main entrance. Slightly to the right of this angle is the murder scene.

negro" was returning to the hotel from an errand when he was stopped by the crowd at Siever's, two blocks west of Johnson's Hotel on the same side of the street. (Today's incarnation is located immediately east of the Chamber of Commerce.) Here, Johnigan was threatened again by the gang, but this time the warnings had the scent of finality. We do not know the exact words delivered, but the implication was that Johnigan would not live to see the sun rise again if he stayed in Marlow. Johnigan had had enough. It was time to leave town. He would take the next train back to Duncan as soon as he picked up his pay from Albert Berch. He continued on toward the hotel, dragging his foot with the frozen ankle.

The time was shortly after sundown.

The mob watched Johnigan continue east on the sidewalk, all the while working themselves into the frenzy common to all such mobs, with voices inspiring other voices, hatred inspiring other hatred, and men turning themselves into savages, exulting in the freedom from restraint. Almost as if it were an organism unto itself, the mob began to undulate, expanding and contracting, moving forward then hesitating, finally beginning a relentless and committed thrust to the hotel. In a telling act, several of the boys stopped to shed their coats along the way, ignoring the cool night air.

Halfway to its goal, the mob was joined by Marvin Kincannon, a maverick who fused into the herd after crossing Main Street at a tangent. He became one with the pulsing organism, perhaps providing its very heartbeat. Curious bystanders in downtown Marlow fell into ranks behind the core agitators, giving the mob its arms and legs as it blended into the night, only to reappear again under the solitary streetlight at the front door of Johnson's Hotel.

J. L. Clark was Albert Berch's right-hand man—driver, delivery boy, general helper, confidant. Short in stature, with a flat-topped haircut adding a few inches to his height, the young man was held in high regard by both Albert and Lula Berch.

On the evening of the murders, J. L. Clark was returning to the hotel from the post office, trailing behind Johnigan. He saw the mob forming at Siever's drugstore, before it began its relentless march. This is how J. L. described it on the witness stand at the preliminary hearing, several weeks after the murders:

Q: About how many were there in that crowd?

A: Twelve or fifteen . . .

Q: What did you hear them saying in that crowd with reference to this negro?

A: Just said they were getting up a mob to go down and get the negro. I did not believe they would as they had been coming up there every night and I did not think anything about it.

Q: Were you up there when that crowd left to go to the hotel?

A: No sir.

Q: How long was it from the time you left the crowd up there until you saw these boys come into the lobby?

A: Twenty or thirty minutes.

By the time J. L. Clark arrived at the hotel, Albert Berch had accepted Johnigan's resignation and written out the severance check. Yet, before Johnigan could make it outside the hotel, he learned that a distinguished guest, the district deputy for the Modern Woodmen of America, was waiting for service in the shoe-shine chair. Going well beyond the call of duty, Johnigan sat down at the feet of Mr. Campbell.

Across the lobby, through the front door, a gang of young men burst into the room.

Albert Berch was sitting on the edge of his bed in the family suite, with Lula and their toddler nearby. He finished entering the check in his ledger, then walked out of the room toward the adjacent lobby, while Lula started to take the baby upstairs. Before going through the swinging door into the lobby's writing room, he was met in the hallway by Walter O'Quinn, a resident of Oklahoma City. Walter had previously lived in Marlow for twenty-five years and had known Al Berch since the latter's arrival in town.

In the hallway, the two men talked for a moment, then headed for the swinging door to the lobby. Prior to entry, however, they were joined by J. L. Clark, who warned them about trouble brewing. The swinging door had a small pane of glass, so the men caught a quick glimpse of the commotion before entering.

"Seven, eight, or 10" men had entered the lobby. Still looking through the pane of glass, Berch and O'Quinn witnessed Elza Gandy yank Robert Johnigan away from the foot of the shine chair and begin beating him with a lead pipe, or perhaps a stick. In response, Berch rushed through the door, followed by O'Quinn, then Clark.

Albert Berch ran toward the melee, striking Elza Gandy with his fist, a single blow that knocked Elza backward over a table. Stunned, Gandy remained sprawled on the floor. Berch turned around to face Marvin Kincannon, who, with pistol already drawn, casually shot Berch in the chest at point-blank range. Berch crumpled to the ground, where he began to gasp for air with an ominous gurgling sound, a mere ten seconds after entering the lobby.

Robert Johnigan staggered into the telephone booth near the shine stand, hoping for refuge. Marvin Kincannon stepped over the dying body of Albert Berch "in pursuit of the negro." He fired his gun into the booth, hitting Johnigan. Then, Kincannon opened the folding door and dragged the porter out of the booth to shoot him again. At least four shots were fired in all, one at Albert Berch, the rest at Johnigan, but only two hit the "crippled negro," neither immediately fatal.

With various witnesses at various vantage points, Walter O'Quinn was one of the few who could see all the shots fired by Marvin Kincannon. At the preliminary hearing, he described the scene:

Q: Did you see Kincannon when he fired the shot?

A: Yes, sir.

Q: That is Marvin Kincannon, the defendant in this case here? (indicating)

January 4, 1924, edition of the Duncan Banner.

A: Yes sir.

Q: How long have you known Marvin Kincannon?

A; I have known Marvin about all his life I guess. . . .

Q: What did Berch hit Gandy with when he came in?

A: His fist.

Q: Did Kincannon stand in the same place that he was in when he fired the shot at the negro?

A: He fired the first shot and then he went over to the booth.

Q: In going from where he was standing at the time he fired the first two shots to where he fired the other shots, did he have to pass over Berch's body?

A: He would have to step over his feet.

Q: At the time Berch entered the lobby, or at any other time prior to the time he was shot and killed, did he *(Berch)* have any weapon that you noticed?

A: No sir.

Q: If he had, would you have seen it?

A: I believe I would.

Q: Now, at the time you entered the lobby, or any time until the negro was shot, did you see him with any weapons?

A: No sir, I did not.

Q: What kind of a looking gun was it, describe it best you can, that Kincannon was using to do the shooting?

A: That is a little hard for me to do to look at it under those circumstances, but I judge about a thirty-eight.

The cross-examination follows:

Q: While you and Mr. Berch were standing there talking could you see into the lobby from where you were?

A: I could not without stooping. There was a little glass in this door— the door was shut and I would have to stoop down to see through.

Q: And while you were standing there talking you would not see anything that was going on in the lobby?

A: I never paid any attention until this boy said what he did to Al.

Q: What boy was that?

A: J. L. Clark, the boy that runs the service car for Mr. Berch.

Q: Now you say Berch ran into the lobby?

A: Yes.

Q: What rate of speed did he make?

A: Just about as fast as a man would rush into a place . . .

Q: Mr. O'Quinn, I will ask you this question. If it isn't a fact that at the time the first shot was fired in the lobby that you were in your own room?

A: Absolutely not.

Q: That is not a fact?

A: No, it is not.

One of the witnesses was J. R. Leppla, a coffee salesman from Oklahoma City who frequented Johnson's Hotel in his statewide travels. Leppla had been registered for about an hour and was seated at the large table in the writing room, along with two other men. Openly divided from the lobby by columns and an archway, the writing room also housed the phone booth and shoe-shine chair.

Leppla testified that "about 15" young men were in the lobby, but since he was not from Marlow, he did not know the boys in the mob or the other witnesses. He admitted that he scampered into the café when the shooting began. However, Leppla confirmed that O'Quinn (the "big fellow") was in the room as an eyewitness, a key point since O'Quinn was the only witness willing and able to recall the entire sequence.

The man in the shoe-shine chair was J. L. Campbell of Norman, Oklahoma. Campbell was fifty-three, with a wife, two daughters, and a son at the time. He had just arrived on the evening train when the incident occurred.

Q: What were you doing?

A: I just walked into the hotel to get my shoes shined.

Q: Was the negro shining your shoes when the difficulty arose?

A: Yes sir, just commenced to shine my shoes, he was brushing them preparing to shine them.

Q: What first attracted your attention that there was anything occurring there . . . out of the ordinary?

A: Somebody got him by the arm and says come on or something like that. . . . I was looking towards this dining room door (when) this shot was fired on the right, and I just glanced from that to my right and seen the man fall in about three feet of me, near the shine chair, and about three feet something near that, and I recognized it as Berch. That was the first shot that was fired, then I began to get out of that chair pretty quick and somebody was in my way, I think this negro was in front of me, I pushed him out of the way and started towards the dining room and four or five other shots were fired.

Traveling salesman O. E. Vandergriff, of Oklahoma City, took the stand, another witness from the writing room. Vandergriff claimed a "poor memory for details" but did recall a "stick or a club of some kind up in the air," held by one of the mob. He escaped the scene as quickly as possible, and by the time he returned to the lobby, it was full of strangers. Nick Byrne, a traveling salesman from Lawton, Oklahoma, was the last eyewitness of those seated at the table in the writing room but added little, as "I made my get away."

Finally, J. L. Clark, the eighteen-year-old aide-de-camp to the Berch couple, took the stand at the preliminary hearing:

"North of the phone booth, there is a little hallway that goes back into the hall of rooms. Berch was standing outside his door, talking to O'Quinn . . . when I started out at the door I saw the boys in the lobby, and I said Mr. Berch, about 10 or 12 . . . and he started running, he says, come on J. L., let's go out and run them away. . . . "

Q: J. L., just tell the court what occurred from then on.

A: Berch run up to Gandy—Gandy was hitting the negro with a stick, looked like about two feet long.

Q: How did it compare with these sticks I have in my hand?

A: Did not look quite as long as those.

Q: And what color was it?

A: Lead color.

Q: Who had the stick?

A: Elza Gandy.

Q: What was he doing?

A: Hitting the negro and Mr. Berch run in there and hit him.

Q: Hit who?

A: Elza Gandy, and when Mr. Berch hit him it just kinda turned him around and as he (Berch) turned, Marvin Kincannon shot him.

Q: How far was Kincannon standing from Berch at the time he shot him, about how far, in your best judgment?

A: About three or four feet. . . .

Q: Now, J. L., getting back to the difficulty in the lobby—When did you first see Mrs. Berch after the shot was fired?

A: The first time I seen her she was kneeling down trying to put her husband's head on her lap.

Q: Was that before you left the lobby?

A: Yes sir.

Q: About how long, the best you can estimate it, was that after he was shot?

A: Just a short time.

Q: Did you know she was in that part of the lobby?

A: No sir, I did not see her enter.

J. L. Clark testified that neither Berch nor Johnigan had weapons, that Kincannon fired all the shots, that he used a .38 revolver, and that Berch made no threatening gestures toward Kincannon after striking Elza Gandy. J. L. then demonstrated to the jury how Kincannon held the gun immediately prior to the first shot.

During cross-examination, Clark testified the following:

Q: I will ask you this, if it isn't a fact that Gandy was standing with his hand on the colored boy or by him and Berch run up and hit him?

A: No sir, Gandy was hitting the negro.

The night clerk, Pete Magnusen, watched the young men as they entered the hotel through the main door of the lobby at the southeast corner of the building. Nine or ten, by his account, entered single file, with Marvin Kincannon in the lead and Elza Gandy in the second position. They walked past the front desk, then back to the writing room. The night clerk hurried to the dining room in search of Albert Berch. He could not find him, and when he returned, Marvin Kincannon was standing in the writing room with a gun in his hand. "Mr. Berch was lying there and Mrs. Berch was down there with him."

The exact time of death for Albert Berch was variably reported, centering around 8:15 P.M. As if to defy the sundown law one last time, Robert Johnigan held on until sunrise, when he finally passed.

The doctor who was called to the scene, C. C. Richards (who had delivered the baby Almarian in one of the hotel's rooms), also testified at the preliminary hearing.

Q: Doctor, did you know Al Berch in his lifetime?

A: Yes, well.

Q: Now, when you arrived at the hotel, doctor, did you see Mr. Berch?

A: I saw him lying there on the floor.

Q: Was he living or dead?

A: He was gasping about his last breath.

Q: How far from where Johnigan was lying?

A: Eight or ten feet.

Q: Did you examine his body, doctor, to ascertain what gunshot wounds, if any, were inflicted on his body?

A: No sir, he was dying. I saw that I could not do him any good when I got there so I went over to the negro.

Q: Did Berch die while you were there Doctor?

A: Yes sir.

Q: And how long after you arrived, or about how long?

A: I judge not over a minute, maybe less than a minute.

Additional testimony at this preliminary hearing on January 4, 1924, came from Mrs. Pete Benight, who ran the café and dining room of Johnson's Hotel. She stated that she entered the writing room to see Mrs. Berch lying prostrate over the body of her husband. "The little baby was there by its mother, too, and I picked it up. It was crying and I took it away from there just so it would be away from such a thing."

The newspapers described how Lula Berch was "witness to part of the affair," but none of the crowd seemed to notice when she actually entered the writing room. According to her later testimony, she was in the Berch suite and had started upstairs when the melee began, turning around to become fourth in the parade through the swinging door, behind J. L. Clark.

And this is how my grandmother summarized the final moment to me, over fifty years later:

Lula entered the room, carrying the toddler, my mother, while gunfire was still blazing. Albert lay dying before her eyes, his shirt blood-soaked. Then, Marvin Kincannon fired a shot at Lula by the phone booth but missed, albeit close enough that my grandmother claimed to have received powder burns on her face. She "dropped baby" and ran to Albert's side for his final breath, while Almarian, unhurt, stood beside her father's head, crying.

At the beginning of this book, I mentioned the strange burial pact that my mother made, orchestrating this threesome into a common plot, even though they were a family but a mere twenty-two months—birthing, sleeping, eating, and working the entire time at Johnson's Hotel in Marlow. On this December night in 1923, the dotted chalk line would surround only Albert Berch, even though the three of them were tightly grouped at the moment of his death, with bullets flying. Eighty-eight years would pass before the burial pact was finalized.

And one last touch for the folklore—my grandmother Lula told me that, in the days following the murders, she found "a bullet hole in Almarian's baby gown," marking the path of one of the errant shots that had been fired. According to later trial testimony, at least one stray bullet would be pulled from the wood in the phone booth. But as for confirmation of the bullet passing through my mother's dress . . .

"Oh, Grandma, did you save the baby gown?"

"No, Alan, I did not."

5

Combing Family Roots

Like a swarm of locusts gobbling up the countryside, nearly forty tornados ravaged the Central and Southern U.S. during a two-week period in 1896, leaving a death toll of 484 in their wakes. The twister that hit Nocona, Texas on May 12, less than ten miles from the Oklahoma border, sent the Combs family scurrying to their "storm cave."

Patriarch William David Combs was a veteran of storms, routinely digging a cave on any property where he and his family landed. Spotting the "cyclone" in the distance, he dropped his plow, ran to the farmhouse to gather his family, and then shepherded them into the hole in the ground. Lula Combs was the oldest sibling, age twelve, and she recalled how her baby sister Fannie began to scream when she could not find her pet squirrel to take with her into the storm cave. Their father pulled the door shut against the cries of little Fannie.

In Lula's words: "Dad held the rope on the door to keep it from blowing off. It was on us and no one can tell you the terrible sound of a cyclone. We couldn't hear the thunder anymore, the noise was too great, but the lightning was so terrible we could see it in the cracks of the door. It looked like fire on the outside. . . . We were all crying and praying. My sister was crying over the squirrel. My dad said Honey, let's don't cry over the squirrel. We are safe is all that matters. She said 'yes but we had sense enough to get out of danger, but my squirrel didn't.'"

The Combs family, huddled in the safety of the cave, included William and wife Arrie, oldest daughter Lula, daughter Nettie, son William Fred, and little Fannie. And while they escaped injury from this 1896 storm, ill winds would continue to swirl around this family.

Years later, Almarian, granddaughter of William and Arrie, would trace the Combs genealogy back to John Combs, who arrived in Jamestown in 1619 aboard the *Marigold,* and in the process of discovery, she landed smack dab in the middle of the Daughters of the American Revolution.

But the story was not so glorious for her grandmother Arrie. Her riches-to-rags story began with wealthy ancestors whose Tennessee plantation was burned to the ground by Union bushwhackers during the Civil War. After the Battle of Shiloh, but before the end of the war, Arrie's grandparents freed their slaves, converted their scorched earth to gold coins, and moved to Arkansas, where her grandfather John David Loving bought one of the few mills in Kingston. Excess gold coins were buried "at night under an old dead apple tree," and this story became a source of endless fascination for our mother when she was a child, given that the burial site was lost and the coins never recovered.

Arella Cordelia Loving was born September 18, 1863, in northwest Arkansas. Neighbors "took her in" when she was orphaned by age eight, but Arrie was not allowed an education, and was treated more as servant than sibling. This might explain why eighteen-year-old Arrie was willing to leap into the arms of sixteen-year-old William David Combs in 1881, moving shortly thereafter to Nocona as subsistence farmers. Lula would write late in her life: "If there was ever a man and woman without a sin in this world, besides Jesus Christ, it would have been my mother and father."

Lula wrote her account of the 1896 tornado in several diaries over the years, her descriptive phrases often repeated word for word. Her education was limited to a few months each year, so spelling is often amiss and syntax tortured, while her handwriting evolves from a row of flower petals to harsh quasi-calligraphy over time, as though the pressure on the fountain pen was mounting. Her most chilling words are found at the beginning of an autobiography that she penned late in life for Almarian. She opens her life story with a summary bang: "Life has been a great disappointment for me."

I still hear those words in my head with my grandmother's voice, but this dismal summation should come as no surprise by the end of this book. Lula's story does not illuminate the art of living—it's a story of survival.

Little Fannie, with her pet squirrel a remote memory, will go on to marry a Great War hero, killed in France. Then, during her second marriage, with one daughter by the deceased husband and pregnant by the second husband, Fannie will discover that her new husband has molested her daughter. Horrified that she is bringing another potential victim of sexual abuse into the world, Fannie will perform a self-abortion using the hackneyed coat-hanger technique. She and her unborn child will bleed to death. Fannie is the only sibling who rests near Lula in the Marlow cemetery.

Brother Freddie will die at age fifty-seven of kidney cancer. He and his wife will be the only family members living in Marlow at the time of the murders at Johnson's Hotel.

Not all the tales arising from that storm cave are tragic, however. Lula's younger sister Nettie will grow up to have a son who, after medical school, becomes the highly decorated two-star general Glenn J. Collins, MD. He will serve as chief of staff of Walter Reed Hospital, deputy surgeon

The Combs family photograph taken prior to the birth of their last child, daughter Jessie, circa 1903, while living near Nocona, Texas. Back row: Lula, Nettie (sister). Front row: William David Combs (father), William "Fred" Combs (brother), Arrie Combs (mother), the ill-fated Fannie Combs (sister), Lucinda Mashburn Combs (William's mother, and paternal grandmother to namesake Lula).

general, and commandant of medical forces during the Vietnam War. His son, Roger, will become a radiologist who will have retired and moved to Florida by the time I begin work on this book.

Demonstrating how the branches of our family grew apart, I had never met Roger even though we were physicians practicing in the same city. When I phoned him in Florida and introduced myself as his second cousin, he remembered "Aunt Lula" and "Grandma Combs," of course. But when I asked him if he had any insight about the murder of Albert Berch, his reply was, "Who is Albert Berch?" He never knew that his aunt Lula had once been Lula Berch and, before that, Lula Garvin.

In her account of the 1896 tornado, Lula offers this closing memory as a twelve-year-old: "The first thing we saw in about 10 minutes after the terrible blow was over, was that squirrel frisking over the stump of the big old cottonwood tree that had shaded our well. No human can tell anyone else what it feels like to come out of a cave, not a scratch, but not one earthly thing left, house and barn, horses, chickens, ducks, turkeys, everything gone except Fannie's little grey squirrel."

After a repeat encounter with a 1905 tornado, the Combs family crossed the Red River and moved north to Indian Territory, perhaps under the mistaken belief at the time that tornados don't cross rivers. They left farming behind, switching to the mercantile business, first in Katie, then in Elmore City. By this time, a fifth child had been born, a girl they named Jessie.

Combs Mercantile thrived in Elmore City through three generations, first with William David, then William Fred (Freddie), then his son Doyle. A branch store was attempted for a while in Marlow, but by the time of the murders, my great-grandparents were back in Elmore City.

I have one quick point about Elmore City, located a little over thirty miles due east of Marlow. In spite of its small size (population 700), in replaying Marlow's brush with Hollywood, this tiny town also prompted a major motion picture. In 1980, a ban on public dancing that had persisted for nearly a century was lifted after pressure from maverick students who had been lobbying for several years, allowing the high school's first prom. Readers may be more familiar with this story as *Footloose*, starring Kevin Bacon in the 1984 version and remade in 2011.

In 1949, William David and Arrie Combs moved to Oklahoma City for the end-stage care of his bladder cancer at St. Anthony Hospital. When he died at age eighty-six, Arrie moved in with Lula at 1805-7 Northwest Twenty-Seventh in Oklahoma City, the new Combs Central. Although the duplex has since been razed, a well-hit homerun over the left-field fence by an Oklahoma City University Star today will land on what used to be Lula's front-yard "storm cave."

Arrie's great-grandchildren, thirteen by my count, remember this remarkable woman well. She was quoted in the *Oklahoma City Times* article covering her ninety-ninth birthday: "I don't yearn for the good old days—television and all these modern conveniences have the good old days beat by a mile. . . . I get a kick out of seeing young folks make love and if girls want to wear shorts that's fine by me. . . . I love basketball, football, boxing, and wrestling. Those first five games that OU played were pretty rough but I'm a Sooner fan and always have been." (For the record, Arrie was referring to the first five football games of 1961, where senior Sooners will remember the shocking start to the season at 0-5; and yes, Bud was still at the helm.) "I'm looking forward to my 100th birthday," she said, "but if I don't make it, it'll be my own fault."

Arrie Combs (late 1950s), as her many great-grandchildren remember her.

Arrie avoided hospitals for her first century, but her series of heart attacks began at 101 and ended at 102. She outlived all but two of her children, Lula and Nettie.

Arrie was sharp until the end. Tiny, terrifically wrinkled, with gray hair always on top in coiled braids, she forever sat a mere two feet away from her black and white TV, hunched over to get the closest look possible. As she watched boxing, this wee woman would send her fists flailing, mimicking each blow. And she was forever jolly. To her great-grandchildren, Arrie was a delight.

For Arrie's oldest daughter, Lula, a gentle smile was the maximum expression of emotion. Piercing eyes met you head on. She was taciturn but not gloomy; cool but not cold; stern on occasion but never angry; always kind but no hugging. And we didn't *dare* ask about her past when we were children, nor her *age,* strictly following Almarian's guidelines.

Later in her life (and Lula lived to age ninety-eight), Lula became more like her mother, chuckling and talking in free association. But there was still a difference—she was in the grip of fear, a powerful anxiety over unmet disasters on unseen horizons. And with a nod to her foresight, or merely the betting odds that come with global disquiet, disasters would follow Lula into her nineties.

After Arrie died in 1965, the number of Lula's visitors dropped precipitously. The matriarch was gone, and ill health hit other family members. The home grew silent, and it is there where Lula's anxiety bloomed.

My great-grandmother Combs was born shortly after the Battle of Gettysburg and died when I was sixteen. I did not attend her funeral. Oddly, my mother readily excused both my sister Susan and me from attending, if not outright discouraging it, as though she wanted to protect us from the specter of death as long as possible. Yet, our younger sister, Dawn, did go to the funeral in Elmore City. Services were held in the Methodist church, a point to be made here as religious denominations will emerge as an issue during the murder trials.

Arrie was buried next to her husband in the Combs family plot in Elmore City, Oklahoma where, some thirty-five years later, standing alone in front of Arrie's grave for the first time, I would experience one of the most remarkable coincidences in my life. But I will leave that for a later chapter.

6

Lucinda Jane Combs Garvin Berch

As a preteen, Lula hated to pick cotton, not because of the labor and pain involved but rather the hopelessness in terms of economics. There was something that crushed her spirit when the boldest dream was a marginal profit but the reality was breaking even, or simply breaking.

Although the Combs family left Nocona, Texas for Indian Territory and the mercantile business, sadly, Lula did not escape with them.

On September 2, 1899, a little over three years after the first tornado, Lucinda (Lula or often Lulu) Combs wed Walter Garvin—a farmer—in Nocona, Texas. My grandmother, at age fifteen, daydreamed herself out of one farm and into the farm next door. The first child of Lula and Walter was named Guy, born in Nocona in 1905.

Lula was not stuck on the Texas farm for long, however. The little family moved to a farm near Marlow in 1906. To be exact, their location was closer to the town of Bray, home to a prominent family of ranchers and farmers named, conveniently enough, Garvin. In fact, Garvin County is due east of Stephens County. And it can be assumed that Lula enjoyed the blessing and protection that came from joining a family with clout.

In 1908, second son Glenn was born in Bray, Oklahoma. Two days before Christmas, in 1909, little Glenn died of diphtheria before reaching his second birthday. Lula never spoke of this event in my presence, and she didn't dwell on it with Almarian either. She slammed the door on this misery, driving it deep into her psyche. While it is only conjecture, in 1913, Lula's sister Nettie likely named her newborn son "Glenn," the future major general, in memory of Lula's heartrending loss.

In 1917, eleven years after their move to Oklahoma, Walter gave up farming and ranching to become a merchant in Marlow. "Combs and Son" became "Combs and Garvin," dealing in dry goods and groceries, which was called a "mercantile" in that era but called Walmart or Target today.

Lula's children from her first marriage (husband Walter K. Garvin), Glenn on the left and Guy on the right.

The best-laid plans of this robust thirty-nine-year-old, however, were not to be realized. Four months after spinning off his own grocery division, Walter Garvin made front-page headlines through a distinction to which no one would aspire—he became the first resident of Marlow, Oklahoma to die in the Spanish flu epidemic of 1918.

The *Marlow Review* announced on October 10, 1918, "Marlow Loses Prominent Citizen." The newspaper described the worldwide pandemic under way and reported:

> [The Spanish flu] claimed as its first victim in Marlow, one of the city's most prominent and highly esteemed merchants and citizens, Walter K. Garvin.
>
> Mr. Garvin had only suffered a few days from the effects of this malady and as he was such a strong robust type of manhood he felt that he could fight off the effects of the disease but pneumonia developed and he became very ill Monday night gradually growing worse until he succumbed to the effects Wednesday at noon.
>
> His death comes as a great shock to his many friends in Stephens County because he was such a splendid specimen of physical strength that his death was unthought of. But it seems as though this new disease works on the strong with the same vigor as on the weak. . . .
>
> He was a member of one of this County's best known families. . . .

Considering the reams of paper that Lula used to document her life, she wrote very little about Walter, nor do we have a single photograph. She did not attend her husband's funeral, for he was not the only one in the family stricken by influenza. Their thirteen-year-old son, Guy, was fighting to avoid death's doorstep, and Lula stayed at home that day to nurse him back to health.

In 1918, the pivotal year in this story, the newly widowed Lula Combs Garvin purchased Johnson's Hotel in Marlow, using her husband's estate. And the question arises: what is a single woman trying to pull off in 1918, running a hotel on the back of zero training and little education?

Women had limited rights at the time, and single women pursuing business were widely condemned. But Lula plunged into her new vocation with gusto. Early on, she leased the hotel to a Mrs. Lucy Chaffin, allowing Lula to attend business school in Oklahoma City. As she later put it, "it was the only education I ever needed."

Upon returning to Marlow, she tried out several restaurateurs to supervise the café, a favorite dining spot for locals as well as guests. The reputation of the café peaked under the direction of the husband-wife team of Pete and Bess Benight, part-time residents of Ft. Worth, Texas, though Pete was a Marlow native. Their display ads in the newspaper included menus for Thanksgiving and Christmas dinners, along with the pragmatic pitch that "it will be cheaper here than to prepare a dinner at home, and think of the good things to eat."

For Lula's first year and a half of hotel management, her primary helpmate was Guy, in whom all her love had been channeled after the deaths of her husband and one son. In her recollections of this era, she described a steady stream of men who came "a-courting," yet she knew herself to be past her prime according to the day, in her mid-thirties, with a near-adult son. More to the point, she had little use for these men whom she saw as motivated to get their greedy hands on her splendid hotel, an enterprise enjoying spectacular success. On December 4, 1919, the front page of the *Marlow Review* reported: "Johnson Hotel To Be Enlarged—24 Additional Rooms, 10 Baths and Other Modern Conveniences to be Added: The Johnson Hotel, Marlow's leading commercial hotel, is to be enlarged and improved to meet all the present day requirements, so stated Mrs. Lulu Garvin, the proprietor. . . . When the above contemplated improvements are completed, it places this hotel on par with any other hotel in Southwest Oklahoma. . . . "

We have no information, not even an oral tradition, as to how Albert Berch swam upstream to surpass the doomed competition. Perhaps his advantage came simply from being a new face in town. His arrival in Marlow had always been shrouded in mystery, and it does not appear that daughter Almarian ever pinpointed the details during her years of research.

The *Marlow Review's* editor at the time was James C. Nance, who will eventually shed his career in journalism, enter politics, and be recognized for his legendary tenure in the state legislature by induction to the Oklahoma Hall of Fame in 1955. As with many pre-Twitter, small-town newspapers, the local "goings on" were reduced to single sentences. For instance, on October 2, 1919, the "local news" gave us this riveting item: "Mrs. Lulu Garvin and son Guy were down from Chickasha visiting friends the first of the week." Apparently, there was no Albert Berch at this point. In fact, my review of microfilm dating prior to the construction of Johnson's Hotel revealed nothing about him until the wedding announcement.

On March 17, 1920, Albert Berch and Lula Garvin were married in El Reno, Oklahoma, two days before Guy's fifteenth birthday. They

Guy Garvin, age fourteen.

honeymooned at the still-standing Southern Hotel in El Reno (which, thirty-five years later, would become the adopted hometown of their daughter and the Hollingsworth family). The *Marlow Review* ran the story along with several other wedding notices, printed in a small font that could easily have escaped detection:

> *Burch—Garvin:* A wedding that came as quite a surprise to the friends of the contracting parties . . . The bride is the proprietor of the Johnson Hotel, and has lived here a long number of years. The groom is employed at the Medcalf Barber Shop. He has only resided here a short time. His home is in Los Angeles, Calif. Their many friends wish them a long and happy life.

This story includes the totality of what we knew as children about Albert Berch—*a barber from Los Angeles*. The article nails the event with understated candor: "quite a surprise to the friends of the contracting parties."

Albert and Lula Berch honeymooned at the Southern Hotel in El Reno, Oklahoma,
the eventual hometown of their daughter, Almarian, and her family

Albert Berch would be dead before their fourth anniversary. But that detail aside, I have to believe, based on the spirited voice in her writings, that this period represented the peak joy in Lula's life. This time around, she had married for love (we insist on believing), plus she still had one dear son, and she owned a blossoming hotel of which she was very proud.

After Lula's marriage to Albert Berch, the hotel's success accelerated. At one point, the *Marlow Review* (always insisting that Albert spell his last name differently) reported: "The announcement has been made by Mr. and Mrs. Al Burch, owners of the Johnson Hotel, that a third story to the building will be added as soon as material can be assembled and workmen started on the project. . . . " The third floor would prove to be only a dream.

I suspect that during this brief slice of time, Lula would have been aghast to know that, toward the end of her life, she would write: "Life has been a great disappointment for me." She had already been through the ghastly deaths of her son Glenn and husband Walter, not to mention sister Fannie with her unborn child, but all was well now. She had suffered her lifetime quota of tragedy, and it must have looked like clear skies ahead, or at a minimum, the odds of clear skies were on her side.

Then, one month after her marriage to Albert Berch, Lula's fifteen-year-old son, Guy, dropped dead on the athletic field. Today, we are all too familiar with this type of story, but in those times, it was unimaginable. From the *Marlow Review*, April 15, 1920:

> **Guy Garvin Died of Heart Failure While Practicing With Schoolmates**
> A great pall of sadness was cast over the entire City early Tuesday afternoon when it was learned that Guy Garvin, the 15 year old son of Mrs. Lulu Burch [*sic*], had died of heart failure while out practicing with schoolmates on the track field at the City Park. . . . He made a few *runs* around the track when he fell, as if fainting. . . . The body was carried to Dr. Ivy's office but it was too late to do anything to revive him. Dr. Ivy and Dr. Dolph Montgomery pronounced death due to heart failure.
>
> The boy's mother was prostrated when news reached her of the son's death. It was so sudden and shocking that it was hardly believable by anyone. Guy was the very picture of health and a good athlete for a boy of his age. He has been an active outdoors boy all his life. He was one of the leading Boy Scouts of the town, and it was nothing unusual to see him with a patrol of scouts doing service of some kind or going out for a hike. . . . He was a manly young fellow much loved by his playmates who idolized him for his kindness and freeheartedness. . . .
>
> Interment was in the Marlow Cemetery.

Lula claimed she immediately arrived at the track field, where she saw the boys trying to revive Guy. Ambulance services were not yet a civic standard, and in order to move Guy to a source of transportation for medical care, she ran onto the field and lifted him onto her back, a remarkable act of strength for a woman only five feet tall. According to Lula's account, she toted Guy to the edge of the field by herself before others joined in. While Guy was likely dead instantly from unrecognized cardiac anomalies, the pronouncement of death did not occur until he had been taken to the doctor's office.

The Garvin family plot in the Marlow cemetery was filling up quickly. We have the graves of Walter, Glenn, Guy, and other Garvins as well. G. T. Garvin and wife Nancy are there, the much older half-brother and sister-in-law to Walter. And then there is the mysterious Roy, a contemporary of Walter whom I assumed, at first, to have been Walter's brother. But it was not so.

Roy was one of the many offspring of family patriarch James Robert Garvin, Sr., rancher from nearby Bray. A side trip in my research led to the discovery that Roy had murdered the husband of his cousin Della in cold blood in 1920, leaving Della widowed with eight children. Roy was released from custody in 1921 after a hung jury and minimal prison time, allegedly through paternal influence. The next time he saw Della (daughter of G. T. and Nancy Garvin), Roy was sitting on a Marlow sidewalk, along with his influential father. With a smirk, he said, "Oh, hello, Della." In response, Della pulled out a six-shooter and emptied it with abandon, the fatal bullet being the one that entered above Roy's right eye. Justice was swift. Jurisprudence was ancient. Della was acquitted under the age-old precedent of an eye for an eye.

One more tombstone is worth mentioning in this sad, but colorful, Garvin family plot in Marlow. This grave may, in fact, contain two bodies. Lula's younger sister Fannie Combs Teel (dead at thirty-one), who died by her own hand while attempting self-abortion, is buried with the Garvins, the only Combs in this particular plot. Fannie, who was so concerned about the gray squirrel in the tornado of 1896, died on December 2, 1921, less than two years after Guy's death.

What agony Lula must have felt packed into this little parcel of land—a husband, a two-year-old son, a fifteen-year-old son, and now a younger sister, not to mention the Garvin in-laws. At the time of Fannie's death, Lula was thirty-seven years old, and she must have been exhausted.

Recalling the biblical Job and his replacement family, Lula's only hope for happiness must have resided in her new husband and her dreams for a new family. Standing graveside at Fannie's interment, Lula was accompanied by her second husband and shining knight, Albert Berch. And the new family was on the way. As she stared at the dirt clods being tossed onto the casket of her younger sister, Lucinda Jane "Lula" Combs Garvin Berch was seven months pregnant with Almarian.

Fifty years later, Almarian would trace the Combs lineage back through the centuries, but she would have no such luck identifying her father's roots. And without a window through which to scrutinize the formative years in Albert's life, one cannot ask the bigger question: why? Why would *you*, Albert Berch, violate a social taboo so powerful as to put your own life, plus the lives of your family, at risk?

Throughout decades of research, my mother's "Berch" files would grow full, but only with dead ends—letters of inquiry to every imaginable source, with "no record of Albert Berch" in response. Her fruitless efforts occurred in the days when snail mail was the only option, today often replaced by a click of the mouse. And as I discovered in the end, it will be the mouse that roars.

7

Albert Berch (L. A. to Fargo to Marlow)

In the 1950s, Oklahoma's iconic writing instructor, Foster-Harris, condensed the traditional smorgasbord of thirty-six dramatic plots into three square meals: happy ending, unhappy ending, and the literary plot. Although many authorities then jumped into the fray proposing different narrative groupings, the most simplistic is the binary notion that all stories can be described as "a hero takes a journey" or "a stranger comes to town." While Albert Berch hogs the title of this book, you must have guessed by now that *Killing Albert Berch* should provide equal billing to Lula, a hero on a journey.

As for Albert Berch, historians have pinpointed the date when Jesus Christ was born with more accuracy than it appears at first glance for this stranger. We have plenty of options to choose from, but the range—ten years—is extraordinary. Online ancestry sources, family records, census records, newspaper accounts at the time of his death, and even his tombstone (provided by my mother) all conspire to keep us in the dark. Why?

In my youth, my sisters and I were advised *never* to ask our grandmother Lula her age. Our mother revealed at the time, to my shock, that even she (my mother) did not know Lula's true age. Lula never had a driver's license. She took the train and rode the bus. Eventually, the truth about Lula came out (born June 3, 1884), and the correct date is on her tombstone. But why all the secrecy, and why are the dates on Albert's tombstone incorrect?

As I heard the story of Albert Berch from my mother through many wash and rinse cycles, I recall Almarian stating that Albert was much younger than Lula (ten years stuck in my childhood mind), possibly explaining why Lula kept her age a secret. Albert's current tombstone claims his birthdate as October 6, 1884 (the same birth year as Lula), but keep in mind that it was Almarian who designed and placed this stone after searching for her father's grave in the 1970s. Lula was still alive when the tombstone was engraved, perhaps commandeering the inscription. I never heard the "ten-year" gap mentioned after my childhood.

As it turned out, the ten-year version was very close to the truth. Newspaper accounts of the murders stated that Albert Berch was thirty-five or thirty-six or thirty-nine when he died; however, this information was likely provided by the widow Lula, who was thirty-nine at the time. In contrast, a popular online genealogy resource lists Albert Weldon Berch, Jr., as born in 1894 in San Diego, ten years later than his tombstone indicates. Additionally, the 1900 U.S. Census lists the six-year-old Albert Berch as a resident in an orphanage in Fargo, North Dakota—a fact known to our family, confirming this is the correct Albert Berch out of many possibilities that arise through an online search.

Time out for a brief discussion on how our family spells the name "Berch." The various spellings of *Berch, Birch,* or *Burch*—or even *Bertch, Birtch,* or *Burtch*—created a research challenge both online and in print. And accurate spelling was not a top priority for journalists of the era. Two or more different spellings might appear in the same newspaper article. However, the official spelling here is "Berch," based on key legal documents and, in the end, Albert's own signature.

Finally confirmed through several sources, Albert Weldon Berch was born on October 5, 1893, making his tombstone dead wrong, not to mention online sources being off by one year. He was nine years younger than my grandmother.

Albert Weldon Berch was the son of Albert William Berch, the father's life every bit as enigmatic as the son's. The senior Berch moved to Marlow with the birth of Almarian in 1922, several years after his son. Other than her father-in-law, Lula barely knew the extended Berch family. Her bits and pieces led our mother down many research rabbit trails starting in the 1970s, and confusion persisted when I joined the scramble decades later.

With ample documentation through birth, wedding, and death certificates, understanding that facts could easily be fudged in the olden days, here is the presumptive truth. Dr. Albert William Berch (called *Albert Senior* here to distinguish him from son Albert *Weldon* Berch) was born March 15, 1866, in Racine, Wisconsin. On June 3, 1893, he married Emma Minerva Robinson, originally from Oregon, though both husband and wife were residing near San Diego at the time. Albert Senior was twenty-seven. Emma was seventeen . . . and pregnant.

Although age seventeen appears on the marriage license, one

*Lula and her new baby, Almarian, standing in
front of Johnson's Hotel and its popular café*

online source claims Emma was only fourteen. Regardless, I have a
supplementary document to the marriage license signed by her mother
that grants permission for Emma to marry. Four months into the
marriage, my teenage great-grandmother gave birth to Albert Weldon
Berch. She died seventeen months later on March 27, 1895, an eternal
teenager, nineteen years old at most. We do not know the cause of death.

Another "fact" we knew in our childhood about Albert Berch, besides
him being "a barber from Los Angeles," was that he had been raised by a
wealthy relative named "Aunt Helen." For some reason, I assumed this
was an aunt so distant, probably through marriage, that I didn't need to
clutter my brain with her story.

In late life, at age eighty-one, Lula logged this information about her
second husband:

> Albert Berch was given to his Aunt Helen when his mother was dying
> just after he was borned. She was very wealthy, had no children of her

own. He was schooled in a military academy. His Aunt Helen's name was Basye. She had one brother, Ned Basye. She married O. J. DeLendrecie, a full blood Frenchman. . . . Aunt Helen also had one sister died with cancer. . . . Albert Weldon Berch was borned in Pasadena, California, Oct 6, 1884, died Dec 17th, 1920 [the day is correct, but the year was 1923], age 39 years, 2 months, 11 days. Funeral Methodist Church conducted by N. U. Stout, Ku Klux Klan.

Lula's lifelong effort to maintain the concocted age of her husband Albert is fascinating, as if the exact number of days recorded for his age might nullify the nine-year blunder on his birth year (1893). The punchline at the end—*Ku Klux Klan*—will be delivered again as the story unfolds. But one correct detail among the errors, critical for both my mother's research and mine, was Aunt Helen's maiden name—Basye. This would hold the key to connecting the Berch and DeLendrecie families, a critical union in the final understanding of this saga.

Returning to Albert Senior, his brief bio in the 1892 Voting Register of San Diego County lists him as a "rancher," age twenty-six, living in the Santa Maria Valley near today's Ramona, thirty-seven miles northeast of San Diego. In contrast to Lula's assertion of "Pasadena" noted above, this is very likely where Albert Junior was born in 1893, though no birth certificate has ever been found. We have but a single photograph of Albert Senior, standing with baby Almarian in front of the café sign at the Johnson's Hotel. His face is lost in shadow, so the only available description comes from this voting registry: five feet nine and a half inches, dark complexion, brown hair, brown eyes.

In researching Albert Senior's life, I drove to the Ramona area, and while my trip yielded no trace of his existence there, one bizarre coincidence occurred in my motel room the night before. I was watching a PBS documentary on the Underground Railroad, and a photograph popped up for a few seconds, incriminating two armed men as slave trackers, with a young African-American female seated between them. One of the men has a pistol pointed directly at the head of the girl. Incredibly, that man is my great-great-grandfather, Jesse Berch, father to the man I was planning to track the next morning.

One can easily imagine how I considered poltergeists as infesting the ancient analog TV. I had only discovered this photo myself a few months before its spooky television debut, housed in the Library of Congress catalog. Two things in the 1862 portrait shout, "What's wrong with this picture?" The first is the fact that the young woman is dressed in her Sunday best. The second is the fact that the other man is also pointing a gun at the same angle as my ancestor, but away from the girl. These are not slave trackers, and the story behind this photo will crack the code to explain why Albert Junior did what he did in Marlow.

After Emma's death, Albert Senior's trail is temporarily lost. Although Lula stated that her husband, as a young boy, "was given to" Aunt Helen to raise, the Los Angeles connection was based on Helen's vacation home at the time, as her primary residence was in Fargo, North Dakota.

Aunt Helen's husband, O. J., founded the landmark DeLendrecie's Department Store in Fargo, North Dakota, the city where the couple kept their principal residence until 1914, when they retired to their home in Los Angeles. The original building for the department store still stands, now on the U.S. National Register of Historic Places and renovated as a commercial complex anchored by Block Six Apartments.

Onesine Joassin DeLendrecie, a French-Canadian, arrived in Fargo in 1879 and opened the Chicago Dry Goods House, then built his famous emporium in 1894, originally called "deLendrecie's Mammoth Department Store." In 1897, he was one of the founders of Fargo National Bank, and in 1898, O. J. and a partner opened another Fargo landmark, the Waldorf Hotel, located across the street from the department store.

We cannot pinpoint Al Junior's location until 1900 when, at age six, he appears in the aforementioned U.S. Census records as a resident of an orphanage in Fargo, along with fifty-six others. At this point in time, Albert Senior is missing to history. Was Albert Junior a problem child, prompting his location oh so close, but oh so far, from the actual DeLendrecie household in Fargo? Or did Aunt Helen choose to keep her distance from the shady Albert Senior by distancing Albert Junior? Or was it simply that the DeLendrecie household was already full? Census records indicate ten people living in the DeLendrecie home in Fargo at the time Albert was in the orphanage, none of whom were children of O. J. and Helen, mostly relatives.

Opened by the Presentation Sisters on September 8, 1897, St. Johns Orphanage, for whatever reason, became the home of six-year-old Albert Weldon Berch. In the search for her roots, Almarian made the trek to Fargo in the 1970s only to learn that the original wood-frame building burned in 1907 and all records had been destroyed. From everything we can tell, though, Aunt Helen maintained a high degree of vigilance over Albert Junior throughout his entire life. And that will bring us back time and again to Aunt Helen.

Given O. J. DeLendrecie's success in business, he was catapulted into the role of a city father. He moved into the national limelight, where he served as vice chairman of the Democratic National Committee during Pres. Grover Cleveland's second term. In 1905, O. J. made headlines again when he purchased the Maltese Cross Ranch, the former property of the sitting president of the United States, Theodore Roosevelt. The president often stated that his transformative years took place on his North Dakota property.

Helen was quite the activist in her own right. In fact, she also purchased land previously owned by Teddy Roosevelt, demonstrating a measure of matrimonial independence that was rare for those times. In *Gateway to the Northern Plains: Railroads and the Birth of Fargo and Moorhead* (University of Minnesota Press, 2007), Carroll Engelhardt describes Helen DeLendrecie as the "suffragette wife" of O. J., who stood tall in the saddle of Fargo, accepting the destitute or orphaned, placing them for adoption, and serving on the school board.

And in her cause to garner the right to vote for women, Helen traveled to Washington, D.C. for the 1898 national suffrage convention. When prominent suffragette Laura M. Johns arrived as keynote speaker to the convention in Grand Forks, Helen was chosen to deliver the response. As more and more historical documents are scanned and placed online, it becomes increasingly apparent that Helen was North Dakota's most active suffragette. She was elected secretary of the Equal Suffrage Association of North Dakota, and she landed its headquarters in the DeLendrecie building.

Helen's influence is rather remarkable for a woman of that era, and she seems to have had her fingers in "everything Fargo." For instance, a newspaper account from Williston, a town across the state from Fargo, reflects her involvement in a brouhaha with the Fargo City Council, where the male members proposed that the police arrest all women who walked a certain street in Fargo on the presumption that they must be prostitutes. Apparently, Helen lowered the boom on the council for their self-righteousness, such that the Williston newspaper stated, "Every honorable man and right-minded woman in the land will heartily join with Helen De Lendrecie in crying, 'Shame, gentlemen, shame.'"

Aunt Helen's religious preference is not clearly stated in any of my sources. In one document, "religion" was requested, but Helen left it blank. A 2012 article in the *Bismarck Tribune* noted that she was "president of the Civic Improvement League and helped raise funds to establish the Unitarian Church in Fargo." Our family folklore held that she was a devout Catholic, a point of later importance. O. J. was, in fact, an active Catholic and helped lay the cathedral cornerstone at Broadway and Sixth Avenue North in November 1891.

When I discovered the missing link that clarified the Berch-DeLendrecie connection, to be covered later, I was elated to the point that I sent emails to family and friends, who had no idea what I was talking about. And then, a few months later, in a skinny file from my mother's research that I had missed in my first run-through, it turned out that Almarian had, indeed, made the connection in her later years, along with the explanation for the "-marian" part of her name. Lula had been foggy about the origins of "-marian" and how we were related to the DeLendrecies. And the question is raised again—how much did Lula know about her husband Albert Berch?

"Aunt Helen" is the only name my sisters and I heard growing up, a woman of critical benevolence for our family, even though we never met her. No wonder: she was buried decades before we were born, resting in peace at Hollywood Forever Cemetery since 1926 in the Cathedral Mausoleum. Even if she did not live as a Catholic, she was interred as one. The cemetery, known then as Hollywood Memorial Park, was the final resting place for many of the stars of early Hollywood, including Rudolph Valentino. He died one month after Aunt Helen, his crypt only a few steps away from Helen and O. J.'s, also in the Cathedral Mausoleum. Thus, Valentino's Ladies in Black have been passing by Aunt Helen's crypt every year since.

Helen died three years after the murder of Albert Berch, and one would wonder whether or not our mother, born in 1922, ever met her. To our mother's memory, the answer was no. However, Aunt Helen would indeed cast her eyes on a young Almarian, enough to alter her life and those of the Hollingsworth children in the cascade that followed the murder of Albert Berch. And yet, until I began work on this book, I did not know Aunt Helen's last name.

As part of her 1970s research, Almarian attempted a pilgrimage to the final DeLendrecie home in Los Angeles. With an address on Kingsley Drive in hand, she journeyed to L.A., only to discover rows of condominiums south of Wilshire, between Normandie and Western. I made the very same trip, albeit via Google Street View, and it only took a few clicks and a few minutes.

I picked up Albert Senior's trail again in the Wisconsin Census of 1905. He had remarried—he thirty-nine, Sarah thirty-four—and Albert

Weldon Berch was eleven, living at home once again. By this time, Albert Senior is no longer a rancher but a doctor. He lists his profession on the census as "Osteopathy," confirming my grandmother's claim that he was a doctor of some sort but "not an M.D."

We do not have evidence that Albert Senior completed his studies in osteopathy, a new discipline at the time. Keep in mind that even the MD degree didn't assure quality education in those days, but this was an era before DOs were fully accepted as medical practitioners in the legal sense, a time when osteopathy believed that nearly all illnesses were related to aberrations in the ropes and pulleys of our bodies.

The information from this census added new geography to our family's history and opened new doors. Albert Senior's parents are listed as being from Wisconsin, Albert's birthplace is Wisconsin, and Sarah was born in Wisconsin.

My grandmother Lula had nothing good to say about the man who became her father-in-law. There is no evidence for this in her written record, but there was plenty of oral history. Albert Senior was "no good, probably a drug addict, not even a real doctor." By my mother's version of Lula's account, "he probably didn't go to medical school, maybe osteopathic school, or maybe he was a dentist who decided to practice medicine instead, but likely alcoholic, and certainly practicing beyond his training . . . mother never seemed to know the details."

After another huge gap in the Berch historical record, Albert Junior showed up in Marlow, Oklahoma, in late 1919 or early 1920, his vocation as a barber confirmed in the local newspaper. As for Albert Senior, he entered the stage at Marlow two years after his son's arrival, presumably in anticipation of the birth of his first and only grandchild, Almarian, the calendar clamoring to make that association.

Albert Senior arrived, however, sans Sarah, and we have no information about her fate, be it death, divorce, or simple departure. Dr. Berch's intent was to launch his medical practice from Johnson's Hotel, the "hotel office" being a rather common arrangement at the time, both for itinerant celebrity doctors making brief appearances as well as permanent medical offices. Our family archives reveal that a primary investor in the hotel was Aunt Helen, who, to our knowledge, never set foot in Marlow. This did not prevent her from writing Albert Junior to make sure that Dr. Berch located his practice anywhere except within the walls of Johnson's Hotel. No explanation was offered, and Albert Junior obliged. Dr. Berch was, however, allowed to live at Johnson's Hotel.

We have a studio portrait of Albert Weldon Berch taken shortly before his murder. This was the only photograph my sisters and I knew to exist, and it is this likeness we viewed in our family home, fixed in a double frame along with Lula's "flapper" photo, located close to our mother's reading chair. The serenity of Albert's face in that portrait haunted me even as a child, where at some level, I understood that catastrophe can strike in a single second.

We must ask ourselves, of course, if Albert was an opportunist, latching onto ownership of Johnson's Hotel by marrying the widowed Lula. As living descendants of Lula, we want romantic explanations at the core, and we want it even if our grandmother was a "cougar" in today's parlance. A steamy answer will come later, but for now, consider this: of Lula's three husbands, she was married to the first for nearly twenty years, the third for twenty years, while Albert Berch was her husband for only four years. Lula chose to be buried with Albert Berch.

We have to consider, too, that in 1963 Lula prepaid a crypt on the ground floor at Rose Hill Burial Park and Mausoleum in Oklahoma City, where she had planned eternal rest *by herself*—until her daughter concocted the Marlow plan. But indulge me a touch of romanticism. In spite of Lula's vow never to set foot in Marlow again after the murders, her remains are with Albert Berch in Marlow soil, along with their only child.

Almarian Berch, born only ten paces away from the spot where her father would be murdered, spent much of her eighty-nine years trying to understand what had led to the tragedy on December 17, 1923. In the end, she didn't know much more than the twenty-two-month-old toddler who had wailed by her father's side as he lay dying. After all those years, Albert Berch remained little more than a stranger who came to town.

8

From Zeitgeist to Kyklos

The killers of Albert Berch and Robert Johnigan had an accomplice, a force without shape or form but an agent that, in its absence, might have allowed both men to live long and fruitful lives. This accessory, exerting a shadowy influence on the murderers, was the spirit of the times.

Whether it's Babe Ruth starting his tenure with the Yankees, or Rin Tin Tin saving Hollywood, or flappers and speakeasies, the Roaring Twenties have become so stereotyped that it's hard to imagine a zeitgeist that is anything but carefree fun. Bobbed hair and short skirts, bootleggers profiting from Prohibition, and a stock market on a wild streak all combine to give us the impression today that prosperity and joy permeated the decade. But did it really?

In Oklahoma, prohibition was written into the 1907 constitution, rendering the Eighteenth Amendment redundant in 1919. Bootlegging and its spinoff crimes were already rampant, and it would be a difficult call to say whether state revenues were greater from nature's oil or from manmade alcohol.

In Washington, D.C., the decade began with Woodrow Wilson in office until 1921, followed by Warren G. Harding, whose sudden death tossed the baton to Calvin Coolidge in 1923. Coolidge reigned silently for most of the decade, handing the hot potato to Herbert Hoover in the nick of time. One brief note about the Great Depression and the Dust Bowl: in all of Lula's many documents, she does not make a single reference to either of these events, possibly reflecting the fact that her difficult life stayed the same course, be it rain or shine, dust or no dust.

To borrow from Wall Street's binary worldview—greed balanced by fear—we can look at the Roaring Twenties either from its lighter side based on greed or its dark side based on fear. As we approach the murders in Marlow, it will be fear that dominates.

Returning to 1918, when Lula bought the hotel, World War I had recently come to an end, so jubilation would have been expected as the prevailing sentiment. Yet, patriotism was still peaking with the late entry of the U.S., so when postwar negotiations deteriorated at Versailles and then the League of Nations flopped, the horrors of the Great War didn't seem so easily justified.

The 1918 Spanish flu pandemic added to the disillusionment. While the newspapers and magazines minimized the first wave of deaths due to influenza to keep up war morale, the deadlier second wave peaked at the end of the war. Then the third wave killed millions more after the war, testing the faith of those in the U.S. who believed that Providence should have spared the Guardians of Democracy.

Then, a nexus of events led to a widespread thirst for "true Americanism," the definition of which originated with "nativists" (not Native Americans, but the nativists who conquered the natives). Before passing judgment on this "true Americanism," keep in mind that some of the fears originated from valid provocations, much in the way current fears were altered by 9/11.

The Bolshevik revolution of 1917 introduced a whole new way of thinking about socioeconomic structure, and proponents in the U.S. openly claimed that America should follow in Russia's footsteps. Overlapping philosophies thrived, including those of socialists, radical labor organizations, anarchists, and—if such a thing exists—nihilists. These ideas were largely attributed to intellectuals, many of them Jewish, immigrating to the United States from eastern and southern Europe. Anti-immigration and anti-Semitism were thusly linked.

Fear wasn't limited to anarchists and their penchant for bombings. Anti-Catholicism reached its peak at the same time. The postwar "true American" movement resurrected the belief that Catholics intended to assume control of the country, starting with local governments and eventually handing the booty to their king in Rome.

Declining morality was also a concern, and the same voices that prompted Prohibition added their chorus to this new "Americanism." For many, it was the end times, and a great call came forth for a return to Victorian standards.

Historically, African-Americans had been the scapegoat for many of society's ills. So when some black leaders aligned themselves with socialism or communism, a double dose of angst fed the fever of hate in many whites. Lynchings became commonplace. Race riots broke out across the country. In the 1920s, these events caused whites and blacks to draw deeper lines in the sand.

Aspiring politicians saw an opportunity to turn the many "anti" sentiments into one pure goal—the "true American." Fire from many Protestant pulpits added to the rising frustration. But no one came close to the impact of one "Colonel" William J. Simmons, who packaged hate through a scheme that capitalized on mankind's love of secret organizations, especially when the secrecy is adorned with rituals, robes, and a cryptic lexicon.

William J. Simmons was a minister in the Methodist Episcopal Church, first in Florida, then Alabama. He dropped his higher calling in 1912 to become a "fraternal organizer," most notably in the Woodmen of the World (WOW). There he obtained his rank as "colonel," his preferred manner of address, having been only a "private" in the Spanish-American War. WOW at the time was a combination fraternal organization and insurance company, with a peculiar perk for its members: a tombstone shaped like a tree stump. (The iconic stump still marks Walter Garvin's grave.) In this era prior to social security or disability, the insurance offerings were attractive, not to mention the brotherhood tossed in as a bonus.

Simmons earned twenty-three degrees in at least seven fraternal orders. While recuperating in an Atlanta hospital from an automobile accident, he had a vision to establish a new fraternal organization, based on the romanticized version of the original Ku Klux Klan, which had formed post-Civil War with a single agenda item—to block Reconstruction. Many Southerners considered the original Klan to be the ultimate savior of the South, at a time when carpetbaggers, scalawags, and "uppity Negroes" appeared to threaten white supremacy.

Confederate veterans founded the KKK in 1865 in Pulaski, Tennessee, before the ink was dry from the signing at Appomattox. It was originally known as the KuKlux Clan, the word "KuKlux" probably borrowed from the Greek *kyklos,* plural for "circle." Details of the founding vary, but six veterans from the South are thought to have organized the Klan, led by the first Grand Wizard, the colorful Confederate general Nathan Bedford Forrest. Most accounts indicate that General Forrest left the Klan several years later, once it became apparent that it had become a terrorist organization. But the historians will have to sort this out, as Forrest was not beyond war crimes himself, assassinating both white and black prisoners during the Civil War, to name one penchant.

Lynching became a staple of the Klan diet, targeting blacks as well as sympathetic whites. A "lynching" is to be distinguished from a "hanging," the former being violence without due process, the latter being the same thing after due process. Not all vigilante deaths were by hanging. But regardless of the methodology, if perpetrators came under scrutiny, all-white juries rarely indicted Klan members, either out of silent sympathy or fear of reprisal from local Klansmen.

The original Ku Klux Klan shrank to insignificance when Reconstruction ended in 1877 with the withdrawal of federal troops. That's the good news. The bad news is that the Klan's goal was then accomplished through the passage of Jim Crow laws and the rise of other groups operating outside the law.

The memory of the original KKK, though, was still fresh in 1915 when "Colonel" Simmons had his epiphany. In fact, a few elderly enrollees had been members of the First Klan, while others were the sons or grandsons of original Klan members. Nearly forty years had passed since the demise of the First Klan, its tactics mostly forgotten and its purpose romanticized by many Southerners.

On Thanksgiving Day in 1915, "Colonel" Simmons and a group of early converts gathered on Stone Mountain, outside the city of Atlanta. They burned a makeshift cross, proclaiming a new organization, chartered by the state of Georgia as "The Invisible Empire, Knights of the Ku Klux Klan, Inc."

A few weeks after this first cross-burning by the Klan 2.0, D. W. Griffith's groundbreaking, epic silent film, *The Birth of a Nation*, was shown in Atlanta for the first time. Simmons surely knew the content of the film and timed his cross-burning accordingly, as the movie had actually premiered ten months earlier. A "fraternal organizer" could not have asked for a better recruiting tool, for the film depicts Klan members as though they were the Jedi Knights of *Star Wars*, saviors of the cosmos. It has been alleged that *The Birth of a Nation* is still used for recruitment into the KKK, but today's Klan is not a single organization as before.

While the movie is sometimes presented as a cinematic masterpiece that incidentally lulled an entire nation into sympathy with the Klan, this is not the case. Several cities banned the movie from the get-go for its overt racism, even in an era when, by today's standards, the overwhelming majority of the population was racist.

The film was treated as a special event in Marlow and Duncan, where it took more than two years to arrange a showing. The *Marlow Review* reported on December 13, 1917:

Mr. Frank Miller, manager of the Pastime Theatre [in Duncan] has announced to the patrons of his show house that he has completed all arrangements for showing of D. W. Griffith's famous and historical photoplay, "The Birth of the [sic] Nation." There is very little to say, in praising Mr. Griffith's great picture, as it has been shown all over the country and has made far the biggest hit of the ages. The theme is derived from Thomas Dixon's famous book on the Civil War and Reconstruction in the Southland, "The Clansman." It will be shown only twice, afternoon and night. The admission for the afternoon performance will be 50 cents and the night show will be a dollar. Special music will be played throughout both performances.

The Birth of a Nation boosted membership in the Klan, but the organization's growth subsequently lagged. Charles A. Alexander, in his book, *The Ku Klux Klan in the Southwest* (1965; repr.: University of Oklahoma Press, 1995), explains that the contagion of the KKK eventually swept the country through a publicity firm in Atlanta that struck a remarkable deal wherein 80 percent of the ten-dollar initiation fee went to their promotional efforts. In Simmons' words, "They made things hum all over America."

Journalists began writing articles exposing the Klan as an un-American racket. Most notably, the *New York World* ran a twenty-article exposé in 1921, and other newspapers followed with their own series. But the national coverage actually resulted in a windfall in membership. Some new recruits simply cut their applications out of the newspapers that had printed them for the purpose of exposing the Klan.

And then, just when one might have hoped for the Klan to die a natural death, the U.S. House of Representatives held hearings on the organization, prodded by concerned constituents. "Colonel" Simmons and other charismatic speakers appeared before the House Rules Committee and heightened the image of the Klan as a defender of the American Way. Congress ended its inquiry without specific recommendations. Many interpreted this as a silent endorsement, whereupon membership accelerated to frenzy, at the rate of 5,000 new enlistments a day.

In spite of attempts to label the organization as "backwoods Southerners," the membership included doctors, lawyers, bankers, businessmen, judges, politicians, and preachers. Two-thirds of the Klan speakers bureau was composed of Protestant ministers. Although membership was meant to be secret, politicians on the demagogue ticket openly boasted of their Klan alliance. Some members ended up in their state's governor's mansion as well as the U.S. Congress. Some statehouses were thought to be controlled by the Klan, or by sympathizers at least. And when it came to geography, the Klan was organized in every state.

The growth of the KKK was beyond exponential; it was parabolic, with 1 million new members in 1923 alone, the peak year for the Klan. Total membership by that time had likely reached 5 million. It is estimated that, at its peak, 20 percent of the adult male population in the U.S. belonged to the KKK. Indiana had the dubious distinction of the highest percentage (30 percent), electing a Klan member as governor in 1924. Being a pro-family organization, the KKK spawned auxiliaries for the wives, and a children's division as well, with white robes and pointy hats for the ladies and kids.

Historical graphs charting the growth of this Second Klan hit the zenith around the time of the Marlow murders. Yet, rather abruptly, this version of the Klan died out, with membership dropping to 30,000 by 1930. Much as occurred with the First Klan, internal dissention was compounded by backlash due to the negative press that covered the terrorists within. Whether or not the Second Klan disappeared entirely is unknown, but membership in the revived splinter groups today is thought to number only 5,000.

The anti-Negro, anti-Jew, anti-Catholic, anti-immigrant, and pro-morality agendas appealed to many. Some, of course, joined for the secret brotherhood and ritual, and perhaps an interest in one or two items on the hate list, ignoring the other agendas. At first, most new members were not exposed to acts of terrorism within their own membership. It was only after an enthusiastic recruit showed promise and was cleared for the "Third Order" that he could participate in the whippings and killings.

In spite of its apparent cohesiveness, the national organization was highly fragmented. Propaganda came down from on high, but the functional unit of the Klan was the Klavern, the group organized by a city or town and its environs. Each Klavern had its own priorities and procedural traditions, to the point that the KKK even at the state level was not an effective umbrella.

Specific to Oklahoma, race relations were comparable to those in states that had been in the Confederacy, even though statehood came nearly fifty years after the Civil War. Lynchings in the early 1900s targeted blacks more and more, largely due to the influx of white settlers from the Confederate states into what had been Indian Territory in the southeast part of Oklahoma. Although estimates vary widely, approximately forty lynchings took place in Oklahoma between 1907 and 1930. Perusing newspapers of that era via microfilm, one is struck by the number of lynchings throughout the region, covered in the news with remarkable equanimity.

In 1920, Gov. J. B. A. Robertson held an Inter-racial Conference to address the issues of lynching, civil rights, and education. Nothing changed, and in 1921, Oklahoma would host what many call the worst race riot in U.S. history. Despite the significance of the Tulsa race riot, I never heard of it during my school years in Oklahoma. I was not alone; few had. The story was not included in the state history books in our schools. No one seemed to talk about it. Then, in 1997, the legislature formed a commission to study the riots, issuing their final report in 2001. A landslide of interest followed, with books, magazine articles, and websites educating Oklahomans about their whitewashed past.

In spite of these stories of racism, some historians maintain that the motivation for many, if not most, Oklahomans to join the KKK was the group's condemnation of moral violators—bootleggers, gamblers, prostitutes, and unfaithful husbands, even if the unlawful were wayward Protestants. After all, there were not many Jews or Catholics in the state, and many towns were all white anyway.

The first mention of the KKK in the *Marlow Review* came shortly after the Tulsa race riot, in July 1921. The topic was the 100th anniversary of the birth of Gen. Nathan Bedford Forrest, covered by the newspaper as an event that would be celebrated throughout the South. An article one month later in the Marlow newspaper addressed possible corruption in the new Klan, with accusations that Imperial Wizard William Simmons had purchased his home with Klan monies. Simmons denied this vehemently, stating that if he were proved a liar, he would slit his own throat.

After the Simmons article, the Marlow newspaper coverage of the Klan accelerated, but without editorial comment, simply relating events. For instance, readers learned that the Klan in Shawnee, Oklahoma, had issued a dictum that "all women of questionable character in the Third Ward" should vacate. One man was whipped after consorting with said women, and "the pulpit and newspapers of that city are backing up the Ku Klux in their effort to rid the city of all undesirables."

The stories move closer to Marlow. "A Negro is Victim of Klansmen" tells of a whipping of a black man in Duncan because "the negro had unfairly whipped a 2-year-old child." This article begins, "All doubts as to there really being a chapter of the Ku Klux Klan in Duncan were dispelled last night. . . . " A follow-up story quoted from the *Duncan Eagle* newspaper, "Rev. Frank Beach, pastor of the Christian Church, while he did not endorse or condemn the Ku-Klux as an organization, did strongly endorse their tenets in his sermon."

The admission that the Klan had officially arrived in Marlow came in a headline on December 1, 1921: "Ku Klux Klan Active in Marlow." A rambling subtitle added, "Wm. Ard is the First Victim of the Ku Klux Klan—Was Captured by Robed Figures and Carried to Secluded Spot Where a Lecture and Whipping is Said to Have Been Administered." This punishment was carried out due to Mr. Ard having been cruel to his wife and adopted children. The newspaper elaborated that Marlow citizens were divided about the new organization, although the general sentiment "on the streets" seemed to favor the Klan.

In 1921, a beloved minister of the Methodists, Rev. N. U. Stout, returned to Marlow as pastor. Accolades appeared in the *Marlow Review*'s November 10 edition: "Brother Stout has endeared himself to his congregation and his friends by his very pleasing personality and his untiring efforts in behalf of all that is good in religion and church work."

On December 22, 1921, the local headline stated, "Marlow Klan Donates $100 to Poor Children." The subtitle told the story: "*Review* Editor Receives $100 in Currency With Instruction to Deliver Same to Ministerial Alliance With Request That it be Used to Bring Cheer to Poor Children of the City."

The money was accompanied by this letter:

> We, the Knights of the Ku Klux Klan of Marlow, Okla., believing in the tenets of the Christian religion and that it is more blessed to give than to receive, ask that you hand the enclosed sum of money to the Ministerial Alliance of Marlow to be used in bringing cheer to the poor children of the city this Christmas. A part of our creed is 100 per cent Americanism; upholding the constitution of the United States; law and order, pure womanhood, and the care of the poor children of America. Please comply with our request, at your earliest convenience. Signed—Knights of the Ku Klux Klan of Marlow.

The *Review* editor, Jim Nance, in passive compliance with the request, delivered the money to Rev. N. U. Stout, secretary of the Ministerial Alliance.

Notably, prayers opened and closed all Klan meetings, hymns were sung, and every Klan had an official chaplain, the Kludd, who guided religious ceremonies at each meeting. Grand Dragon N. Clay Jewett's goal for the Oklahoma Klan was to make sure that each Kludd was an ordained minister.

The Klan was careful to perform public acts of charity and to involve itself in civic activities and politics. The morality issue played well for all strata of society, resulting in very little class distinction among members of the Klan. "Klannishness" was a virtue. Trading business and political favors among members was the norm. White sympathizers to racial equality were considered un-American, and these "n----- lovers" were to be treated the same as, or *worse* than, blacks.

If extremist members ever got carried away, wherein an act of intimidation ended up with inadvertent murder, then the Klan had a strategy in case judges and prosecuting attorneys were not "Klannish." According to this scheme, the Exalted Cyclops, i.e., president of the local Klavern, would suspend the membership of anyone in the Klan called for jury service so that they could testify honestly, hands on Bibles, that they were *not* Klan members. My source here is Howard A. Tucker's monograph, *History of Governor Walton's War on Ku Klux Klan: The Invisible Empire* (Oklahoma City: Southwest, 1923). I've included this tidbit for background, given my later discovery of a quote from the Exalted Cyclops from Marlow who denied any involvement by members of the Klan in the murders of Albert Berch and Robert Johnigan, or in the due process of the law that followed.

DeBarr Hall, on the North Oval of the University of Oklahoma, was named for Edwin DeBarr, PhD, originally from the University of Michigan. He was one of the most popular professors on OU's original faculty and a vice president of the university. He was also the Grand Dragon of the Oklahoma Realm of the Imperial Knights of the Ku Klux Klan, serving until 1923 when the Board of Regents suggested he might want to bow out of that position.

The Klan in Oklahoma peaked at an estimated 100,000 to 150,000 members in 1923, plummeting to 1,500 by 1930. Some historians pinpoint the month of December as the absolute zenith of Klan membership, the very month of the Marlow murders. At its heyday

The KKK near Drumright, Oklahoma, 1922 (Courtesy of Tulsa Historical Society)

in Oklahoma, an estimated 10 percent of the adult male population joined the Klan, compared to 5 percent for the country as a whole. In August 1922, Klan candidates swept primary elections in both parties, putting the Invisible Empire in control of many county and municipal governments. In *The Ku Klux Klan in the Southwest*, Alexander claims the Klan dominated the Oklahoma legislature in the early 1920s, having thoroughly infiltrated the dominant Democratic party, as well as the Republicans.

Historians struggle to arrive at the truth about individuals and their KKK membership status. Many were Klan sympathizers without ever joining. Others joined early on, until they realized the dark side. Then, anti-Klan forces had a tendency to label all of their opponents as Klan members, while Klan members often boasted, right or wrong, that prominent individuals had been secretly initiated (President Harding, for example).

In Oklahoma, rapid-fire accusations of Klan membership were leveled against any and all political opponents by one of the most colorful characters in state history. This energetic personality, who tried singlehandedly to stop the Oklahoma Klan in its tracks, was the fifth governor of Oklahoma and the first to be impeached and removed: John "Jack" Calloway Walton.

9

King Jack

John "Jack" Calloway Walton was born in Indianapolis, migrating to Oklahoma Territory in 1903 as a contractor in civil engineering, though some sources state more specifically that Walton was a "sewage plant builder" with all the metaphorical trappings therein. He was described, not necessarily by his friends, as "thick set, of medium height, with college-cut brown hair, the rounded, fleshy face of the politician, large protuberant eyes, and a weak mouth."

Walton was impeached and removed from the office of governor less than a year after his term began in January 1923. The impeachment process was not unique for Oklahoma. Before Walton, the state had only four governors, three of them threatened with impeachment by hostile legislatures, while the fourth, J. B. A. Robertson, missed impeachment by a single vote.

Jack Walton was living in Oklahoma City in 1907 at the time of statehood, working his way up as commissioner of Public Works, then mayor of OKC until his election as governor. Originally a Populist, he gravitated to the Democratic Party when the former party's influence waned.

Walton was mostly interested in building alliances that would send him to the governor's chair and beyond. Even his close aides, reflecting on the saga years later, found him to be a bundle of perplexing inconsistencies. Most historians today, however, simply pigeonhole Walton as a prototypical demagogue. But at this time in history, with Klan enrollment mushrooming, it seems the vacancy for chief demagogue would have called for a Klansman. Therefore, this is the question that scholars ask: "How did Walton's only anchored political position evolve as a fight against the Ku Klux Klan?" Most would argue this answer: "Out of desperation, to save his own neck."

In an article written by Scott Cooper for the *Oklahoma Gazette*

Jack C. Walton, fifth governor of Oklahoma (Courtesy of Oklahoma Department of Libraries)

newspaper on September 5, 2007, titled "Klan Clash," Walton is portrayed as the typical charismatic orator with little to back it up, a Huey Long without savvy. Fond of campaigning while surrounded by a party atmosphere, Walton thusly earned one of his several nicknames, "Jazz Band Walton." Oklahoma historian William Savage, Jr., is quoted in the article as saying this about Walton: "He was really a stooge for leftover Socialists from the beginning."

As mayor of OKC, Walton supported the meat packers who went on strike, making him a man of the people. The Farmer-Labor Reconstruction League had a different nickname for Walton, "Our Jack," and they backed him for the 1922 gubernatorial bid. The KKK neither endorsed nor opposed Walton at this point, supporting the current view that Walton's eventual stance was a last-minute life raft to save himself. Certainly, he did not run for office on an anti-Klan platform. Yet, a few early actions in Walton's career suggest an anti-Klan proclivity that, upon his election as a Janus-faced governor, might have been hidden from the Klan-led legislature, where he wanted to make friends.

In his book on Walton, *History of Governor Walton's War on Ku Klux Klan: The Invisible Empire,* written at the time of the events, journalist Howard A. Tucker noted, "Walton opposed the Ku Klux Klan as mayor, and notified members of the police force that no Klansmen would be allowed on the city payroll in his department." Interestingly, Tucker published his book prior to Walton's impeachment, stating on the inside of the cover page: "compiled largely from my personal acquaintance with Governor J. C. Walton, while a newspaper writer, from the time he entered politics in Oklahoma City in 1917 and from sworn testimony taken before the military courts while Oklahoma was under martial law."

In the *Gazette* article, Larry O'Dell, a research specialist with the Oklahoma Historical Society, shared similar views as William Savage, Jr., concerning Walton: "I'm surprised he stood up to the Klan the way he did because he shifted in the wind so much." In fact, when Walton took office, he appointed several Klan members to his administration, including the state health commissioner. But political allies one day can become enemies the next, and soon, charges of corruption began to gather at Walton's feet.

A repeated accusation against Governor Walton was his penchant for granting pardons to criminals on a scale not seen before, with alleged cash payments for the absolution of sins going to his appointees or even himself. The numbers were impressive. By the fall of 1923, more than

250 pardons had been granted, though some of these were commuted sentences from death row to life in prison, considered by enemies of Walton as full "pardons." Claims were made that Walton was pardoning some criminals before they reached the state penitentiary. As a result of this apparent moral laxity, the Oklahoma Klan became united in its hatred of Jack Walton. Historians believe that whippings and beatings escalated during this period as a "call to justice" in order to counter a wild-eyed governor who had invented his own form of indulgences.

Great uproar also occurred when Walton announced his intent to raise his own $5,000 salary to $12,000, plus a gubernatorial discretionary spending account of $200,000. The former Populist favorite now enjoyed a personal butler, was riding around in a chauffeur-driven limousine, and, to top it off, engineered the purchase of a $48,000 mansion under unusual circumstances involving a loan from a man who would later become Oklahoma's tenth governor, E. W. Marland.

Oil magnate Marland was so intriguing in his own right (marrying his once-adopted daughter, long before Woody Allen was born) that his colorful life spawned the August 6, 2012, announcement of a major motion picture—*The Ends of the Earth*—to star Jennifer Lawrence and backed by the Weinstein Company. Officials with the E. W. Marland Estate Foundation were not so star struck that they couldn't see Hollywood tampering a little too much with the facts, and the Weinstein project went silent. Instead, what emerged was *High Stakes: The Life and Times of E. W. Marland*, a one-hour documentary, coproduced by Scott Swearingen and Steve Herrin, premiering in 2016.

Walton's purchase of the Caldwell mansion in what is now the Heritage Hills section of Oklahoma City would become Article IV of the impeachment hearings. The item failed eighteen to twenty-three, most believing that this particular charge collapsed only due to the power and wealth of the future governor, E. W. Marland.

Two months after Walton's ouster, my grandmother, the newly widowed Lula Berch, will be granted her first audience with Jack Walton by "camping out" on the steps of this mansion.

The story of Walton's final downfall is complicated, made more so by conflicting accounts that reflect the vantage point of the particular author. One rich source is a senior thesis submitted to the History Department of Princeton University by John Hunter Montgomery, dated April 11, 1962, in "partial fulfillment of the requirements for the degree of Bachelor of Arts," titled "Oklahoma's Invisible Empire." Written forty years after the fact, and perhaps unbiased, it must deal with the fading memories of those interviewed.

The second reference is more focused on Jack Walton's story, a 287-page manuscript titled, "Oklahoma's Hundred Days," by Aldrich Blake, then of Laguna Beach, California, dated June 12, 1957, and housed at the Oklahoma History Center. Also writing long after the fact, Aldrich Blake was not impartial—as chief advisor to Walton, he was a central character in the story.

Aldrich Blake was a protégé of Thomas Gore (grandfather to Gore Vidal and a distant relative of the Al Gores, Sr. and Jr.). Blake had been campaign manager for Oklahoma senator Thomas Gore in 1920, then became Governor Walton's private secretary. Importantly, Blake was truly anti-Klan, and many believe that he coaxed Walton into his anti-Klan stance as part of his own personal agenda, a skill that wheedling "yes men" have perfected throughout the centuries.

In June 1923, not yet six months into his tenure, Jack Walton imposed martial law in Okmulgee County, sending the National Guard to stop mob violence. Two months later, he did the same in Tulsa, both times allegedly to squelch Klan activity. Yet, it was Walton's suspension of habeas corpus that rankled observers the most, adding to the mutterings for impeachment.

Walton went directly to his public, accusing the KKK of obstructing his efforts against mob violence. He also demanded that Klan members quit wearing masks. His efforts worked, at least temporarily. Newspapers were prompted to investigate alleged atrocities by the Klan, and the hypocritical actions of a "moralizing" group were exposed. Emboldened by his victory, Walton banned all KKK parades and demonstrations. The KKK fought back, reminding the public of Walton's record of pardoning criminals, while allegedly pocketing bribes in the process.

From the 1957 memoir written by chief aide Aldrich Blake, we have these words to consider, along with possible hyperbole:

> Before Walton declared martial law in Tulsa, none of us knew the Klan's numerical strength in Oklahoma. Also unknown to us at the time was the fact that it already controlled most of the judges in the state, possessed a powerful bloc in each branch of the legislature, and that it counted nearly all the prosecuting attorneys, police chiefs, and sheriffs in the state as among its members. The Klan's popular strength lay in the county seat towns and cities. Most of the Protestant ministers had joined. A great

many politicians and businessmen, often just to go along with the crowd, already were in. In addition, thousands of people had been attracted to the Klaverns by sheer morbid curiosity. And, once in, these people did not dare to get out!

Within a few days after Walton suspended the writ of habeas corpus, N. Clay Jewett, the new Grand Dragon of the Oklahoma Klan, emboldened by the widespread denunciation of Walton in the press, announced that Klan parades would be held throughout the state on the night of September 12, 1923. According to Aldrich Blake, Jewett asserted that Walton "never could break the power of the Ku Klux Klan in Oklahoma." Blake also notes that the *Daily Oklahoman*, the primary newspaper in Oklahoma City, was strongly opposed to Walton and that the governor's response to this snubbing was to pledge that someday he would start his own newspaper. (In fact, the *Daily Oklahoman* was both anti-Walton and anti-Klan.)

Blake writes that in a speech at Madill to a "wildly cheering crowd," Walton said, "The unspeakable and damnable outrages accredited to masked bands upon the helpless and defenseless citizenship of Oklahoma have until now gone unpunished. Not a single instance can you find where the culprits have been required to face criminal trial. . . . Ninety percent of the floggings, or midnight tar and feather parties, murders and other beastly and brutal assaults upon both men and women have been done by parties wearing masks."

Then, one can understand how Walton became his own worst enemy as he continued in a soft voice: "No doubt you have read in the stinking newspapers that the Grand Dragon has announced that a lot of Klan parades are going to be held. I have no objection to these parades if no masks are used. Put on your 'hardware,' boys, and the first Klansman you see coming down the street wearing a mask, shoot, and shoot to kill!" The governor paused again as the tense crowd waited for his parting shot: "You know, there is a big difference between being a Grand Dragon and a governor, for it so happens that the governor has pardoning power. If any of *you* kill one of these masked Kluxers, don't bother to write me. Just phone collect, and I'll wire you a pardon!"

Although not confirmed, Aldrich Blake claimed there was never a demonstration of mask-wearing Klan members in Oklahoma after that. This offers one explanation as to why, a few months later, there would be no white robes, no hoods, and no masks worn in the murders of Albert Berch and Robert Johnigan. Then again, we will see that the Marlow massacre, if not a spontaneous combustion of reckless youth, might have been subcontracted with great care to preserve anonymity. Still, the wearing of masks was a major issue nationwide, seemingly a surrogate focus for the whippings and beatings that many observers refused to acknowledge.

In his closing comments at Madill, Walton announced, "I have crossed the Rubicon. It is a fight to the finish. If necessary I shall arm every man in the state who is opposed to the Klan empire. The burden of this fight is falling on me and Aldrich Blake."

Open warfare, including whites battling whites, was anticipated, and the entire nation turned its eyes to Oklahoma. In September 1923, after a grand jury investigated his shady machinations, Governor Walton declared martial law in Oklahoma County, where national guardsmen took control of the police station, city hall, and the county courthouse. Most sources claim that this move, in effect, placed the entire state of Oklahoma under martial law.

Speaker of the House of Representatives was William D. McBee from Stephens County, home to Marlow and Duncan. In a coincidence of geography, when considering the Marlow murders about to unfold, McBee was the chief architect of the plan to stop Jack Walton. Naturally, McBee was labeled "Klan," though Montgomery's 1962 thesis includes interviews with former Klan members who deny McBee was ever a member.

McBee did his own share of documenting the events of the day, writing *The Oklahoma Revolution* (Oklahoma City: Modern, 1956) and serving as an active member of the Oklahoma Historical Society. In the midst of this heightening feud, Walton, in one of his last official acts as governor, squelched a planned KKK march in Stephens County. The legislature was out of session at this point in the crisis, but Speaker McBee ordered an emergency session, and sixty-four members of the House of Representatives arrived in Oklahoma City on September 25, 1923.

In response, the Oklahoma Army National Guard's Forty-Fifth Division leader, Gen. Baird Markham, issued an order "forbidding the gathering of pretended sessions of the legislature to meet in the capitol or anywhere else." At the time, no governor of any state had ever sought to disperse a duly elected legislative body using armed troops. When Speaker McBee tried to organize the group in a federal building, Governor Walton telephoned Pres. Calvin Coolidge, who, in his trademark laconic style, considered options and rendered a summary "no." Governor Walton turned the capitol into an armed encampment, surrounding it with barbed wire and machine-gun nests, with troops stationed to turn legislators away. In essence, Oklahoma was on the brink of a statewide civil war.

A *Daily Oklahoman* headline read as follows, using the archaic term *solons* for the legislators: "Solons Yield to Bayonet Rule." The article stated: "The iron heel of Waltonism, personified by the six-shooter and bayonet, stamped down upon Oklahoma City Wednesday when an armed cordon of national guardsman was thrown around the capitol at daybreak."

Before he was impeached and removed from office, Jack Walton kept his word about starting his own newspaper. Charlie McCloud, a socialist supporter of Walton, began editing and circulating *Jack Walton's Paper,* a weekly that was supported by voluntary contributions to the "Anti-Klan newspaper." McCloud published a tally of Klansmen in the House: at least 67 of the 107 members were Klan, 12 were opposed to both Walton and the Klan, and the remaining 28 supported Governor Walton to some degree.

The petition to pursue impeachment continued, and when the statewide vote was set for October 2, 1923, Governor Walton threatened to use the military to stop it. By one account, he also threatened to retaliate by pardoning all the convicts in the state prison system.

Then, Aldrich Blake conceived a plan that was pure win-win, for his own purposes at least. Walton should resign to avoid the inevitable guillotine about to befall the governor, but with the proviso that Walton's anti-Klan legislation be passed in its entirety.

Walton agreed . . . at first. The next morning, Aldrich Blake discovered in the newspaper that Walton had fired him. Other advisors to the governor had pointed out that, if he followed Blake's advice, instead of becoming the national hero that Blake was envisioning, Walton might end up in jail. Then, Walton swung his axe into the neck of another top advisor, Ernest T. Bynum, prompting the *Daily Oklahoman* to respond with this headline: "Wanted A Goat." The newspaper mocked Walton for firing his two chief aides, and then recommended that King Jack's head should roll, not those of his most loyal subjects.

Impeachment was approved in a landslide vote. On October 23, Jack Walton was suspended. On November 19, he was removed from office, deemed guilty on eleven counts. Blake wrote in his memoirs, "On November 20, 1923, exactly the 100th day of the Klan War—there were both cheers and tears on Oklahoma's political front. The King's head had rolled."

Historians note that Walton's stand against the Klan was largely ineffective during his term. Afterward, however, the legislature considered all of his recommendations, though only the "unmasking" provision made it into law as State Question 123. Aldrich Blake wrote,

"15 of the country's leading metropolitan dailies agreed that Walton had been an incompetent leader in a worthy cause, exactly what Ralph Pulitzer told me in New York."

The conflict had turned the "Invisible Empire" into a highly visible political force, which had an ugly wing of terrorism. Many had been ignorant of this until the light was shone on the organization by a frantic politician whose back was against the wall.

Walton was nearly oblivious to the sentiments against him, it seems. He never gave up on politics, forever branding his opponents as "Klan." He served on the State Corporation Commission and tried to run for governor again in 1934 and 1938. He didn't come close. He practiced law in Oklahoma City, where he died at age sixty-eight, buried in OKC's Rose Hill Burial Park.

An additional reference source for Governor Walton is worth noting—the extensive files generated by my mother, Almarian. Included is a treatise titled, "The Controversial Candidate of the Farmer-Labor Reconstruction League," as "partial fulfillment of the Masters of Arts Degree in Journalism at the University of Oklahoma," signed in 1976 by the chairman of the Graduate Committee, OU professor Jack Bickham.

The "Controversial Candidate" is John Calloway Walton. From Almarian's many files, and drawing upon a faded memory of my own, I believe it was her intent to write a book about Governor Walton. Judging from the labels in those files, her proposed title was to be *King Jack*. In one passage, she throws up her journalistic hands and declares that Walton's "innermost thoughts are an enigma."

One generation earlier, Lula also documented her feelings about Jack Walton. Her bias, given her experience, was so powerful that she never acknowledged that Governor Walton had been removed from office. In contrast to Almarian's highly organized, professional files addressing this puzzling character, Lula's newspaper clippings are pasted randomly into popular magazines that served as backbones for her scrapbooks. She collected Klan articles from any source, any state, any event. And when writing about her encounters with ex-Governor Walton and his subsequent support to be described shortly, she never applied the "ex-" prefix to the word "governor." She believed that Walton would eventually be exonerated and returned to his rightful place on the throne.

Who could argue with Lula's personal slant? As it turned out, King Jack probably saved her life.

10

Seven Defendants Dwindle to Two

Funeral-home directors Garland Smith and J. F. Callaway arrived to pick up the bodies. "Things were really in a mess down there," reported Callaway. The undertakers prepared Berch's body for removal, while local newspapers stated that Robert Johnigan, barely alive, was taken "elsewhere."

Later, in courtroom testimony, Callaway would acknowledge that he had "taken things" from the pockets of Albert Berch, including several long cartridges, and turned them over to a woman he did not know. Incredible as this act may seem, given crime-scene forensics today, this "tampering" barely raised an eyebrow at the time. Whether or not the testimony was drawn from Callaway to bolster claims that Kincannon acted in self-defense is not apparent. And no attempt was made to pinpoint the mystery woman who allegedly took the cartridges. Surely, J. F. Callaway would have known and recognized Lula Garvin Berch, who had lived in or near Marlow for seventeen years. The cartridges are never explained, perhaps because it was commonplace for men to have cartridges in their pockets in 1923 small-town Oklahoma.

With Albert Berch's body on its way to the Callaway funeral home, Robert Johnigan taken "elsewhere," and blood still drying on the tile floor, a simple question comes to the mind of any crime-scene aficionado—where are the police?

Oddly, the police did not appear. Perhaps more accurately stated, the night-watch policeman did not make it to the scene (in all but one account). The solitary officer on duty admitted that he heard the noise and commotion, but did not respond because "a bunch of boys had been shooting off cap guns."

This glossy excuse was good enough.

Other law-enforcement authorities arrived promptly, notably the Stephens County sheriff and the county attorney.

Now, the plot is thick and ready to be stirred.

It is easy to dismiss the horrible events of December 17, 1923, as "a group of boys got liquored up and things got out of hand." And while it would seem that young men who are out on the town would be carrying flasks of bootleg liquor, alcohol is never mentioned: not in the newspapers, not during trial, not even in later accounts by my grandmother . . . nowhere. The only accusations of liquor-induced behavior will be applied by prosecuting attorneys to two of the unindicted witnesses, but as for the boys and young men in the mob, it is never discussed. One might argue that bootlegging was so rampant at the time that no one was willing to walk down that road for fear of implicating judge, jury, and much of the population. Nevertheless, I make this alcohol point only because of its conspicuous absence.

And where alcohol escapes easy blame for vile behavior, widespread accusations of Klan involvement began immediately, and my grandmother fueled that perspective with vigor. Lula's world turned black and white after the murders, and if you agreed that Albert's death had been a gross injustice, you were safe from Lula's judgment and wrath. On the other hand, if you felt that Albert Berch brought his death upon himself, or contributed to his own demise in even the tiniest way, you were a card-carrying Klan member.

Given that the Klan was reliably shy about membership rolls, we cannot confirm who carried a card and who did not. However, Lula was not shy about singling out H. R. Gandy, night-watch policeman, and she was willing to announce his Klan association to anyone, anywhere. She further claimed that he winked at his son, Elza Gandy, with knowing reassurance at the son's trial, an accusation that made headlines.

Without police pursuit on the night of the murders, Marvin Kincannon had plenty of time to escape. Witnesses reported that he drove away with "three or four others in a small automobile." For a while, he hid at the home of his uncle, Tom Kincannon, but left there and was missing for days. During this time, Robert Johnigan died of his injuries, so when the arrest warrant was issued for Marvin Kincannon, it was for two murders.

Four days later, Kincannon was still missing. At one point, journalists cornered County Sheriff Brigham Young, quizzing him as to how Marvin might have eluded capture. The sheriff gave a hackneyed answer: "Nothing to say for you durn newspaper fellers now." The headline to the story in the *Marlow Review* would read, "Young Kincannon and His Pals Succeed in Escape."

While Marvin was still missing, seven other arrests were made, the targets being the young men who actually entered Johnson's Hotel lobby, while those in the mob outside were considered curious bystanders. Those arrested were: Elza "Buddy" Gandy, Ollie Lloyd, Byron White, Fred Stotts, Homer Thompson, Ellis Spence, and Frank Cain. The gang was collectively referred to as "boys" or "young men," with Fred Stotts the only exception, being a man in his forties and, notably, Marvin Kincannon's father-in-law. Most sources state that Marvin Kincannon never married, but this was not the case.

Frank Cain was subsequently released, even though at least one witness adamantly maintained Frank was present at the scene. A young man named Herman Stout was arrested in Duncan but was freed after a supporting alibi. With the release of Frank Cain, the total dropped to six defendants, with primary suspect Marvin Kincannon bringing the number back to seven.

A few days later, accompanied by a cousin and his brother Dewey, Marvin Kincannon sauntered into the Stephens County Courthouse, walked the steps to the top floor, and surrendered to jailer Otis Holder. In this pre-Miranda era, the county sheriff took first crack at the suspect,

Johnson's Hotel with outside decking, as it appeared in 2011. The door facing the street corner is where the mob entered the night of the murders.

with the *Duncan Banner* stating: "When Sheriff Young attempted to question him at the jail this morning the boy said: 'I have been advised not to talk to anyone about it and I am not going to talk.'" He never did.

On December 28, 1923, Marvin Kincannon was formally charged with the murders of Albert Berch and Robert Johnigan, though he did not enter a plea. The *Duncan Banner* reported that, as the charges were read, "Kincannon stood nonchalantly in front of the bar of justice, a rather don't care expression over his face, apparently unconscious of the graveness of the charges being read by the county attorney."

Kincannon and Gandy were held without bond, while those complicit in the lobby scene were released ($8,000 each). Several weeks later, after the preliminary hearing, Judge M. W. Pugh would free Gandy on a $15,000 bond. Kincannon would remain in jail until trial.

The preliminary hearing was held before Stephens County judge Eugene Rice, beginning January 4, 1924. The *Duncan Banner* would describe the courtroom as crowded, stuffy, and sweltering, in stark contrast to the mist and sleet outside. One journalistic phrase—"a rather clammy something seemed present"—nailed the ambiance through ambiguity.

Through a series of legal maneuverings to which we are not privy, Marvin Kincannon was ordered to stand trial in the spring session of Stephens County Court not for two murders in a single trial, but for Berch in one trial, then Johnigan in a second, this being a new twist on the concept of "separate, but equal." Elza Gandy would stand trial apart from Kincannon, charged only in the murder of "the crippled negro" and absolved of any role in the murder of Albert Berch.

Lula was beside herself, outraged that Gandy would not stand trial for the murder of her husband as well. But that wasn't the last insult to her sensibilities. Before the next year was over, all charges would be dropped against the five accomplices who entered the lobby as part of the intimidating gang.

Two weeks before Kincannon's trial, on April 4, 1924, the *Duncan Banner* announced that Judge M. W. Pugh had disqualified himself as trial judge, and the position would be assumed by Judge Will Lynn. We have no information as to what was behind that decision, but keep this action in mind, as associations among town leaders will gradually evolve.

On April 11, 1924, the Oklahoma City newspaper, the *Daily Oklahoman*, claimed that court proceedings were "expected to attract the largest crowd ever in attendance at a court case in the city [Duncan] as all parties connected with the affair are all well known throughout the county."

On April 18, Judge Lynn sat on the bench over the course of three days while nearly two hundred veniremen were scrutinized before the attorneys could agree on twelve men to serve on the jury and decide the fate of Marvin Kincannon. State's attorney Paul Sullivan asked for the death penalty. The defense attorneys, Joe E. Wilkinson and Ben Saye, argued self-defense. After all, Albert Berch had cartridges in his pocket, and the Negro rushed Marvin Kincannon with an open razor that apparently no one saw but Marvin. When this approach failed, the defense switched to "insanity."

The trial of Marvin Kincannon is next on our horizon. But as of yet, I have not buried the victims.

Interment of Albert Berch was at the Marlow cemetery. As for Robert Johnigan, newspapers stated only that his battered body was taken "elsewhere," but court testimony will reveal his burial as taking place in Ardmore, Oklahoma.

The funeral of Albert Berch must have been an unforgettable event for those present. The details we have today are contained in a Memorial Record booklet given to Lula. For whatever reason, Lula allowed someone else to record the details, as the handwriting is not hers.

A. W. Berch's birthplace is listed as Los Angeles; we have his "passed away" location at Johnston (*sic*) Hotel, Marlow; and we have his age at the time of death—let confusion reign—at thirty-eight years, eight months, and nine days, officially adding almost nine years to Albert's life. A short note then states: "Killed in a gun battle that ensued over a negro brought from Duncan to Marlow to work as porter, Monday, 8:30 p.m. at Johnston Hotel . . . by Marvin Kincannon."

Services for Albert Berch were held Wednesday, December 19, 1923, at 11:00 A.M., officiated by Rev. N. U. Stout of the First Methodist Church. Song selections included "Nearer My God to Thee," "Jesus, Lover of My Soul," and "Death Is Only a Dream." Albert Berch was "rendered" (eulogized) by Mrs. T. T. Eason and Mrs. Red Clayton. Just two pallbearers are listed, raising the question as to whether or not these were the only two men willing to risk reputation (or worse) in support of Berch. Pallbearer T. T. Eason is listed as an oilman, while his co-bearer, Harry Jarboe, is listed as a permanent boarder at Johnson's Hotel.

Floral offerings were by:

L. C. Jones—Washington
L. A. Birmingham—Ft. Worth

_____ Kelsey—Ft. Worth
Bessie Benight—Marlow
Mr. and Mrs. Tom Cox—Marlow
Mr. and Mrs. Clyde Stanton—Marlow
Mrs. John O'Quinn—Marlow
Mr. and Mrs. Fred Combs (Lula's brother and sister-in-law)—Marlow
Mrs. Chafin—Duncan

The other pages of the Memorial Record are left blank, perhaps reflecting a dead man with few friends willing to acknowledge themselves as such. Then, an unimaginable notation appears under "Memoranda," located between the lists of renderers and pallbearers:

> Pastor says: "For we are consumed by Thy anger. This man must have angered God to be took away so suddenly." Wife ran from church and did not return.

Lula Combs Garvin Berch had stormed out of her own husband's funeral.

In spite of this shocking event, the Marlow newspaper reported that "Rev. N. U. Stout conducted the services and paid many high tributes to the character of the deceased man."

Reverend Stout would go on to play a pivotal role in the building drive for Marlow's current First Methodist Church, constructed shortly after the murders.

"The pastor was Klan, don't you see?" Lula would explain to me over fifty years later. Indeed, the Klan was a common denominator in many of the odd things that took place both before and after the murders. It explained why Albert Berch's "permission" to hire the "negro" from the city leaders was a trapdoor for a man with a noose around his neck already, why the police looked the other way, and why it took three days and over two hundred candidates to find a jury in the trial of Marvin Kincannon. It explained why, upon hearing that Albert Berch was raised in a Catholic orphanage or had a rich Catholic aunt, the natives grew restless, especially when Berch refused to sell them the profitable hotel. Robert Johnigan wasn't the only target of the Klan. In my grandmother's version of the events, the stranger who came to town, Albert Berch, was Enemy Number One. And if this seems a stretch, well, a smoking gun to support Grandmother Lula's contention will emerge.

For Lula, the murder of her husband was an assassination, planned well in advance. Newspapers quoted her as demanding the electric chair for Kincannon, the man with the gun. Within days of Albert's funeral, even before the preliminary hearing, she was knocking on the door of the newly impeached and removed governor of Oklahoma, volunteering as a one-woman crusade to bring down Oklahoma's Ku Klux Klan.

Within three weeks of the murders, the story of Albert Berch would appear in towering headline print—"KLAN MURDER SAYS WIFE"— in Jack Walton's newspaper, the *National Anti-Klan Weekly*. While the murders and ensuing legal proceedings were covered by regional newspapers, with spotty national coverage as well, none were so bold to subtitle the story as did ex-governor Jack Walton in his newspaper, with the shocking allegation: "POLICE PERMIT MURDER."

Lula's crusade was under way, and the cascade would follow.

11

According to the Newspapers

The courtroom transcripts served as my primary source for legal proceedings with one exception—Marvin Kincannon's murder trial, as the records have been lost. Those blanks are filled in by a scrapbook assembled by Lula. The brown leather cover is inscribed with gold ink in her shaky handwriting: "Daddy's Death + Almarian Berch." Inside, brittle pages serve as scaffolding for newspaper articles glued securely in the 1920s. But with the adhesive giving up and letting go, the yellowed clippings now flutter free between the pages like pressed leaves.

Initially, newspaper coverage was sparse. The *Daily Oklahoman* placed the story as a blurb on page eighteen the morning after the murders. Even the nearby *Duncan Banner* did not consider the story worthy of front-page coverage, announcing the crime on page two. However, as details emerged, font size grew and placement moved front and center.

While newspapers might not capture precise testimony in context, they do provide interpretation that is missing from legal transcription. As for determining the exact source of these stories, we are hampered by the fact that Lula often trimmed away the name of the newspaper, as well as the date. Here are excerpts from friable newsprint, bolstered by microfilm review, starting in the days that followed the murders and continuing through the trial of Marvin Kincannon.

Widow Wants Youth to Pay Death Penalty (no newspaper identification or date)—"I want him to go to the electric chair," she sobbed in an interview Wednesday. "If the laws of the land do not mean that a person should pay with his life for the taking of human life then we might as well not have any laws." The county attorney, Paul Sullivan, agreed and asked for the death penalty. Mrs. Berch said that she lived in constant fear of being killed at Marlow and now is completing arrangements for the sale of the Johnson Hotel. "A threat has been made against my life since the preliminary hearing by a member of the mob," Mrs. Berch said.

"The first week in February I was warned they were coming after me. I was told one of them remarked my husband was a negro lover and that their work was only half done. Soon after the warning several persons came by and shots were fired at the hotel."

Two Are Dead After Fight in Lobby of Hotel—Marvin Kincannon Alleged to Have Led in Firing; Race Trouble Behind Fray (*Oklahoma City Times*, three days after the murders)—After the story clarifies that the mob members were not wearing masks, this follows: "His father, Albert Berch, Sr. who is a well known physician here, admitted Tuesday that young Berch had been warned to dismiss the negro. Considerable sentiment exists against Berch for bringing the negro to Marlow, a non-negro town, the county officers say."

A key point in this case dealt with whether or not Albert Berch had been fairly warned, and here we read that Berch's own father played into the hands of the defense. Was this an innocent blunder? Recall that Lula had palpable antipathy for her father-in-law, never fully explained.

Another article (unidentified and without the headline) states, "Mrs. Berch denied Friday afternoon that Berch had been warned to get the negro out of town. She asserted permission had been given by several of the town's leading business men for the negro to live there. 'Reports that Mr. Berch ignored a warning to get the negro out of town are going to handicap us in our prosecution of the persons guilty of this murder because it will put public sentiment against us,' she said."

The article continues, "Marlow's unwritten law, exemplified by prominent public signs bearing the command: 'Negro, don't let the sun go down on you here,' caused the death of Berch, and the fatal wounding of the first negro who has stayed here more than a day in years." Within hours of bringing Johnigan to Marlow, Berch "received an anonymous communication ordering him to dismiss the porter at once and drive him from the city. Berch ignored the letter."

Marlow Slaying Occurred After Business Men Had Backed Hiring of Negro (newspaper unidentified, January 4, 1924)—Although newspaper photographs were infrequent at the time, this article is headed by a coarse likeness of Lula. "Johnigan was brought by the Birch's [*sic*] from Duncan. 'He had an excellent reputation there and was a fine old negro,' Mrs. Berch said."

In the article, Lula claims to have won approval from business leaders before the hiring, as well as "a number of people" who said it would be okay. She reiterates that, in contrast to Albert Senior's comments in the newspapers, Albert Junior received no death threats, anonymous letters, or warnings before the murders.

Klan Angle in Mob Case Is Mystery (no newspaper identification or date)—"What part has the Marlow Ku Klux Klan played in the death of Al Berch, Marlow hotel proprietor, and Robert Johnigan, Berch's negro porter, and the subsequent hearing now in progress there? While the klan has not been mentioned in the testimony offered at the preliminary hearings of Marvin Kincannon [et al] . . . this angle is freely talked by spectators at the trial. Klan and Anti-klan sentiment is strong at Marlow."

And the trial begins. . . .

Kincannon Jury Finally Completed: Defence Suddenly Switches from Self Defence to Insanity (*Duncan Banner*, no date)—In early testimony, Mattie Kincannon claimed that her brother fell from a trapeze in his youth and was practically unconscious for several hours, and in her opinion he had never been right since. (Note: many senior citizens in Marlow today were taught as children by schoolmarms Mattie Kincannon and her sister Lizzie.)

And in the same article, this tidbit: "The Ku Klux Klan organization in Stephens county is taking no part in the trial of Marvin Kincannon. Eugene Bryce, exalted Cyclops of the Duncan klan, said Thursday when asked to deny or confirm court house rumors that the organization was lending moral support to the cause of the youth who is charged with the murder of Al Berch, Marlow hotel man. 'The klan is taking no part whatsoever in the trial,' the cyclops said. Furthermore, 'Kincannon is not a member, none of those who were charged with being in the party was a member, neither were the fathers of any of the boys members, as has been charged,' he said."

With a touch of irony, the flip side of this *Duncan Banner* clipping reveals a "down-home" column, where it is noted that "a Duncan girl has written a song entitled, 'Daddy Stole Our Last Clean Sheet and Joined the Ku Klux Klan.'"

Jury Secured and Kincannon Goes to Trial (*Duncan Banner*, April 18, 1924)—This issue is historically unique, with "Johnson Hotel" stamped in ink at the top of the front page to denote ownership. "Swinging away from the attempted effort to prove self defense for the killings, the defense . . . devoted their entire efforts to an attempt to show a temporary mental derangement of the defendant at the time the crimes were committed and a dozen witnesses were used in this attempt."

The defense attorneys summarized Marvin's insanity with these

April 18, 1924, edition of the Duncan Banner, *covering the start of the first trial*

examples: at seven, Marvin ran away from home; at eleven, while imitating the stunts of a trapeze performer, he fell and inflicted injury to himself; at twelve or thirteen, he refused to assist his brother, who had fallen into a deep hole while swimming, and when asked why he didn't help, he "laughed, and replied he didn't know why"; at fourteen, he had "bumped his head and began beating a post with his fists, would run away when called by an older relative, then other times be normal and friendly, and be in constant trouble at school."

The article continued, "Then, Dr. R. L. Montgomery, mayor of Marlow, testified that the mother of the defendant was a low mentality, although not entirely insane or without a mind capable of being controlled. As the family physician, he knew of this condition of Mrs. Kincannon at the time of the defendant's birth or soon thereafter." (Note: Marvin's mother had died ten years earlier, thus sparing her from the "low mentality" descriptor.) Marvin "had been up before" Dr. Montgomery, the police magistrate for Marlow, on multiple occasions. "Dr. Montgomery stated, 'I think his mind was subnormal.'"

During cross-examination, Dr. "Dolph" Montgomery admitted that Marvin had passed the army medical examination after the war and that this was "a very stringent and strict examination." Seemingly cornered, Dr. Montgomery explained that Marvin's "mental affliction was apparent only at intervals."

In sharp contrast to mayor-magistrate-doctor R. L. "Dolph" Montgomery's statements, Dr. C. C. Richards, the Marlow physician who had delivered baby Almarian and who had answered the call to attend to Berch and Johnigan at the crime scene, testified that Kincannon was completely sane.

The newspaper then reveals a coup for the prosecution.

"State Springs a Surprise: Something of a sensation was sprung during the closing moments of the taking of testimony when the state called to the witness stand Dr. D. W. Griffin, medical superintendent at the state hospital in Norman, who testified and that in his opinion Marvin Kincannon was perfectly sane."

Dr. Griffin was the first superintendent of what was later called Central State Hospital in Norman, a position he held from 1902 to 1950. Today, the psychiatric facility is named Griffin Memorial Hospital.

The article describes the circuslike atmosphere: "Not only is the district court room packed with spectators but the corridors of the building on the three floors are crowded. Women with less than a year old babies are seen in the crowd; white headed men and women shoulder for places of vantage that they may hear and see all, and when a vacancy occurs in the ranks of the rabble a score of leg-weary human beings perpetrate a center rush for the position."

D. W. Griffin had been seated in the audience throughout the trial, observing all witnesses as well as the defendant, Marvin Kincannon. A sub-header in the article says it all: *Defense Is Dealt Crushing Blow by Testimony of Dr. Griffin.*

"Griffin knocked the prop out from under the insanity plea when he told the jury that in his opinion the young slayer of Al Berch was sane on the night of December 17 when he fired the shot that killed the hotel man. After the conclusion of Griffin's testimony, the county attorney said, 'That's our case.'"

The defense replied, "We have no more witnesses." Thus concluded twenty-four hours of testimony, a duration of time shorter than what had been spent in seating the jury.

A *Daily Oklahoman* article reported, "The jury seemed impressed with Griffin's statement relative to Kincannon's testimony. The superintendent of the asylum has been a specialist in nervous and mental diseases for more than a score of years. He has been on the staff of the asylum since 1898 and . . . an instructor in nervous diseases in the University of Oklahoma. Upon taking the stand, he said he had been a silent observer of Kincannon's actions in the courtroom since the beginning of the trial and had listened to the boy's testimony on the stand."

Defense attorney George Womack asked, "Isn't it true that in certain cases of insanity the patient is very cunning?"

"Yes, sometimes they are quite cunning," he said, "but if the cases are carefully studied we can find the abnormality. The insane criminal makes so many outstanding blunders that his insanity is easy to detect. He does not work with others. He works alone. After he commits a crime he stands out boldly and does not often flee."

Marvin Kincannon took the stand shortly after his sister had testified as to his mental condition. The *Daily Oklahoman* described it like this: "His entire testimony was given in a low husky voice and he kept shifting in the chair, placing his hand to his face as he answered the questions. Once or twice when the prosecutor shot a question at him he flared up and snapped back a reply, his black eyes blazing."

"Don't you know that this poor old crippled negro, Johnigan, never did a thing in the world to you except if he did come at you with a razor as you say?" asked Sullivan.

"Well, that's enough, isn't it?" Kincannon hurled back.

"A hush fell over the courtroom as Kincannon outlined his actions on the night of the tragedy. Prognosticators bet on a not guilty verdict [or] all the way to the electric chair, while many believed a verdict would not be possible." So said the newspapers.

The verdict came after five hours of deliberation, and Marvin Kincannon was found guilty—not for murder but first-degree manslaughter. As the verdict was announced, Marvin appeared cool and unconcerned, one elbow on the table, cheek resting on hand, and "black eyes snapping, but without the twitching of a muscle or a particle of change in color to denote that the verdict was of any concern to him."

Prosecutor Paul Sullivan was "displeased," noting, "If he is guilty in the murder of Albert Berch, then he should receive life at a minimum, or even the death penalty." Defense attorneys Joe Wilkinson and Ben Saye were equally outraged and immediately filed a motion for a new trial (denied).

Kincannon Is Found Guilty; Marlow Slayer Sentenced to 25 Years in Prison; May Not Appeal Case (*Daily Oklahoman*, April 19, 1924)— Correspondent Harold Mueller wrote, "The verdict was reached after five hours of deliberation. J. W. Davenport, Comanche merchant, was foreman of the jury. Kincannon took the verdict silently and showed little change from his stolid demeanor of the trial. . . . Paul Sullivan, county attorney, said the youth probably would be tried on the other murder charge in July. The others who are charged with him in the

Johnigan case likely will not be tried until October. They are expected to file petitions asking that they be tried separately.

"During the morning Kincannon lay on a cot in the Stephens county jail, his 20-year-old wife, Ada, sitting beside him, waiting for the verdict of the twelve men. Two sisters and two brothers were gathered about him to keep him company during the trying hours while the jury deliberated. Now and then the youth patted his wife on the back, stroked her arm and then she would let her hand rest in his a moment.

"Kincannon was not talkative. 'I'll be glad when it's over,' he said. He refused to pose for a picture, but said he would consent to have a photograph taken with his wife if acquitted."

There would be no photograph, not even a mugshot from the McAlester prison. As for other trials to follow, only Elza Gandy would face a jury, and this would be for the murder of the "crippled negro," Robert Johnigan. Kincannon was never tried again, a remarkable lapse given the scene at the phone booth in the writing room.

Testimony from the preliminary hearing had been inconclusive as to the exact cause of Johnigan's death, be it bullets (by Kincannon) or blunt trauma to the head (by Gandy). Without modern forensics, but with plenty of politics, it was decided to put Gandy on trial for Johnigan alone. His acquittal was more likely, apparently allowing full blame to be placed for both murders on the already-convicted Kincannon.

The brown leather scrapbook with gold letters from a trembling hand on the cover contains more than newspaper clippings related to the murder. Lula included a smattering of motivational pieces as well, aphorisms and inspirational sayings that, long ago, filled newspaper space where today's astrology columns sit. For example, one cartoon series is labeled "The Cheerful Cherub," from the *Daily Oklahoman* dated March 8, 1926, two years after the murders. This rhyme is the caption for a cherub and its nearby puppy:

> When I am feeling sad I find
> I'm looking backward in my mind
> For sorrows never really last
> Unless we won't let go the past.

For Lula, the past would not let go of her, nor would she let go of it. Instead, they would be locked in a bleak embrace.

12

Kincannon to the Pen, While Gandy Goes It Alone

Lula Berch's blood was still boiling from the first trial when the second one began. Even with Marvin Kincannon behind bars at the Oklahoma State Penitentiary in McAlester, and knowing that a "not guilty" verdict had been a real possibility, Lula saw the crime as a double assassination, premeditated. The only "closure," acknowledging the anachronism, would have been the electric chair for Kincannon, which, conveniently enough, was located at his current house of detention. In 1924, the electric chair was enjoying its peak popularity nationwide, having just surpassed the old-fashioned method of execution that had served so many for so long—hanging.

The man who had pulled the trigger on both victims was now in prison, but there were still loose ends, primarily what to do with Elza Gandy. After all, Gandy hadn't laid a hand on Berch. In fact, it had been the other way around. Charges were never filed against Gandy for the murder or manslaughter of Albert Berch, even as an accomplice.

Legal maneuverings began right away. Elza Gandy requested that he be tried separately (granted), and throughout his trial, the other young men in the hotel lobby that night were still listed as defendants for their own upcoming trials. Importantly, Oklahoma law at the time excused these defendants from serving as witnesses at the Gandy trial.

Yet, because Gandy was not charged in the Berch murder, he was free to testify in Kincannon's trial, where he took much of the heat for his buddy. Then, for his own trial, perhaps believing his prior testimony could not be entered as evidence, Gandy's testimony will turn on a dime.

While this strategy didn't work so well for Gandy, it proved glorious for the other defendants, as all charges against the lobby "bystanders" were dropped after the Gandy trial. Thus, these key eyewitnesses never had to testify against their buddies, nor did they face trial themselves. At the time of the Gandy verdict, the *Duncan Banner* noted, "There are

5 other defendants charged with participation in the killings but their cases do not appear on the court docket for trial and court officials could not say when they would be called." In fact, they were never called. In the end, we have Kincannon tried alone for killing Berch and Gandy tried alone for killing Johnigan.

Given limited records today, it is difficult to theorize how the judicial process might have been engineered behind the scenes to result in minimal jail time for the fewest possible number of defendants. Nevertheless, as any good conniver knows, the key to success is to move the pawns without generating a paper trail.

A word about offensive words is in order before presenting the testimony from the Elza Gandy trial. Today, the "N-word" has been thoroughly expunged from proper language. After reading the courtroom testimony related to this story, however, I'm convinced that in 1924 rural Oklahoma, the word had not yet undergone the metamorphosis into vulgarity. Attorneys and educated witnesses on both sides used it, always interchangeable with "negro," sometimes both used in the same sentence. Furthermore, today's historians are conflicted as to whether or not the word should be carved out of historical accounts. I likewise struggled with whether to record testimony as printed in the legal documents or whitewash the language. I made my choice to write the word as *n*-----.

And so we begin.

Elza Gandy's trial for the murder of Robert Johnigan occurred during the 1924 fall session of the Stephens County Court in Duncan, Oklahoma. District Judge Will Lynn presided, with County Attorney Paul D. Sullivan and Assistant County Attorney J. H. Long. Additional assistance to the State came from Bond & Lewis, of Duncan. As for the defendant, it was Joe Wilkinson and Ben Saye of Duncan, the same attorneys who had defended Marvin Kincannon.

Gandy pleaded not guilty. The jury was empaneled with the same difficulty as had been encountered in the Kincannon trial. When finally assembled, the all-male jury included no residents of Marlow. (A list of jurors is available on the website that accompanies this book.)

In his opening statements, prosecutor Sullivan recounted the events of the murders as known, with the following conclusion:

"The testimony will disclose other things that I have not mentioned to you but it will show that Gandy 'ribbed' the bunch up, got them together for the purpose of going there, furnished the gun to Kincannon and that he first committed an assault on the old negro and the negro's live [*sic*] was taken in that killing. Gentlemen of the jury, if our testimony bears out this brief statement, we think we will be entitled to a verdict of guilty. I thank you."

Testimony largely duplicated what had been given in the preliminary hearing, including the many inconsistencies among eyewitnesses. For instance, some heard three shots, while others heard five or more. Some saw a stick, others a lead pipe. Some saw Kincannon attack Johnigan before shooting Berch; others did not. Also, great effort was spent trying to establish whether or not Berch or Johnigan had brandished any weapons.

One witness, Homer Steele (not to be confused with defendant Homer Thompson), followed the mob in a crowd of "fifteen to eighteen," most of whom were more curious than passionate about the cause. Having viewed the scene from the sidewalk outside, he testified that Marvin Kincannon entered the writing room first and started fighting with Johnigan. According to Homer, Kincannon grabbed Johnigan by the throat. Johnigan fought back. The prosecutors accused Homer of heaping extra blame on already-convicted Marvin Kincannon, as it was known from prior testimony that Kincannon's initial interaction with Johnigan was so brief that most eyewitnesses didn't even catch it.

Another witness who had looked through the lobby windows from the outside was young Johnny Morgan. He testified that Kincannon started the ruckus with a quick jab to Johnigan's ribs—the only contact by Kincannon against Johnigan, initially at least. Morgan then added a new twist to the story, claiming that some of the boys did indeed buy firecrackers at Siever's drugstore, helping to support the fragile excuse of the night-watch policeman (Elza Gandy's father), who claimed he didn't check out the popping noises at Johnson's Hotel as they sounded like firecrackers or cap pistols.

No one raised the possibility that the firecrackers might have been an intentional diversion to provide an easy out for the night-watch policeman. Some of the mob at the hotel even thought that Kincannon and Gandy had set off firecrackers in the lobby—that is, until Berch fell to the floor. Near the end of Morgan's testimony, he supported a key point in the prosecution's claim by stating that he and several others saw Gandy wielding a stick of some sort during the march from Siever's drugstore to the hotel.

For the first time in any of the proceedings related to the murders, a Mrs. John Green testified. As a bystander, she had noted Elza Gandy, Ira Acre, J. R. Taylor, and J. L Clark (Berch's right-hand man) as part of the group at Siever's. She testified it was Elza Gandy who hollered to the group, "All right, let's go," followed by, "Come on; there is no backing out." She began trailing the mob in her car out of curiosity, but before parking near the hotel, she heard gunfire and sped away. The revelation that Berch's man, J. L. Clark, was "with the mob" raised eyebrows and became a new pivot point in the trial.

Remarkably, there was not a single witness who saw Marvin Kincannon's weapon until he brandished it in the lobby of the hotel. The fact that the mob had gathered at night removes some of the mystery here, or perhaps Kincannon had the weapon concealed before he joined the mob en route. However, most testimony suggested that a transfer of the weapon to Kincannon had occurred. Harry Stotts testified that Jasper Simpson told Stotts that he heard Gandy say to Kincannon on the night of the killings, "Take this," the implication being that Gandy was talking about a gun (the objection was sustained).

J. L. Clark lived at Johnson's Hotel. With a flat-topped haircut and close-set eyes, he resembled 1950s TV comedian George Gobel, more suited as lackey than conspirator. Lula considered him a trusted friend. As he had done at the preliminary hearing, J. L. testified about the crowd at Siever's: "They were talking about going to the hotel and getting the n-----." Someone asked another why they were waiting, and the response was, "We are waiting on Kinney" (Marvin Kincannon). With that, J. L. Clark testified that he returned to the hotel and told Albert Berch that trouble was brewing. As he was warning Berch, though, J. L. looked through the small pane of glass in the swinging door leading to the writing room and saw the gang. Elza Gandy was hitting Robert Johnigan with something that looked like an iron pipe, reportedly two inches wide and about two feet long.

During cross-examination, attorneys sought to make the case that J. L. Clark had fueled the fires on both sides of the battlefield: "Didn't Berch tell you to go up the street and steer the bunch of boys down there so he could beat up on them?"

"No, sir."

The defense attorney then provided a detailed account, including witnesses who claimed J. L. Clark worked as a mischievous catalyst, telling both sides that the other was looking for a fight. Clark vehemently denied it all. Clark then testified that after the murders he moved to

Oklahoma City, where he was "jerking soda" at the Winter Garden Dance Hall on West Fifth Street.

Mrs. Pete Benight lived in the hotel and ran the café and dining room, separated from the lobby by French doors. She testified that she was sitting on one of the stools at the counter when she heard gunfire. She ran to the writing room, saw the gun, and then ran back to the dining room until the gunfire ended. When she returned to the lobby, Berch was "practically dead, but the negro asked me to get him a drink of water." The two bodies were lying close together. The mob was backing out of the lobby.

Several witness recalled the exit of the mob in the same fashion: backing out in a *V* shape, then scattering once outside. Kincannon was the last to leave, serving as the "point" of the *V*, backing out with gun in hand, still facing the crime scene.

✯✯✯

Testimony from the widow, Lula Berch, came next.

Lula had been in the Berch suite, headed upstairs, when she heard J. L. Clark enter and announce, "There is a mob of boys in the lobby." Albert Berch had written the severance check for Johnigan only a moment earlier. "I grabbed my baby and ran in behind them," Lula recounted.

Q: What did you see?

A: By the time I got to the door, I seen a fight of some kind.

Q: Who was fighting?

A: The first person I recognized was the Gandy boy. He had hold of the negro and I seen there was a scuffle.

Q: Did the Gandy boy have anything in his hands?

A: Yes sir, something.

Q: What was he doing with it?

A: When I seen him, he was not doing anything with it. I seen my husband rush up and hit him with his left hand and—let me see—the Gandy boy was in this position (illustrating) and he [Berch] hit him like this (illustrating) and turned around with this leg like this (illustrating) facing Kincannon and Kincannon killed him. He fell against [Walter] O'Quinn and on to the floor. I had baby in my arms and I seen I couldn't do anything so I put her over here (indicating) and I took his head in my lap and seen he was dying.

Q (State's attorney): How long did he live?

A: I don't know. Probably three or five minutes.

Q: What else did you see after the shooting of your husband?

A: I didn't see anything.

Q: What was your condition?

A: I guess I was crazy. I don't remember anything after I saw husband was dying.

Q: Where were you when you next recall anything?

A: I was in my bed room with the doctor standing over me. . . .

Defense attorney Wilkinson handled the cross-examination.

Q: You have moved to Duncan and have been running the Belmont since then?

A: Yes sir.

Q: I will ask you if on the 22nd day of July, you and one Stillwell O'Neal were not convicted in the police court of Duncan, on the charge of keeping rooms where immoral women were kept?

A: We was not.

Mr. Sullivan: We object to that as being incompetent, irrelevant, and immaterial.

The Court: Is it for the credibility of the witness?

Mr. Sullivan: It is a police court.

Q: You will say you were not?

A: It was thrown out.

Q: I will ask you again if you wasn't arrested and taken to the police court and counsel represented you and the case tried?

A: I wasn't arrested.

Q: You went to the police court didn't you?

A: Yes sir.

Q: And had a trial?

A: Yes sir.

Q: And the judge found you guilty?

A: Yes sir.

Q: And addressed a fine against you?

A: Yes sir, but then threw it out of court.

Q: You are certain that his records show that case has been disposed of?

Mr. Sullivan: We object to that if the court please.

Q: Was you there when it was thrown out?

A: I have got his word for it.

Q: You was tried and convicted was you?

A: I didn't know we was trying that case here.

Q: Stillwell O'Neal was staying with you and—

A: He was not staying with me. He was manager of that hotel. I wasn't even there and wasn't running the Thompson.

Q: But you and he were tried at the same time?

A: Yes.

Q: And both convicted. That is all.

Sullivan took over on redirect examination.

Q (State's attorney): As long as Al Berch was living to take care of you was you ever in any trouble?

A: I was not.

Q: Since his death you have had to get along the best you could, have you?

A: I sure have.

Q: You stated that you had a rooming house here [Duncan]?

A: Yes sir.

Q: That is called the Belmont?

A: Yes sir.

Q: I will ask you this. Did you stay there, running that hotel yourself?

A: I did not.

Q: The hotel was just in your name?

A: That was all.

Q: Was you responsible for the travelers that came there?

A: I was not.

Q: Were you there at the time of the occurrence?

A: No sir, I was not.

Q: Did you have anything to do with anybody coming there for immoral purposes?

A: No sir.

Q: That is all.

Walter O'Quinn, a key witness in the Kincannon trial, then testified that Al Berch had expressed a desire to borrow O'Quinn's pistol. O'Quinn had the impression that the Clark boy and Albert Berch had had a prior conversation that led Berch to suspect trouble was brewing. However, O'Quinn didn't have his pistol with him.

O'Quinn was the only witness among the crowd who actually saw Kincannon draw his gun and fire, so the questioning was intense for him during cross-examination by Wilkinson. The defense attorney first established that O'Quinn was "in business" with a Mrs. Collins. Then Wilkinson continued:

Q: In what hotel?

A: We had the Belmont.

Q: Was that before or after Mrs. Berch was running it?

A: She has run it since.

Q: I will ask you if about the 20th of August, you was here and you were arrested at Mrs. Berch's rooming house here, and you were arrested with or in the company of Lucy Collins and brought before the police court of the City of Duncan and tried and convicted, you and her together?

A: And I appealed the case—

Q: You were convicted?

A: Yes, I was convicted in the City Court.

Q: And that is the lady with whom you ran this hotel?

A: Yes sir.

Q: I will ask you if you have been convicted of any other crimes and served a term or paid a fine?

A: No sir, I never served a term.

Attorney Wilkinson then proposed that O'Quinn had been arrested for gambling on multiple occasions, a charge O'Quinn repeatedly denied. Then Wilkinson threw a grenade:

Q: I will ask you if you are not under indictment for bank robbing—

Mr. Sullivan (State's attorney): Just a minute.

The Court: Sustain the objection. You will not consider that question at all, gentlemen.

Q: I will ask you this. At the time this killing occurred in Marlow . . . at the time the first shot was fired, you wasn't up in a room playing cards with Cass Graham, Bill Lucile and a boy named "Cozy" and another man?

A: I absolutely was not and I don't believe they will say so either.

Q: That is all.

Sullivan took over on redirect.

Q: Mr. O'Quinn, this occurrence down here in the police court, did they try you before a jury or the police judge?

A: Just before the police judge.

Q: Did you ever know of a police judge in Oklahoma, acquitting a man for anything?

A: I never did.

★★★

After the prosecution rested, Wilkinson introduced witnesses for the defense with this opening statement (excerpt): "We expect to show that to many of these town boys . . . a negro in the town of Marlow was a curiosity, something like an elephant coming to town, and this bunch of boys knew that this negro was there and were talking about going to have some fun out of him, and they got some firecrackers, there was no thought of anybody being hurt, and they went down to have some fun out of the n----- at the suggestion of this jitney driver that works there [J. L. Clark]. We expect to show that this man Berch was trying to run this n----- over the people of Marlow. It was a town that was a white man's town and they didn't want any n----- there. . . . I am not going to undertake to relate all of the testimony; I am just giving you a short statement of it. . . . I think we are in a position to say that we have a right to ask you to return a verdict of not guilty as to this defendant. He went down there—he is not going to deny that, and he is not going to deny that he went inside, but all that happened to him—he got knocked down and then he got out. That is all that happened to this kid. I don't know why Berch hit him first but he did and then went after the other fellow and got shot. . . . I think that you will believe that Berch's and the colored man's death was caused by the actions of Berch instead of this defendant."

The first defense witness, Charlie McReynolds, testified that he and Ernest Calhoun heard J. L. Clark encourage the group to "have some fun with the n-----." Furthermore, both men testified that Clark delivered threats indirectly from Berch, who had allegedly instructed Clark to steer the mob to the hotel, whereupon "he'll take care of the lot of them, and if he [Berch] can't do it alone, he has plenty of backing." McReynolds and Calhoun agreed that this conversation took place one hour before the shooting.

On cross-examination, Sullivan explored McReynolds' drinking history, as well as the libation habits of his co-witness, Ernest E. Calhoun (one of two Ernest Calhouns serving as witnesses), pointing out that neither man could recall anything accurate about the time sequence in the case, nor could they identify J. L. Clark or anything about him.

Q: You already had had so many that you didn't know which way you were going, hadn't you?

A [McReynolds]: I don't think so.

Q: That fellow Calhoun had had right smart to drink before that, with you, hadn't he?

A: He didn't ask me and I didn't ask him.

A long line of witnesses followed, some of whom had been in the lobby that night, some on the street, some corroborating conversations, some not. The focus of the defense was not so much what happened in the lobby but what was said earlier at Siever's, trying to tag ringleaders other than Gandy. Someone, possibly Gandy, declared immediately prior to the killings, "Watch out for Kinney [Kincannon]. I've seen him get out of tight places before," insinuating that something more than firecrackers was afoot—that perhaps a loose Kincannon would be following his own script.

Then Gandy took the stand.

Elza Gandy was twenty-two years old at the time, single, and living with his father, H. R., who was variously described as a lawman, night watchman, and policeman. No information about the mother was included in the trial proceedings, other than she lived "elsewhere." Elza worked "pulling some bolls for a fellow west of town." In his testimony, Gandy stated that he came to Marlow with Jack Derdgan and Homer Steele. Later, Frank Cain joined them. They migrated from Siever's drugstore to the bakery, got a drink, got a shave at Joe Calhoun's barbershop, then headed over to the wagon yard. There, near Citizens National Bank, Elza testified that he met J. L. Clark (the catalyst, according to the defense strategy), who said that "there was going to be a bunch of boys at the hotel shortly and he said if I seen any to come on down there and we would have some fun."

Then, Elza described returning to Siever's with Cain and eight or ten others, specifically Frank Moore, Byron Wright, and Ollie Lloyd. Once the mob began its march to the hotel, Gandy happened to notice Marvin Kincannon angling toward them from across the street. Kincannon didn't actually join the group until "just before" they got to the hotel, the implication being that there was no time for Gandy to have passed a gun to Kincannon.

Q [Wilkinson]: While you were in the lobby, what did you do?

A: Well, I walked back through by this writing table and I walked from the west side clean around the writing table. . . .

Q: Did you go up to where the n----- was?

A: I walked up about three feet of him.

Q: What did you do if anything?

A: Not a thing . . .

Q: What occurred next?

A: The next thing I knew somebody said, "Get the Hell out of here," and hit me just about that time.

Q: What effect did it have on you?

A: I fell over on the table, the writing table and about the next thing I knew I started to get up some way and couldn't hardly make it and I pushed my hand on the table and there was a shot fired and when they done that I went for the door.

Elza Gandy then claimed that he exited the lobby, stopped by the tailor shop to pick up a pair of his trousers, and "went on home."

Sullivan's cross-examination initially allowed Gandy to claim that he simply went along with the crowd. Sullivan then reminded Elza of his testimony in the Kincannon trial, when he admitted that he and Frank Cain went to get two sticks before going to the hotel. (Charges against Cain were dropped early on.) After Sullivan read the testimony from that trial, Gandy denied making the statement. Sullivan then read more testimony where Gandy had claimed that he only wanted the stick to "carry around." Again, Gandy denied the words. Sullivan quoted further from the earlier trial: "I found my stick in front of the blacksmith's store." Gandy denied ever having said such a thing, once again.

Sullivan continued reading: "Question: 'You went to the hotel and took the stick with you, didn't you?' Answer: 'Yes, sir.'" Then, back to the trial at hand, Sullivan asked the same question, but the response was: "No, sir."

It didn't stop there. Gandy's entire testimony flip-flopped from the Kincannon trial to such an extreme that one has to question his legal coaching. Given that the same set of attorneys defended both Kincannon and Gandy, what was the strategy? Perhaps it was: "Do everything we can to get Marvin off the hook, then once that is done, we'll get Gandy off as well. No one will care when we change the answers to the same questions."

As an aside, when the county attorney referred to Robert Johnigan as "crippled," Gandy replied, "Not so badly."

Q: He had to drag that leg when he walked, didn't he?

A: No, he got along pretty good.

Q: Pretty good for a crippled negro?

A: I have seen them get along worse, Mr. Sullivan.

Sullivan then returned to the most important point in the Kincannon-Gandy interchange as related to the murders—did Gandy provide Kincannon with the murder weapon? If so, Gandy should have been charged as an accessory to the murder of Albert Berch.

Q: I will ask you if . . . you didn't give him (Kincannon) the pistol that he killed them with?

A: No sir.

Q: Do you remember that Kincannon testified that you did?

Mr. Wilkinson: We object. That is improper.

The Court: Sustain the objection.

Mr. Wilkinson: We move to instruct the jury not to consider that.

The Court: You will not consider that question, gentlemen.

Mr. Wilkinson: Mr. Sullivan knows better than that.

The Court: Never mind any of that.

Gandy then offered an account of his role in the writing room, where he claimed to have wandered about for five minutes or so, apparently doing nothing.

Q: What did Berch hit you for?

A: I guess because I was the closest one to him. That is all I know. I was the closest one to him.

Sullivan proceeded to read more testimony from the Kincannon trial, but Gandy stonewalled it by claiming said questions were never asked, that instead, the transcript was faulty. In response, Sullivan called J. R. McAtee to testify, the official court reporter for Stephens and Grady counties. McAtee transcribed the testimony, in shorthand, for *State of Oklahoma v. Marvin Kincannon* in April 1924. Sullivan instructed him to read, not from the final longhand, but from his original shorthand, over the objections of defense attorney Wilkinson. The account from McAtee confirmed the version being read by Sullivan as accurate, leaving Gandy's testimony profoundly self-incriminating.

In his instructions, Judge Lynn told the jury they had three choices— murder, manslaughter in the first degree, or justifiable homicide—and he provided detailed definitions for each. Instruction #14 made this clear: "The Law is that if two or more persons conspire to commit a felony and death occurs in the prosecution of the common object, all are guilty of murder, and if two or more persons conspire to commit a misdemeanor, and death happens in the prosecution of the common object, all are guilty of manslaughter in the first degree."

Instruction #14 clarifies why most of the testimony dealt with the details as to what happened at Siever's drugstore in the hours/days before the murder, rather than the details of the murder itself. If the intent was only to "have some fun," then the deaths are manslaughter in the first degree, but if the intent of anyone was to commit a felony, assault and battery or worse, then all are guilty of murder. And while this may explain the "manslaughter" concept in 1924 Oklahoma, this does not clarify why Kincannon was tried only for Berch and Gandy only for Johnigan.

The judge then reminded the jury that Kincannon had already been convicted of manslaughter, not murder, so it should be the same for Gandy (in so many words). If, however, the jury believed Kincannon acted alone and should have been convicted of murder, then Gandy did not have to be convicted at all. Alternatively, if in doubt about murder or confused about any of several allegations, such as Gandy as a ringleader, providing the gun, or beating Robert Johnigan, then the jury should find for manslaughter in the first degree.

Furthermore, "Albert Berch had the right to employ as his porter the deceased Robert Johnigan, and the deceased Johnigan had a right to accept such employment and live in the town of Marlow and at Al Berch's hotel so long as he obeyed the laws of the state . . . and, that Al Berch had a lawful right to protect the said Johnigan against an assault of any persons, or to prevent the said Johnigan being run out of the town of Marlow while he was at his hotel and on his premises. . . . "

Long, an attorney who had assisted the prosecutor, was well under way with his closing argument when the court reporter showed up late, leaving us without record for the initial few minutes. (Apparently, court sessions in 1924 Oklahoma began on time, no matter what.) Long noted the shady testimony of all those who had minimized the role of premeditation. He also pointed out the failed attempts to blame the entire episode on delivery boy J. L. Clark, who apparently was a very believable witness in his denial of ever having egged the gang on. The defense had used every trick in the book to paint J. L. poorly, even smearing him as currently employed in a "dance hall," when everyone knew that "some of Oklahoma City's finest attend that dance hall."

Long took great pains to point out how Gandy's entire testimony changed subsequent to the Kincannon trial. Originally, Long supposed, Gandy was trying to help his friend, assuming he would get off like the others who had stood by in the lobby, but now that Gandy's life was on the line, he had switched. Then Long appealed to the sympathy of the jurors:

I am assuming Gentlemen, that they were not expecting to kill Al

Berch or Robert Johnigan in the first instance but you see what the result was Gentlemen. You saw that little woman as she took the witness stand. . . . You gentlemen know whose hands have robbed her of protection. You gentlemen know who robbed that infant of its protection. You gentlemen know that women are dragged down to the depths of Hell by such things as that. Don't let that condition cause you to go wrong in this case Gentlemen. . . .

[The mob] in front of Siever's Drug Store, they went there for the unlawful purpose of driving this negro out, and all I ask in this case is justice, and I know that every one of you jurors want the verdict that you render to be that. Let it be a verdict that you can face that old negro woman with [Johnigan's wife, Lizzie, was in her forties at the time] and say to her, "I have done the right thing." Let it be a verdict that twenty years from now, when that child [Almarian] grows up and you men face that child, that you can face it with and say, "I have done my duty."

Ben Saye, in closing arguments for the defense, clarified the charges and reminded the jury that killing Albert Berch was not the issue of the day. Gandy was on trial for killing Johnigan, not Berch.

Saye argued, "If I am not mistaken in what he [Long] said, the whole tenor of his speech was to criticize some of the things we asked Mrs. Berch. He appealed to your sympathy because of her and the fact that there is a child alive. I say to you now that I believe I have as much respect for Mrs. Berch as the County Attorney or any gentleman who sits on that side of the table, but you are not trying her . . . what has that to do with determining whether or not Gandy is responsible for that killing?"

Saye then tried his hand at blurring the boundaries—if you say Gandy is guilty even though he did not kill Johnigan directly, then so is the mob outside. "Why draw the line based only on those who went inside?" It doesn't matter that Gandy talked out of both sides of his mouth in two different trials—neither version should convict him since he didn't directly kill Johnigan any more than the rest of the mob did.

Saye continued: "I honestly believe, if Mr. Berch had not rushed in that lobby and knocked that boy down in that manner, he [Berch] would have been alive today and so would the old n-----. . . . I say to you that I don't think under that evidence, that there was anybody hit that n----- on the head. The physical facts that they have brought before you don't prove it. . . . Now, where is the conspiracy in this case and if there was a conspiracy, who conspired? . . . I think I am warranted in saying that they will ask you to give him four years for being where he had not right to be, but are you going to do it? You make him an ex-convict; you make him an outcast for life, and for what? Did he conspire to murder Robert Johnigan? Did he conspire to murder Al Berch? Don't you know this boy's surprise when Al Berch came in there and knocked him down? . . ."

Ed Bond, helping to close for the State, delivered a twenty-seven-page oration, sprinkled every few paragraphs with "I have no personal feeling in this case, no not none." Then he would spew forth a fountain of hyperbolic passion that, today, is as unsettling as it is inspirational. After defending the word "n-----" as of African origin, he proceeded to describe his own background in Kentucky, the nobility of his father's slaves, and how they were loyal to the South throughout and even after the war, protecting the women and children while the men were fighting. Attorney Bond also detailed how someone set fire to his house in 1908 because he had a "n----- family" living on his land, helping him work his property. After describing the God-given paternalistic obligation of the white man, Bond pulled out all the stops to sway the jury in recognizing the obligation of the law to treat blacks as equal to whites. The oration lasted *one and a half hours*. Excerpts follow.

"Robert Johnigan was shot that night, nobody disputes that, he was killed while at the feet of [J. L.] Campbell, doing the work they couldn't get a white boy to do. He was shot that night and as he saw the dawn breaking, his soul took its flight and went to the other shore, and some day the defendant's soul will go the Great White Way and I would love to see what transpires. . . .

"Go to them and ask them how Al Berch ran his hotel in Marlow and if they don't tell you that they were running a fair, square, decent place and I will stop right now and tell you to turn this man [Gandy] loose. . . . They [the boys] said they wanted to have a little fun! I imagine it must have been funny to that woman there, when she stood by the grave of her husband and heard the clods beating on the coffin of her husband as they put him away forever. . . .

"Doctor Richards testified that the negro had a lick on his forehead. Somebody hit him there. What did Elza Gandy go there for? What did he tell Kincannon, 'Here, take this' for? He never explained it. He never denied it. Then he said, 'Watch Kinney, I have seen him get out of tight places before.' Elza Gandy knew that he had a gun in his pocket and he knew that Kincannon would use it. . . .

"That was Al Berch's misfortune. He felt it was his duty to protect this old Robert Johnigan and he went out and he did it like a man and he gave his life for Robert Johnigan, and then it costs Robert Johnigan his life too. I wonder if these lawyers for the defendant can do that? If they would stand up and say, 'You can't do it. I must protect him and I will give my life in doing it?' That was what Al Berch did, Gentlemen. Al Berch was no 'slouch' of a man I can tell you. . . .

"Had Robert Johnigan hurt that boy? No, he was shining shoes and these boys walk in there, but do they call Berch and say, 'We don't want this n----- to stay here?' No. They don't consult Berch at all. They walked in there and when Al Berch came out they turned on him and shot him and he lays there with his wife and baby on his breast listening to the death rattle in his throat. . . . But that woman there lost the support and protection of her husband that night and they come and tell you it was all a joke! That is the grimmest joke I ever heard any man tell. We just want to have a little fun so we can go into your home and blow out your brains. . . .

"I have no personal feeling in this case, but are we going to uphold the laws or make a travesty of them as was done in Chicago, where Leopold and Loeb took a boy and hammered his brains out and then the judge said they should not be hung. . . . I say to you that Oklahoma is ahead of Illinois and we are only sixteen years old. I wish they had had a jury of Stephens County men instead of that judge and he had given them a dose of Oklahoma justice . . . instead of a judge letting them off because they happened to be nineteen years old. . . .

"If they can do that and escape the penalty, then we just as well tear down our court houses, close our churches, and raise the Dragon of Hell instead of Old Glory on the top of our courthouses. . . . Yes, they wanted to have some fun. They say, 'Take it in that way.' They ask you fellows to look at it as a joke. . . . It is horrible—the most horrible thing that ever happened in Stephens County, and you Gentlemen know it. . . .

"Elza Gandy knew that Kinney was going to get out of that tight place before they went there. Do you think the people of Marlow approve of that? That night a shame fell over the town of Marlow for the good people have told me so. It was a blot upon the town where they have as good people as any town in the State of Oklahoma. They say this is the greatest disgrace that ever befell the town and they hope and want the jury to do its duty. . . . I would like to know if in Stephens County there is one man so low, so depraved, that he would say, 'I think you done the right thing when you went there and killed that n-----.' . . .

"Gentlemen, I don't believe there is any man on earth that is so hard that he don't sometimes think of the Master up there, waiting, and having to look him in the face and answer some questions about his life here. What did Johnigan do that night when his soul winged its way up there? He went up there, and the Master said, 'What are you doing here?' and Robert Johnigan's soul answered, 'Marvin Kincannon and Elza Gandy came to the hotel where I was working and started to fight me and they shot Mr. Berch and then they shot me. I ran in the telephone booth but they shot me in there and dragged me out and shot me again. That is the reason I am here.' And then what do you think the Lord is going to say, 'You are a negro. They had a right to do it'? No! He will say, 'Robert Johnigan, come in. You did nothing in the sight of God that is wrong. Your soul is as pure as a white man's.'"

When the ninety-minute soliloquy ended, defense attorney Wilkinson began his closing statement. Once again, he questioned the character of J. L. Clark and Walter O'Quinn, then blamed the whole affair on Albert Berch, who, in spite of an impeccable track record in Marlow, ostensibly had motives of his own that had backfired. Wilkinson also remarked on the sympathy that had been paid to the two widows, but he reminded the jury that there is nothing like a "mother's love," and that the jury should be thinking of poor Mrs. Gandy and the fact that her son would be facing prison time.

Sullivan offered the final argument for the State:

> You have no evidence in this case in any way that smirches the memory or the conduct of Al Berch in his life time . . . all you have heard in this case was conceived in the minds of Joe B. Wilkinson and Ben Saye and it didn't come from the witness stand. It is not the best evidence. Now, we find Al Berch, the owner and proprietor of the leading hotel in Marlow, Oklahoma. We find that it was a respectable hotel. Why do I say that? You could see by the class of people that told you from the witness stand that they made that their stopping place when making that town, that first class people frequented that hotel. . . .

Sullivan also reminded the jury that over the past year, people had plenty of time to discredit Robert Johnigan. And if there had been a single count of criminal activity, it would have been brought forth. But no one could come up with one negative word about Robert Johnigan. Yet, there had been "talk on the streets" of "running Johnigan off" from the day he arrived. Sullivan reminded the jury that shining shoes is something whites won't do. But instead of appreciating this fact, Gandy was outraged by Johnigan's presence in Marlow. Sullivan also referred to defense witnesses as "booze hounds," and as for McReynolds and others implicating J. L. Clark as a sly instigator working both sides, "you can look at them in the face and tell what kind of cattle they are." Sullivan admonished the jury to remember that the "act of Kincannon is the act of Gandy."

The jury was confined to quarters and rendered their verdict ten minutes later:

"We, the jury, drawn impaneled and sworn in the above entitled cause, do upon our oath find the defendant Elza Gandy guilty of manslaughter in the first degree and fix his punishment at confinement in the penitentiary for a period of 7 years. [Signed] G. W. Young, Foreman."

Elza Gandy was ordered to serve seven years in the state penitentiary at Granite, Oklahoma, a different prison from the one at McAlester, where Marvin Kincannon was already serving his time.

Two weeks after the jury verdict, the *Duncan Banner* described a visit to their town by N. Clay Jewett, the Grand Dragon of the Ku Klux Klan of the realm of Oklahoma, where "around a thousand klansmen and klanswomen were said to be present." "A magnificent banquet was served, much of the food being brought in from the country by members

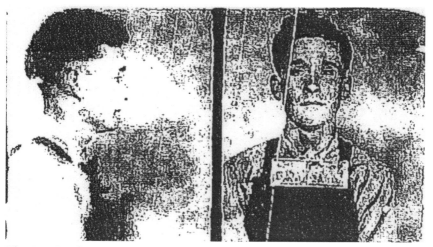

Elza Roy Gandy, age twenty-four, two years after the murders. This mugshot was taken at the state penitentiary at Granite, Oklahoma. (Courtesy of Oklahoma Department of Corrections)

of various lodges of the county. Mr. Jewett's visit had no political significance, according to local officials of the klan."

At the time, there was no evidence that linked the KKK to the murders of Albert Berch and Robert Johnigan.

In spite of the "victory" for the prosecution, the defense had already won the lion's share of the contest in that no charges were ever filed against Gandy as an accessory to the murder of Albert Berch. Furthermore, Gandy's seven-year sentence for "manslaughter" had been measured differently from the twenty-five-year sentence to Kincannon for the same crime against a white man, while both sentences ran well below the electrifying consequences for murder.

Nevertheless, given the pervasive mood of the times, one can argue that it's remarkable that charges were filed at all, and even more remarkable that convictions were obtained. So, when it comes to delivering the wreath of roses in victory to either the prosecution or the defense, we should consider that the only floral wreaths in this story belong on the caskets of Albert Berch and Robert Johnigan.

13

A Trip to Oklahoma's Supreme Court

As a character entering the story later on, I need to squeeze in for a moment to explain discovery of the trial transcripts, which were nowhere to be found in the Stephens County courthouse. These transcripts eluded my mother's lifelong research—and thank goodness, after the shocking discovery that, after the murders, Lula once paid a fine in police court for providing rooms in one of her hotels for "immoral purposes." Whether there's a fire or not, just the smoke is enough to choke you. Even I gasp, and I'm two generations and decades removed from the events.

Without the transcripts, there would have been gaping holes in this story. The key to their discovery came from one brave woman who claimed a life-insurance policy on her husband after the murders. That individual was not Lula Berch. It was Robert Johnigan's wife, Lizzie.

Early in my research, when I Googled a variety of key names and places related to the Marlow murders, only two links popped up, and they popped up again and again no matter how I asked the question—one for Elza Gandy and one for Lizzie Johnigan. The Gandy link was to a legal website tied to the Oklahoma Court of Criminal Appeals, where his conviction was upheld. Had this been the only link, I probably would not have pursued it, given that the pertinent information was already online elsewhere. In summary, the Gandy case was appealed on November 22, 1924, and decided in the Oklahoma Court of Criminal Appeals on May 15, 1926, a year and a half after Gandy was sent to prison. The lower court actions were upheld.

Several points of contention were made, most notably when the county attorney had asked Gandy if he gave the gun to Kincannon. When Gandy answered, "No," Sullivan then asked in reference to the earlier trial: "Do you recall that Kincannon testified that you did?" The objection from the defense was sustained at the time. As it turns out, Kincannon did not say this in his own trial, at least not in those exact words.

Still, the irregularities were not enough to throw out the conviction, so it was final. "The court was zealous in according the defendant a fair trial. The judgment of the trial court is affirmed. Doyle and Edwards, J.J., concur."

Gandy stayed in prison, for a while.

Although this first Google link was self-explanatory, the Lizzie Johnigan connection to an Oklahoma Supreme Court case was not. In fact, it was not even clear from the online information how Lizzie was related to Robert. But the gist of the case had something to do with an insurance policy from Lincoln Health and Accident Insurance Company and its death benefit that had not been paid to the beneficiary. Perhaps I could finally learn something about "the crippled negro" through the court records, given that my family knew next to nothing, not even his name. My childhood recollection of the story was that the black man had been beaten to death, while one of my sisters remembered that he had been shot. As it turned out, we were both right.

From the available information online, my guess was that the surviving widow had not been paid by the insurance company, prompting her to take the case to the state Supreme Court after failing to garner justice in the lower county court. At the same time, it was the only lead I had for Robert Johnigan, and I needed to chase down those legal documents, if they existed.

I met Justice Yvonne Kauger of the Oklahoma Supreme Court many years ago when I served as the surgeon for her mother. Appointed by then governor George Nigh to the Supreme Court in 1984, Yvonne had served as chief justice from 1997 to 1998, and was still serving as justice at the time I began work on this book. So, when I asked her if records from the 1920s were still accessible, she went to work excavating the archives, with the help of her aide, Derek Smalling. The result went far beyond my expectations. In order to review the Gandy and Johnigan cases back then, the original trial transcripts had been sent to Oklahoma City for the appeals process. These original documents had never been returned to Stephens County.

With the dust blown from the covers, I now had access to Gandy's original trial transcript from Stephens County, along with his appeal. As for Johnigan's insurance case, the Supreme Court had relied on the documents from the preliminary hearing in Stephens County, so this transcript had been hibernating in Oklahoma City for nearly a century as well. Because Marvin Kincannon did not appeal his case, his transcript was never sent to Oklahoma City, leaving it as the only missing document.

Justice Kauger had been encouraging me to come to Oklahoma's capital complex anyway, in order to tour the newly renovated court building, as she had been instrumental in the renovation of the old Oklahoma Historical Society building into the Supreme Court. Given that I would not be able to take the original transcripts out of the building, I could review them on site, while Derek Smalling began the arduous task of scanning the myriad pages into digital documents.

For those of us who attended grade school anywhere near Oklahoma City, a field trip to the Wiley Post Building southeast of the State Capitol was standard, where the state's historical museum was formerly housed. The neoclassical style that dominates Washington, D.C. was borrowed for the buildings of the Oklahoma complex, all of which surround the landmark oil well on the grounds. For the past thirty years, Yvonne Kauger had worked on her dream of building a new home for the historical society, now at the Oklahoma History Center, while moving both the Supreme Court and Court of Criminal Appeals into the stately building that bears likeness to the high court in D.C.

As I entered the building on a pleasant day in January 2012, I recalled the childhood field trips, while also calculating that fifty years had passed since my last visit. As it is now a high-security building, I waited in an antechamber filled with Native American art until Justice Kauger came downstairs to greet me and begin the tour. Many of the original murals had been preserved, along with marble staircases and much of the interior design, including the art-deco auditorium that remained much as I remembered. Justice Kauger is an adopted member of the Cheyenne and Arapaho tribe of Oklahoma and an aficionado of Native American art. As we toured, she named the artist of every piece, including an abstract teepee by Choctaw artist Derek Smalling, who was upstairs busily scanning documents.

During our stroll through the halls of justice, we knocked on the door of another Supreme Court member, Douglas Combs, who would later serve as chief justice. Justice Combs and I were fraternity brothers at the University of Oklahoma, and if his last name sounds familiar, yes, we are distant cousins. During Almarian's research in the 1970s, she linked her Combs lineage to that of the Combs family in Shawnee, Oklahoma. Her Elmore City clan was from the Tennessee branch, the latter from Kentucky. Justice Combs was surprised to learn that I was there on "Combs business," writing the story of Lula.

Then, we knocked on the door of Vice-Chief Justice Tom Colbert, who had expressed to Justice Kauger a special interest in my story. He was eager to know more, hoping someday to read a finished work. Tom Colbert, by the way, is the first African-American to serve on Oklahoma's

Supreme Court. Nearly one year subsequent to our meeting, he was sworn in as the chief justice.

We ended our tour in Justice Kauger's office, where the original transcripts were waiting for us while Derek continued copying nearby. Although the court records were not yet a hundred years old, it seemed as though I was caressing broken tablets found at the base of Mount Sinai. Over the course of my research, two main forces breathed life into this murder story—the photographic history and the exact words spoken by the main characters. On this day, it was the words at work. For the first time, I heard the words of the characters involved in the murders— witnesses, perpetrators, victims—all speaking in their own tongues. Most touching was hearing Lula's crackly voice and country grammar, resurrected, speaking not as a grandmother but as a bereaved widow.

Justice Kauger had become intrigued by the story, so we began to read together, each picking a transcript. We sat on opposite sides of her desk, reading silently while flipping pages. With each new revelation, we spoke aloud. The newspapers had not come close to providing this rich detail. I was awash in new information.

Then, from the transcript that Justice Kauger was reading, she unearthed the death scene as described by my grandmother. Realizing the power that this discovery might hold, she pushed the transcript across her desk to me, saying, "Here, you ought to be the one to read this."

After being buried for so long, Lula's words sprang from the pages. She described how she held Albert Berch's head in her lap, realizing the horror of what had happened and that he had only minutes to live. With the death rattle in his throat, all dreams of life anew vanished with a flicker, while nearby, my nearly two-year-old mother wailed. I never imagined that such a moment could be reanimated through lost words.

I left the Supreme Court building with many pages copied, the remainder arriving a short time later from Derek via email, allowing me to scrutinize them over an extended period. In terms of discoveries made per unit of time, nothing came close to the nuggets contained in these documents.

But what about Lizzie Johnigan? She had started it all, posthumously blowing the case wide open by prompting my trip to Oklahoma's Supreme Court. What was the nature of Lizzie's lawsuit that sent it all the way to the top? I had assumed that she was denied benefits and that she pursued justice. It seemed odd, though, for an African-American woman in 1924 to be this assertive, especially a woman whose husband had recently been murdered simply for being black. As it turned out, I was wrong. It was not Lizzie who pushed the case to the Supreme Court of Oklahoma.

14

Where Have You Gone, Robert Johnigan?

Three months after the murders, Lizzie Johnigan filed a lawsuit in District Court, Stephens County, Oklahoma, represented by Bond & Lewis, the same firm that would assist the county attorney in the prosecution of Elza Gandy. The defendant was Lincoln Health and Accident Insurance Company, a business that was refusing to pay death benefits to Robert Johnigan's widow (as I had suspected . . . so far). M. W. Pugh, the judge who had recused himself in the Kincannon trial, was the presiding judge for this case in Stephens County.

Before a jury, Lizzie testified that she had lived in Duncan since April 1, 1921. Working as a cook, she usually lived in the home of her employer. Her husband, Robert Johnigan, did the same, often working as a porter and living wherever he worked. At the time of the murder, Lizzie was the live-in cook at a home located at Third and Sycamore in Duncan.

Robert's most recent job in Duncan had been night watchman at the cottonseed-oil mill. Lizzie stated that Albert Berch and J. L. Clark came to Duncan to hire Robert, offering him higher pay as a porter at the hotel in Marlow.

Newspaper accounts had claimed that Robert was taken to Duncan after the assault at Johnson's Hotel, while some accounts merely noted "elsewhere." Robert did return to Duncan, after he had died in Marlow. Lizzie testified that she was with Robert from 9:00 P.M. the night of the attack until 5:30 the next morning, when he died in a room at the hotel. No other official rendering seems to have captured this point—both men died at Johnson's Hotel.

Although not an eyewitness, Lizzie testified that her husband had been struck with an iron pipe to the back of his head and shot. Whether it was a stick or pipe remains uncertain, but I'd been told "pipe" as a child, so it is interesting to note that this version was circulating early. Without referencing where she and Robert had lived prior to Duncan, she noted on the stand that Robert was buried in Ardmore, Oklahoma after preparation for burial in Duncan. Robert Johnigan was forty-five years old at the time of death, hardly "old," the descriptor that was used often with "crippled."

The reason why Lizzie Johnigan was on the stand becomes clear.

Q: This policy is for $1,000.00, with a weekly indemnity of $10.00. Have you received any of that money?

A: Not a nickel.

Lizzie described the wounds that she nursed throughout the night. "Underneath his left breast, one right in the hip here, and there was a lick on the left side of his head right here (indicating the back of the head). I rubbed the spot on his head all night." She noted powder burns surrounding both of his gunshot wounds. She also described how she was frightened to enter the hotel that night after the attacks, given that the word had already spread about the racial motivation. She stopped within a stone's throw of the hotel at the "gin house" near the railroad tracks and waited for the crowd to disperse. "Rufus Black was with me and he called up to see if there was any danger for us to go over there. Mr. [Brigham] Young (county sheriff) answered the telephone and told us to come on."

The exact mechanism of Johnigan's death tripped up the legal process during the murder investigation, with criminal charges arbitrarily assigned according to bullets (Kincannon) versus bludgeoning (Gandy). However, in this trial involving the widow Lizzie, the precise anatomy of the murder became fodder for the legal interpretation of wording in the exclusion clause of the insurance policy.

Dr. C. C. Richards had arrived at the hotel within minutes after the shooting, his testimony in the insurance trial being the same as in the criminal trials, leaving the exact cause of death open ended.

Another recognized authority on causes for death during this era was the undertaker.

Q: Now will you tell the Court there Mr. Woodward [a Duncan undertaker] in your own way what bullet wounds you found on his body when you were preparing it for burial, if any?

A: I found one in the left breast and one in the right thigh.

Q: The one in the left breast, did that bullet pass entirely through his body?

A: Yes sir.

Q: Did the one in the thigh pass entirely through?

A: Just a flesh wound.

Q: In your best judgment, Mr. Woodward, was the one in the breast, is that the bullet wound that caused his death?

A: Yes sir.

(Note: The bullet was fired by Kincannon, who was never tried for this crime.)

Given the paucity of information we have about Robert Johnigan, I'll include a few lines of testimony by Lizzie Johnigan at the Gandy trial. This is the only reference that provides information about the disability that seems to have defined Robert.

Q: Was he crippled or not?

A: Yes sir, crippled in one leg.

Q: What was the matter with his leg?

A: He was shot when he was quite a boy, here in the ankle. . . .

Q: Was his leg—tell the jury how he walked.

A: He dragged it, he couldn't bend his leg. He dragged it when he walked like that, all the time when he walked.

Q: Do you remember who shot him in the ankle?

A: Yes sir, he told me John Love shot him. They were raised together, just kids. . . .

Q: Accidentally?

A: Yes sir, accidentally.

On December 9, 1924, in the original insurance trial held in District Court of Stephens County, a jury of twelve "impaneled and sworn in the above entitled cause do upon our oaths find for the plaintiff and fix the amount of her recovery at $1,000, with interest at 6% from March 20, 1924."

Remarkably, the jurors had decided in favor of Lizzie Johnigan.

Lincoln Health and Accident Insurance Company, through Walter E. Latimer, attorney for the defendant, promptly filed a motion for a new trial. Judge M. W. Pugh ruled against the motion, whereupon the defendants appealed to the Oklahoma Supreme Court. Indeed, it was the *insurance company*, not Lizzie Johnigan, that pushed the case to a higher court and then into my hands eighty-eight years later.

Avoiding the legal jargon, the question at stake could be summarized as follows: Robert Johnigan had purchased a $1,000 life-insurance policy that covered accidental death, but in the eyes of the insurer, when one examines the facts of the case, *his death was no accident*. In fact, Bob Johnigan fully understood that negroes were not allowed to live in Marlow, and he had been adequately warned that his life would be in jeopardy if he moved there. Yet, upon confirmation of this fact, he refused to leave Marlow. Thus, he contributed to his own death.

In Latimer's words, "He had warning and was forewarned of said killing in plenty of time to have avoided same by leaving said town, which he should have done in the interest of peace and harmony, and to save his life, and by reason of the above conduct on his part the said killing was not accidental, according to the terms of the policy . . . " (statement filed in District Court, Stephens County, April 1, 1924).

The stack of legal documents relating to this case is thick, indeed. And there are so many exclusions written into the insurance policy that it makes one wonder if any manner of death would have qualified for coverage.

Yet, on April 13, 1926, over two years after the murder of Robert Johnigan, the Oklahoma Supreme Court rendered their decision with one dissenting vote (J. Phelps), the judgment being signed by C. J. Branson. Plaintiff Lizzie Johnigan received a judgment of $1,000, with interest at the rate of 6 percent per annum, from December 18, 1923 (the day of Robert's death) to the date paid. Lincoln Health and Accident Insurance Company was instructed to make payment to Lizzie Johnigan within twenty-four hours.

In reviewing the decision of the Oklahoma Supreme Court, one is struck by the care with which this case was addressed. There were two interpretations of the wording of the exclusions, no doubt, but the Court described in detail how carefully the wording had been made, almost as if the insurer wanted it to be ambiguous to allow any conceivable interpretation. The Court even pointed out the use of a single comma that was highly suspicious as a ploy to leave doors open to multiple interpretations. The bottom line, though, was this: Robert Johnigan took out an insurance policy that covered accidental death, and his death was an accident, at least from the standpoint of the insured and the beneficiary.

A copy of the original policy, issued November 27, 1922, more than a year before the murders, was included in the documents I received from the Oklahoma Supreme Court. The weekly premium was thirty-five cents. Weekly indemnity was ten dollars. Ironically, the company logo was a picture of Abraham Lincoln, and their motto was: "A Square Deal To All." The company is no longer in business.

I am somewhat embarrassed to note that at the time of my mother's burial in the Marlow cemetery in 2011, I did not even know the name of the black porter who had been murdered along with my grandfather. It wasn't that I forgot. I simply never heard the name from my grandmother or mother. Nor had my sisters. On the way home from the interment, though, my wife and I stopped at the Marlow Chamber of Commerce. A patient of mine from Marlow had mentioned that a town museum had opened and that it contained a scrapbook dealing with the double murder at Johnson's Hotel. I was directed to the museum by Debbe Ridley of the Chamber of Commerce, who, as it turned out, had organized the scrapbook.

Thumbing through the pages, I was overwhelmed by how little I knew regarding the murders and their aftermath. However, most striking was the realization that I knew nothing about the porter and that his descendants, if any, could also write a book about this double murder from their perspective.

Unfortunately, the name of the porter, as listed in various newspaper accounts, was Bob Journegan, Robert Jonigen, Robert Johagin, and so forth. For a good while, I was completely stymied in my efforts to learn more simply because I couldn't get an accurate handle on his name. And it was here that Lizzie came to the rescue. It was here that a Google search led to the Oklahoma Supreme Court case, which included the legal name of the deceased as Robert Johnigan. Then, of course, Lizzie's case led to the bulk of information related to the murders and trials through the lost transcripts. So, here's to you, Lizzie Johnigan. And to continue splicing lyrics from Simon and Garfunkel—where have you gone, Robert Johnigan?

Armed with the proper spelling and birthdate, the name of his wife, and their whereabouts after 1921, I assumed that the murders from the perspective of the Johnigans would be easy to assemble. But it was not so.

Given the fact that Robert was buried in Ardmore, Oklahoma, it was intriguing to discover "Robert and Lizzie Johnigan" as African-American residents of Ardmore in the 1920 U.S. Census, recalling that Lizzie testified that they moved to Duncan in April 1921. This particular Robert in 1920 listed his occupation as a "driver," while Lizzie worked as a domestic. They had two children living at home—Henry, who would have been ten at the time of the murders, and Josephine, age seven. Two older children lived nearby with cousins—Vada, about fifteen at the time of the murders, and her sister Lillian, age thirteen.

However, cross-checks to make sure this was the same couple who lived in Duncan led nowhere. Importantly, Lizzie never mentioned children in any of her testimony, nor did attorneys mention fatherless children in drawing juror sympathy. In contrast, the prosecution frequently referred to the toddler, Almarian Berch, as "fatherless."

Why not assume it's the same Johnigan couple and call it quits? Besides the absence of any reference to children in the trial records, Robert's age isn't a perfect match. Granted, from what we've seen about the age of Albert Berch, it's clear that one could pick and choose an age during this era, then stick with it—or change it.

From the insurance policy, we can gauge Robert to be forty-five, but the Robert from the U.S. Census would have been about forty-one. A point in favor of these two Roberts being one and the same is the fact that Robert's birthdate is listed "about 1882," giving some leeway. And while it's compelling to say "case closed," and assume that the murdered Robert and his wife had descendants who also inherited this saga as part of their family history, there are still loose ends.

Anyone involved in genealogy research appreciates the fact that old-fashioned footwork is still needed to supplement online efforts. While performing some of this footwork at the Oklahoma History Center, leafing through records from Stephens County in the 1920s, I happened across one Lizzie Johnigan, age thirty-nine, getting remarried to a much younger Grant Platt, age twenty-nine, in Duncan, Oklahoma. In cross-checking her age, it was identical to that of the Lizzie of the 1920 census, who was born in 1885 and married to a Robert Johnigan . . . with four children.

So, if you were to ask me whether or not I believe I have found the correct Johnigan family, I would say, "Yes, I *think* so."

Lizzie testified that Robert Johnigan had been buried in Ardmore. I made the assumption that he would have been buried in a segregated cemetery at that time. So, imagine my surprise to discover that Ardmore, a town of 25,000 today, has twelve cemeteries designated as African-American. Granted, some are quite small and might be considered family plots rather than cemeteries. Nonetheless, genealogy warriors, fortunately, have traipsed through these cemeteries, recording the names from readable headstones at each site. Only one, Clearview Cemetery, the largest, had Johnigans listed—twice.

So, on a chilly and windy day in March 2012, I spent an afternoon doing footwork, literally. I walked the rows of Clearview Cemetery for hours, captivated by the mixture of modest gravesites alongside lavish tributes. A large proportion of graves were unmarked, while others had creative monuments born of destitution, such as a pool of concrete poured directly onto the ground, with names and dates written with childlike fingertips.

The two Johnigans were easy to find, but there was no way to link them to Robert. And once I realized the large percentage of graves with no markers at all, I saw the futility of searching the other eleven African-American cemeteries. The readable names had already been posted online. Finally, a public-records office for the Ardmore cemeteries had no written logs of the burials from the 1920s.

So, in the end, I had to ask, "Where have you gone, Robert Johnigan?"

And that was how this chapter ended after my first draft. Nonetheless, two years later, as I was polishing this manuscript, I decided to check the online ancestry service one more time. Much to my surprise, someone had opened a "private member story" for Robert Johnigan that was tagged to a newspaper article titled, "7 Held for Murder." This web-based feature allowed one-way communication from me to the anonymous party who had established the link.

When I received a reply, it was not from a Johnigan descendant. It was from (follow closely now) a neighbor who had helped out an ex-significant other who was still very close to a family of Johnigan descendants in Minnesota. As it turned out, this significant other had opened the online option to help the Johnigan family discover their roots, only to stumble upon a newspaper account of the murder of one of their ancestors. The Johnigan descendant involved at this point had never heard about the murders and was so disturbed by the discovery that he asked his significant other (before becoming ex-) to drop all genealogic pursuits and never mention the murders to anyone in the family. This approach worked fine, until I came along.

The ex-significant other was so taken by the story of the murders, and the fact that a book was being written about the saga, that he took it upon himself to inform the Johnigan descendants of their heritage. Widely spread—primarily in Minneapolis, Kansas City, and Oklahoma City—the Johnigan descendants *had never heard about the murders*, even though many had been raised by the aforementioned children of Robert and Lizzie.

To say they were stunned is an understatement. And in one of the most remarkable moments in the course of my research, I placed a phone call to the "hub" of the family of Johnigan descendants, our voices bridging the two families after ninety years, albeit ever so briefly. With the name "Johnigan" married away years ago, they have asked to remain anonymous. That said, I was able to confirm that I had correctly identified the Johnigan family living in Ardmore, Oklahoma in 1920 as the same Robert and Lizzie Johnigan of the Marlow murders. Through the ex-significant other, I was also able to learn some details about the four Johnigan kids as adults, all now deceased.

Even though the descendants had been completely shielded from the story of Robert's murder, a strong message had been handed down through the generations—"do not live in small towns . . . always make your home in a metropolitan area." No explanation for this curious advice was ever given to the Johnigan descendants.

15

Lula's Crusade in the Aftermath— the First Obsession

At the time of Albert Berch's burial, Lula could not afford a headstone. She would need every penny to survive. Although she had been prospering at the time of the murder, cash flow took a nosedive. Few dared to stay at the hotel as guests. She was desperate to leave town, but finding a buyer for the hotel would not be easy, at least in the immediate aftermath.

She intended to exhume and move Albert's body out of Marlow to be close to her, wherever she settled and died, another reason to forego purchase of a headstone. So, the only marker on the Berch plot was a small metal placard staked into the ground, the last name scribbled on paper under a celluloid cover, misspelled as *Birch*.

Lula wrote:

> I was left almost penniless after the funeral. My husband had bought a small interest in a little, shabby hotel in Duncan, one that you gave room and board by the week or month. O what a workhouse! There was a woman running it who was ill and was going to quit, so I decided maybe I could take it over and keep a roof over my baby's and my head, so I took over this job. I stayed with it one year. I was chambermaid for 20 rooms, helped do the cooking and dishwashing and in the meantime had to have my baby operated for abscess of the mastoid. This was a year of grief, work, and worry, and finally the man who owned three-fourths of the hotel bought my interest.

In another account, she recalled in 1965, "No one would stay at the [Johnson] hotel, so after leasing the furniture, I kept my personal belongings, took my baby, and left town. This was 41 years ago. The other murderers have never been tried. Some of them are old men with blood still on their hands on account of following a mob."

Here's where the story turns icky, or ickier, for Lula. In a letter found in a cardboard box in the Hollingsworth attic, written more than a year

129

after the murders, on stationery from the Doss Hotel in McAlester, Oklahoma, an anonymous author describes sinister activities that involve Lula's father-in-law, Albert Berch, Sr.

The handwriting in this letter matches nothing else in my archives. I suspect that it was written by one of the detectives who helped Lula in her fight for justice. From one of Lula's logbooks, we know that a detective was commissioned to travel to McAlester in order to meet with Marvin Kincannon in prison to try to solve the mysteries surrounding the murders, most notably, the name of the alleged mastermind. Even though the letter below does not relate to that particular interview with Kincannon, the fact that it is anonymous, originates from McAlester, and is written by a man with a mission supports the notion that this is one of the hired detectives. Furthermore, the letter refers to an individual (illegible, but suggestive of *Reeves*) who is teamed up with Lula in this pursuit, perhaps a lead detective. The letter is dated May 12, 1925, while Lula is living in Duncan. Here is the letter in its entirety, with my notations in brackets.

My Dear Mrs. Berch:
I wrote you a rather long letter from Holdenville [Dr. Albert Berch moved there after the murder of his son], this were about my interview with "Dr. Berch." Also wrote Uncle Jim [unknown person] a letter telling him to ask you to show him the letter. The more I think of that matter the more I am impressed with the idea that you and [name illegible— Reeves?] ought to get *some one* to pump the "Dr." for more information. If I were going to be around him I would soon found out who the special *7 boys* were that were selected to go down and "run the n----- off," also who it was that sent them. I gathered that it was "some one else" other than these first ones who arrived and put the *rat* in who did the killing. [The author of this letter transitions here to a later incident at the hotel.] He frankly told me that it was the "best citizens of Marlow" who went with him to the hotel that night for the purpose of killing you—That these citizens remained outside while he went to your room for that purpose. And that it was only "because of the child looking up at him so appealingly" that he desisted. [Although there is some pronoun ambiguity here, the compelling interpretation is that "he" is Lula's father-in-law, restraining his intent to commit murder.]
If the Dr. is not a "Klux" he is very friendly to them. When I suggested that from reading the newspaper accounts I gained the impression that the Klan was behind the boys, he denied its responsibility for that act— only the "best citizens of Marlow" were responsible. He told me there was

no regular KKK organization at Marlow then or now, but admitted that a goodly number of the best citizens of Marlow belonged to that organization [this double-talk is not explained, and it appears that the comments that follow are quoted from Albert Berch, Sr.]: "Although I had never joined them I was very friendly and admitted that I had noted a wonderful effect for good brought about through their influence in many localities." And now listen—it was then that he told me that Klan *was behind* the Carter affair. "Not the organization, but some of the most influential and younger members of the Klan at Marlow were behind the man made by that man Carter soon after the killing of my son." The man was made for the "purpose of running off those two whores at the hotel and to keep *that woman* from disposing of the property to an undesirable party."

There is not one bit of doubt in my mind that the good *Dr.* was one of the planners of that Carter affair and that they intended going further but got cold feet when they found [J. W.] Simpson [deputy sheriff, Stephens County] on the job. Looking back now I can see the whole plan just as the Dr. narrated it to me. Of course, I cannot suggest a way for you and [illegible—Reeves?] to proceed. You can work that out yourself. If I were around Holdenville any length of time I could get the whole thing from him. That is, unless he found out *who I was*. If he did that I might have to "git up git" to dodge the wrath of some of those "best citizens" myself. One thing bear in mind all the time—the Dr. knows every single man and every bit of evidence in your Carter case to date. Sincerely yours, X.

Now, it becomes easier to understand why Lula loathed her father-in-law. Throughout all the years of my mother and grandmother telling this murder story, they never mentioned Dr. Berch's possible role in the saga. Until my mother died and my research began, I was not even aware that my great-grandfather ever lived in Marlow. The only reference to his name was with regard to the accusatory opinions held by Lula—he was not a "real doctor," and he was a "drug addict or alcoholic or both."

The role of Albert Senior in this story would be a tale in and of itself, yet we have no more information other than what is contained in the letter above. But recall that, after the murders, Albert Senior told the newspapers that his son had been fairly warned to get the negro out of Marlow. That remark, criticized openly by Lula, has a different ring to it now.

The second bit of intrigue from the letter is the "Carter affair," occurring at some point after the murders. After my initial reading of this letter, I made note to track down any information about a "Carter affair" that I could find, as the name was unfamiliar to me. While I came up empty-handed during my first year of research, the name Carter, as the father of Oklahoma icon Pearl Carter Scott, will surface again, lending new meaning to "your Carter case" from the Doss letter.

So who hired the detective(s) mentioned above, if Lula was "almost penniless"? Enter the ex-governor of Oklahoma, Jack Walton. By "ex" I mean "newly impeached and removed from office." While the family folklore told us that Lula "camped out" on the steps of the governor's mansion until he agreed to talk with her, I doubt that's how it went. My guess is that ex-Governor Walton tripped over himself, and perhaps Lula as well, to interview a "victim of the Klan." Motives aside, no one can deny that Jack Walton, by this time, had transformed himself into a Don Quixote, jousting the Ku Klux Klan while dreaming of his own return to political office in Oklahoma.

The current governor's mansion was not built until 1928, so our family lore is actually referring to Governor Walton's stately home at 431 Northwest Seventeenth Street, at the corner of Walker, in the Heritage Hills section of Oklahoma City. The circumstances surrounding the purchase of this home, as noted previously, were dragged into the impeachment charges, but later glossed over due to the stature and power of the seller, future Oklahoma governor E. W. Marland.

The Library of Congress lists *Jack Walton's Paper, the National Anti-Klan Weekly* as being in existence for one year (1923), and perhaps only one issue. However, I have a copy of volume 1, number 11, discovered in the excavation that took place in El Reno after my mother's death. This issue was published January 6, 1924, three weeks after the Berch-Johnigan murders and at the same time as the preliminary hearing in Stephens County.

I suspect that Lula rained down like manna from heaven for the ex-governor, providing the centerpiece for Walton's next edition. With a multileveled headline, her story dominates the front page and inside as well. The article begins with a brief editorial; I provide here excerpts from the subsequent account:

"Shoot Dear Daddy! Never Come Back!" Cries Baby
KLAN MURDER SAYS WIFE
Grief Stricken Mother Drops Child, Rushes to Aid Prostrate Husband
Police Permit Murder
"My husband, without a moment's warning and unarmed, was not murdered by a mob of sons of Marlow klansmen—he was massacred. I

saw him shot down as I held our 22 months old baby girl in my arms. As I dropped the child to run to him and hold his head, Marvin Kincannon fired a shot over my head. . . . I saw only one gun which Kincannon used. The rest of the mob were armed with iron pipe which they used in knocking the porter in the head. Kincannon fired the gun from his shoulder, killing my husband instantly. As I cried and plead for him [husband] to speak to me, he breathed his last. Baby darling cried: 'Boy shoot daddy! Dear Daddy never come back no more.'"

So said Mrs. Lulu Berch, widow of A. W. Berch who was killed by a mob at Marlow, while he was peaceably operating his hotel and on his own premises. Berch had been a town builder, having spent over $50,000 in ___ting [unreadable] and furnishing one of the best hotels in the state compared to small towns.

"My husband had been accused of being an anti-klan and a Catholic," continued Mrs. Berch. She was in Oklahoma City Tuesday, to see Governor Jack Walton and spent more than an hour at the Walton home. . . .

"The Ku Klux Klan deprived me of everything in life, in taking my dear husband's life," she said between sobs, as she told her pitiful story.

Like hundreds of others who have sought aid from Governor Walton, since he was stripped of his power by the Ku Klux Klan legislature—Mrs. Berch's plea is almost in vain.

[Lula continues:] "Most of the mob members are sons of klansmen who belong to the Marlow klan. It was twenty minutes before any city officers arrived at the place and all members of the mob had fled. I am told, that the city officers knew that the massacre was to take place; that one of the officers passed by while the mob was on the way to the hotel. The city officers are klansmen. The son of the city night watch was in the mob. I have no confidence in Speaker McBee—I believe he is a klansman. Had it not been for the fact that Sheriff Brigham Young is a strong anti-klansman, and for the quick work of Deputy Sheriff J. W. Simpson, all of the mob would have escaped and perhaps gone unpunished. . . . Statements published—that my husband was killed because he fought to protect the porter, are false [note: Lula maintained that her husband had been the primary target and that the Klan had used the porter as an excuse to murder Albert Berch]. Before my husband's death we were offered $55,000 for the hotel property and it is worth $60,000. . . . The Ku Klux Klan has boycotted the hotel ever since it was built."

Stephens County is the home of Speaker McBee of the house of representatives. McBee was one of the leaders who demanded that Governor Walton be impeached because of his fight against the Ku Klux Klan. Stephens County klansmen were threatened with martial law because they wanted to stage a monster masked parade. Walton was ready to send soldiers, when the klan informed Sherriff Young, that they would abide by the governor's orders. McBee then issued the call for the meeting of the legislature which was dispersed by the militia.

Speaker McBee, after declaring that he "was opposed to the klan," failed to sign the bill prohibiting trespassing by mobs on private property of klansmen or others—which was voted by both house of the legislature. Oklahoma is without any anti-klan legislation at present, as result of Speaker McBee's failure to act.

The Walton newspaper is filled with stories from across the nation concerning Klan activities, though the focus is on Marlow. Another article headlined *Klan Policeman Winks at Crime While Son Leads Murder Mob* tells the story of H. R. Gandy and his son Elza Gandy.

Then, tucked away in a corner, sits a headline not much larger than the print: *Acting Governor Is Opposed to Klan, Says*—leading to an announcement that M. E. Trapp declared, "I am opposed to any secret order which keeps its membership rolls secret—that includes the klan, make sure of that."

While Trapp's anti-Klan sentiments had been suspected, this speech in Muskogee, Oklahoma removed all doubt. State Question 123 and its Initiative Petition would be launched under Trapp's auspices before he became the official governor, a proposed law "requiring the filing and recording of the names and addresses of officers and members of all secret organizations in the office of the county clerk of the county of their residence," as well as other provisions intended to weaken the Klan. This State Question 123 will resurface as a smoking gun as this story transitions from true crime to investigative journalism decades later.

Lula's account in Walton's newspaper is noteworthy, as she first mentions the one bullet shot over her head but later mentions two stray bullets that came close to her, one of these leaving powder burns on her face. There is no mention of the hole in the baby gown. Was this an omission? Or did Lula add this to the story later when she found a hole in the toddler's gown? The exact number of bullets fired varied greatly in court testimony, but there is complete agreement on at least one stray bullet, and perhaps two or more. So the family folklore of the bullet hole in our mother's gown lives on.

Jack Walton's Paper *(vol. 1, no. 11), Sunday, January 6, 1924, only two days after the preliminary hearing for the accused murderers and three weeks after the murders*

Former governor Jack Walton didn't stop with the newspaper coverage, however. When Lula told him of the death threats made against her, and bullets being fired into the hotel after the murders, Walton sent detectives to protect her in Marlow as long as she lived in the hotel. And he hired others, perhaps a team of detectives, to define the connection between the Klan and the murders. Lula wrote in one of her accounts:

> Governor Walton sent a detective to the penitentiary to interview Marvin Kincannon to see if he would say it was the KKK who planned the murders. He told him he talked only to business men about the deal and he [the detective] would have to find out for himself if they were KKK. He said he only talked with one man and this man told him what to do and how to do it and who to kill and told him we have plenty of money to get you out of trouble. The detective talked with some 27 men who had made bond and who was citizens of the town. But these boys were coached so thoroughly they wouldn't tell a thing. They sneered and hooted at the detective. They said we have plenty of protection and plenty of money.

In the end, very little came from Lula's determined efforts, other than the satisfaction of knowing that she had pursued possibilities to their limits, and that she had been helped by her esteemed Governor Walton. Who can blame her for lionizing the disgraced governor? At the lowest point in her life, after such a series of tragedies and now the murder of her husband, the only person willing to aid Lula in her fight for justice was "King Jack." And though she moved on with her life, we shall see the ceaseless failure of that weak bromide, "Time heals all wounds."

16

For the Rest of Her Life

Lula was enamored with property and real estate for the rest of her ninety-eight years. Without too much psychobabble, it could be argued that the wounds she had suffered from the loss of her first family, and now Albert's murder, were sublimated into bricks and mortar, that is, stuff that would last.

She owned a series of hotels in Duncan, prompting this memory after the murders: "Lived there [the Thompson Hotel] 2 years after Al passed away . . . Bought furniture Bonair Hotel 1925, kept it 3 months. Buff brick, 40 rooms. Traded equity for furniture in the American Hotel, 30 rooms. Kept it 6 months. Sold. Bought the lease on BellAir. Kept it 3 months . . . " (and so forth).

Regarding Lula's quest for financial security during the Roaring Twenties, keep in mind that there were no federal welfare programs, no unemployment benefits, no disability, and no social security. Some states and charitable organizations funded "public relief" programs, but she refused these avenues.

Lula was a natural at real estate "flipping." Her profit margins, however, were lean. In fact, she teetered on the brink of insolvency. Eschewing "relief," Lula finally admitted the need for help, recognizing the only source of wealth in her extended family—Aunt Helen.

Family lore told us this: with toddler Almarian in tow, as proof of Albert Berch's legacy, Lula boarded a train and headed for Los Angeles to visit the one great bastion of riches to which she might have access— Aunt Helen DeLendrecie, the surrogate mother of Albert Berch. By the time of Albert's murder, Helen and her husband, O. J., had retired from Fargo, North Dakota to what was then a plush section of Los Angeles, with silent-screen stars as their neighbors.

Helen had originally listed Albert Weldon Berch in her will as a minor beneficiary among many. But his death, coupled with baby Almarian's existence, prompted the elderly woman to rewrite her will and establish a trust for my mother's education. This trust paid for Almarian's boarding school and college education, with enough left over to make a down payment on her first home after marriage to my father.

Lula's financial doldrums proved to be unrelenting, and it is very unlikely that Almarian would have made it to the University of Oklahoma without Aunt Helen's backing. While dissecting sharks in her comparative anatomy class, Almarian met my father, and the history of my immediate family began. Dad always quipped, "I liked her comparative anatomy."

The trip to Los Angeles to show the baby Almarian to Aunt Helen proved to be true upon scrutiny of the *Marlow Review* microfilm. However, the exotic journey made the local news *prior* to the murders. So in contrast to my family's version, it was not a trip made out of desperation after all but a time of peak joy for the Berch couple. Still, before her death in 1926, Helen adjusted her will for the new baby.

To our knowledge, money was never transferred directly from Helen to Lula after the murders to help with general expenses. Also, there was one catch to Aunt Helen's educational trust money, according to Lula. Almarian was to be raised Catholic, with the somewhat obscure coupling of religion to boarding school. And here's where the religious confusion begins. I had always believed that Albert Berch was Catholic, reinforced by the fact that Lula kept a crucifix prominently displayed in her home. As a child, I learned from my mother three reasons for Albert's murder: 1) he would not sell the hotel to the Klan, 2) he was Catholic, and 3) he hired a black man against sundown laws. Note that in the 1950s and 1960s, even Almarian believed that her father had been Catholic.

So, the first time I read in the 1924 newspapers that Lula claimed an error on the Klan's part in believing that Albert was Catholic, it made no sense. In fact, Lula was correct. Albert was not Catholic, nor was Lula. If the citizens of Marlow got that impression, it had to do with his early years in a Catholic orphanage or perhaps his reference to a "rich Catholic aunt." In fact, Aunt Helen may have been Catholic more in the sense of charity and social duty, given that she helped establish a Unitarian Church in Fargo. That said, her crypt is squarely planted in a Catholic mausoleum. The only confirmed Catholics in the family turned out to be Uncle O. J. and Almarian.

Aunt Helen's strategy might have been for Almarian to get the best education possible in that day and time, which was often through the Catholic Church. Regardless, it made a Catholic out of Almarian, for a while. She was raised in various Catholic boarding schools in Oklahoma, primarily in Chickasha. And she and my father, Francis W. Hollingsworth, were married in the Cathedral of Our Lady of Perpetual Help in Oklahoma City. Eventually, Almarian defaulted on her commitment, renouncing her Catholicism to become a card-carrying Presbyterian in order to raise a family of predestined Protestants.

With Helen being such a powerful influence on our family, it is remarkable that I didn't know her last name until I began work on this book, nor did I know why we called her "aunt." Another question brewed: why was Lula so willing to surrender her daughter to Catholic boarding schools? The answer, as always for Lula, can be traced to real estate and oil leases.

After Albert's murder, Lula began working in the city of Duncan at Reynolds Real Estate, where she spent a great deal of time "driving around the area" with the brother of the owner. Harry Reynolds was a World War I veteran who had settled in Duncan after the war, having spent most of his prewar life in Pond Creek, Oklahoma. On April 23, 1927, Lula and Harry were married by a justice of the peace in Stephens County, a little over three years after Albert's murder. My sisters and I knew Lula only as "Grandma Reynolds," a widow.

What seemed to Lula as mild "nervousness" in Harry at the time of their marriage, thought to be a form of "shell shock" after the Great War, grew into a medical nightmare, sending Harry all the way to the new clinic in Rochester, Minnesota where the Mayo brothers were staking their claim as the top spot in the U.S. for medical care. The nation's leading expert on thyroid disorders evaluated Harry there and diagnosed him with Graves' disease, or thyrotoxicosis. Sadly, he was considered inoperable due to the heart damage done by years of an overactive thyroid gland that had flogged the cardiac muscle into permanent fatigue. Today, his illness would be managed with relative ease, but for Harry and Lula, the torture would continue for over twenty years. A stroke due to the related hypertension did not have the decency to end it for Harry, turning Lula into a full-time nurse, shaving, feeding, and bathing her husband. His death from unrelated lung cancer was perhaps a welcome event for both Harry and Lula.

My sisters and I knew nothing about Harry's illness until shortly after our mother's death, when we stumbled onto a bounty of files related to his condition. In these, Lula chillingly described in detail Harry's mental meltdown, leading him to the brink of suicide. In fact, this tangential tale of uncontrolled Graves' disease and its psychiatric manifestations was so compelling that I was sidetracked into a new chapter, called "What's the Matter with Harry?" that I placed online, so as not to depart from the main story at hand.

Harry's bizarre affliction aside, he and Lula, early on, were drawn to the fact that many folks in the area were getting rich in the oilfields. In 1919, Erle P. Halliburton had started an oil-well cementing business in Duncan, Oklahoma, incorporated in 1924, and by the time Harry and Lula considered entering the business, Halliburton's company was well on its way to becoming an international powerhouse.

Oil was so easy to access after a field had been identified that "wildcatters," those speculators who poked random holes in the ground, had stories that rivaled those of the California Gold Rush. Lula, of course, had been listening to the oilmen talk during the glory days of Johnson's Hotel and had already ventured into wildcatting during her marriage to Albert Berch. Opportunity knocked, and Harry and Lula responded by liquidating their real-estate assets and plunging all $6,101 of their personal "wealth" into drilling projects.

Lula and Harry worked in the oil patches, a nomadic existence, traveling from wellsite to wellsite and often living in tents. This was "no place for a young girl," so Almarian, five years old at the time and endowed with the educational trust from Aunt Helen, was sent to boarding school, where she lived nine or ten months out of the year. In the summers, she joined her mother and stepfather as a junior wildcatter.

Contrary to what one might feel for a five-year-old separated from her mother, by her own account, Almarian loved school and the other kids. This would not last, however, as the Great Depression prompted many dropouts from boarding school, and the social buzz was silenced. As Almarian grew older, she realized that there was "another world out there," and she wanted to participate.

From our childhood on, Almarian told us that "Harry and Mother were wildcatters who struck oil several times, but had leases taken away from them and never made a dime." That pretty well sums it up.

Lula and Harry were two-thirds of Cruce Oil, and in one of her writings, Lula describes her early days at Johnson's Hotel and how she got swept away by oil fever after she "learned the business by listening" to the oilies staying there. Already familiar with real-estate transactions, Lula discovered that mineral and drilling rights were a new ballgame. She describes meeting a retired judge and wealthy speculators from

Wichita Falls who prompted her entrée as an oil woman: "There was a shallow field that was producing at that depth, and a geologist said the chances were almost 100 percent this acreage [640 acres] would produce at the same depth. So, it proved true."

But things did not work out in the end. The events that followed occupy many files, complete with court records and fodder for another book entirely. The controversy centered around the fact that Cruce Oil held a "lease in escrow," a common approach at the time wherein multiple provisions had to be met before the lease could be taken out of escrow—a defined timeframe for geologic survey, for a functioning drilling rig, and for the nebulous requirement of oil with "commercial productivity." One can easily imagine that the advantage went in the direction opposite the wildcatter, thus relegating this particular financial product to the waste bin of history. Cruce Oil was one of the victims of the "lease in escrow" trickery, prompting long and complicated courtroom proceedings.

On the witness stand, Lula was the primary voice for Cruce Oil. And she spoke in roughneck language with the geologic expertise of a dilettante, insisting that high-quality oil had been discovered and retrieved, while her opponents spun their version of oil admixed with sand and water.

A critical point in the trial, however, dealt with a drilling deadline to maintain the unconventional "lease in escrow." At the midnight hour, a drilling contractor agreed to proceed by handshake with Lula, to be finalized later in writing. Lula wrote:

> But old lady luck was against us. Two days before we would start drilling again one of the landowner's sons ran into him [i.e., the contractor who was prepared to save Lula's investment] with his car and killed him instantly [*remarkably, there were no accusations of murderous intent*]. Such a shock. No one but someone who had a fortune tied up in one man will ever know. Then, the big court fight began. The lease owners sued us for cancellation of contract. We begged. We had an attorney plead. . . . I know you will be surprised when I tell you they beat us in court. They gave those leases back to the farmers and not one thing did they let us reserve. So we appealed to the Supreme Court. It stayed in court 5 years, then was thrown out of court because it was not presented right . . . opportunity had knocked, but we opened the wrong door.

Lula's nomadic life with Harry took them from town to town, oilfield to oilfield. Subsequently switching to unoiled real estate, they occupied their properties during renovation, claiming at least thirty different residences in Oklahoma City alone. Lula would flip around a hundred properties, continuing into her nineties.

Harry Reynolds died of lung cancer at age fifty-nine on January 22, 1947, an end to his chronic suffering from thyrotoxicosis but unfortunate timing. He had hoped to live long enough to see Lula's first grandchild and his first step-grandchild, a birth that would occur eighteen days later with the arrival of my sister Susan—one final pleasure denied Harry, after a lifetime of misery.

A few years later, Lula's closest sibling, brother Fred Combs, died of kidney cancer. Then, her father died at age eighty-six. After these deaths in close order, widow Arrie Combs and her thrice-widowed daughter Lula moved in together on one side of a duplex at 1805-7 Northwest Twenty-Seventh in OKC. They purchased it in 1953 and rented the other side. They would live together at the duplex until Arrie died in 1965. Lula stayed there alone for another fifteen years, until poor health forced her to El Reno for her final two years.

As one might predict, the duplex had a "storm cave." But this hole, installed by Lula, was unique. The entry door was located on the front porch. For this property alone, Lula recorded a series of fifteen renters at one point, plus thirty additional tenants over many years in the garage apartment at this same site.

Lula documented many bizarre experiences as a landlady. As she writes about maintenance problems, deals broken, dollars spent, pennies made, all at multiple sites at considerable distances, one fact is not readily apparent—Lula never had a driver's license nor owned a car. As it turns out, she drove some as a young woman before licensure became a law, but by the time she reached Oklahoma City, where she worked her numerous properties, she walked or rode the bus.

★★★

A typical deal for Lula yielded a few hundred dollars' profit, while a major coup landed her a few thousand. In 1951, Lula wrangled the largest trophy in her case, flipping the Avon Hotel in Guthrie after a mere seven days, at a profit of $4,000. She gave Almarian $500 and a new set of tires. Lula would boast that she had her buyer on the line for the Avon even before she had closed on her purchase.

Her writings also include recollections of her many oil leases, a farm in Madill, a café in Duncan, along with long lists of every tenant who lived in her rental properties, several hundred names total. Mixed in her logbooks are aphorisms, important dates (especially family deaths), and handwritten contracts using the language of lawyers.

One of the most common themes in Lula's writings concerns troublesome tenants, including threats against her life as she collected rent. An ex-con threatened her with a butcher knife in one story, while an ex-partner did the same with a shotgun, in both instances Lula talking the men out of their rage. For someone whose life was gripped by anxiety, she seems to have been wearing a suit of armor when it came time to "make the deal."

After Arrie died in 1965, Lula's writings betray two all-consuming emotions—fear and loneliness. She began living alone, without children, spouse, or parent, for the first time in her life. She wrote frequently about her private sadness, but no one had access to her diaries until after her death.

One Christmas card to a friend was found in a heap of postmortem memorabilia, written by Lula though never mailed, inviting the woman to come live in the adjacent duplex. A footnote by Lula in red ink points out (to herself?) that she failed to mail this letter because she was out of stamps, and by the time she had stamps, Christmas had come and gone.

On November 27, 1966, one year after Arrie's death, Lula (age eighty-two) chose to be baptized at Trinity Baptist Church in Oklahoma City. Writing now as the son of an ex-Catholic, and considering my grandmother Lula's lifelong plight, I long to bring back indulgences, or at a minimum, praying for the dead. Regardless of the exact ticket to Heaven, Lula deserves a pass.

Beginning with their marriage in 1943, my parents helped Lula in many ways, though not in the early days. In fact, Lula assisted them financially while my father was an intern in the days when the salary was fifty dollars a month, in addition to free room and board. However, as time went on, the tide turned toward Lula, and she preferred her gifts as upgrades on her property.

Lula's wintertime lamentations, as recorded in her diary, were more intense when my parents were on extended ski trips, leaving her to write about the cold and the snow and the ice and the untold tragedies that were taking place every second as automobiles slid off the slick highways, killing the passengers and the innocents nearby. But there was always one thing to worry about no matter what the weather—property.

In a letter to my mother, judged to be written in the late 1960s, Lula outlines her strategy to turn a house into a duplex. After providing construction details, she transitions to worry: "It will rent for $150 a month instead of $90. . . . I stay awake nights figuring how to meet actual bills, not being able to do what I want to do. I have had all the partnerships I want. I want to be my own boss. [Note: Lula is in her eighties as she writes this.] I will be happy again if I can do as I please, even if I do have to economize to the point of not having the niceties of life as most people call it, and being so lonesome sometimes, or all the time I am not busy, that I get sick to my stomach."

At this same time, Almarian launched her own search for roots, that is, the Combs and Berch genealogies. Much of Lula's writings are in response to Almarian's request for information. In one of these letters, Lula, in her eighties, tells her daughter that Albert and Lula's wedding took place in El Reno. Lula called it a "coincidence," given that this town had become the Hollingsworth home. Lula goes on to grumble about her new renter in the adjacent duplex, who doesn't pull her share of the work. In fact, she does no work at all. She pays for "half of the food, but eats three-fourths, then she'll drive to the store for cigarettes, but won't take me anywhere," Lula writes. "Maybe it's just as well. She has had 2 heart attacks since last year, and she could have one more while driving and kill us both."

Lula goes on to describe a terribly cold winter, and how lucky her three grandchildren are, all of whom were living in California at the time, keeping in mind the problems there with "floods and mudslides." She predicts the impending death of my father, who has had heart surgery by this time, and "statistics show that you never live more than 8 to 12 years after heart surgery." (He would live twenty-three more years.)

In a letter to a niece, Lula wrote this about her daughter:

> Almarian is close by, that is, they drive it in 30 minutes. She comes over almost every week on Tuesday, that's Francis' day off, as I told you she is what she calls herself a freelance writer and is selling her stories. Two weeks ago she sold her article to *Orbit* put out by the *Sunday Oklahoman*. The article was about keys. I told her anyone who could write a story people would read on as dull a subject as keys should be proud of herself. I'll try to be careful not to be so long writing next time. I love you, Aunt Lula.

In August 1975, when Lula was ninety-one, her photograph appeared on the front page of the *Oklahoma City Times*, as part of the headline story: "Hospital Worker Found Slain Near OCU Campus: Body bound with cord, police say." Lula had stumbled upon the body (one of her renters), and this gave her a front-page headshot, her first since the murders at Marlow. No one in 1975 would have suspected that she had been a central figure in one of the most compelling stories never told about early Oklahoma.

Almarian, newly anointed as a writer through her master's degree in journalism, asked Lula to describe the body-finding episode for a planned article that might generate greater interest than the debut story on keys. In a thirteen-page written account filled with hyperbole and malapropisms, Lula reveals that it was a crime of revenge by a murderous roommate who had buddied up to the victim with the plan to kill all along. The motive: the victim had once testified in court, sending a family member of the killer to prison.

An excerpt from Lula's version: "I leaned over all this pile of rubbage to get it off and it was a wood bed low to the floor, and in order to do this, I had to move some of the quilts and My Lord to Heaven when I moved this, my face was only about 5 inches away from this corpse who, as it turned out, had been dead since Sunday and this was Tuesday and he had been choked to death with a one-inch electric cord, hands bound behind his back, his legs and feet bound from things down to his toes . . . he had been dead so long he was mortified."

Three years later, when she was ninety-four, Lula was robbed and beaten. She wrote several accounts of the tag-team thugs—the initial hit by a "white boy," then the purse-stealing and beating by a "colored boy."

Her diary tell us,

> Until 2 years ago, I still cleaned, papered, and painted, still had apartments, but I got robbed at 4 o'clock daytime at 17th and McKinley. I was almost beat to death, was unconscious. Then 17 days in the hospital, then daughter's home 2 months. I lost all the cash I had—no use to go into that but I had brain damage and broken bones and now my daughter writes most of my checks as my arm and thumb is so numb or paralyzed you can see how I scrawl my letters. I have a heart condition but I feel like I have personally helped a lot of people and hope I can still be of benefit to others. . . .

Shortly after her recovery from the assault, Lula fell and broke her

Hospital worker found slain near OCU campus

Vietnamese are forced into camps?

WASHINGTON (AP) — A House subcommittee chairman said today that U.S. military men beat and drugged 13 Vietnamese in Thailand to force them into going to refugee camps at Guam instead of returning to their homeland.

Chairman Joshua Eilberg, D-Pa., of the House immigration subcommittee said that if the Air Force cannot give a full explanation he will conduct hearings on the incident.

Eilberg is presently at Guam with members of his subcommittee and announced through his Washington office that he has interviewed 12 of the 13 Vietnamese.

He said they were among 65 people who fled to Thailand but then changed their minds and asked to return to Vietnam.

"After being threatened by Air Force officers," Eilberg's announcement said, "52 of the Vietnamese agreed to go to Guam. The 13 who did not were then threatened first with jail and then death if they did not go to Guam."

The announcement quoted Eilberg as saying he was told that "the 13

Lula Reynolds, 91, tells officers of finding body. (Photo by J. Pat Carter)

Body bound with cord, police say

By Wain Miller

The body of an Oklahoma City man was found bound with electrical cord in his ransacked apartment today in what police said was apparently a murder.

The victim was identified by police as William J. Wallace, about 30, a nurse's aide at St. Anthony's Hospital.

Mrs. Lula Reynolds, 91, said the man had rented the one-room efficiency apartment from her two months ago but that she had seen him only a few times since then.

She said she found the body after going inside the apartment atop her garage at 1805½ NW 27 to investigate because the man was 30 days behind in his rent and had been ignoring her notes and a telephone call to the hospital requesting payment.

"I unlocked the door and looked inside, and, oh, it was the worst mess I ever saw, with papers and clothes and whiskey bottles scattered everywhere. You couldn't hardly walk over them.

"Well, I thought he must have left, and I had put this new mattress in there," Mrs. Reynolds continued, "and I wanted to see if he had ruined that, too.

"So I went over to the bed and pulled up the cover, and there he was, not two foot in front of my face.

"But if you've never stared a corpse in the face unexpectedly before, you can't imagine what that's like.

"I'll tell you I like to have died, and I got out of there as fast I could, tripping around over all the mess."

Mrs. Reynolds went to another of her apartments, where Norman Na-

Lula makes the front page of the Oklahoma City Times *on August 12, 1975, at age ninety-one, having discovered a murder victim in one of her apartments*

hip. The convalescence after a "hip nailing" was complicated, but she was finally able to use a walker. My parents bought her a home in El Reno in March 1980, a few blocks away from theirs. Lula, by then ninety-six years old, stayed there for eighteen months before moving into the Hollingsworth house on Ellison Avenue. "Everything wore out at once," Almarian wrote, adding "mentally, she was pretty good until she went into a coma, three days before the end."

Lula Combs Garvin Berch Reynolds died on June 29, 1982, in her honeymoon town of El Reno, Oklahoma, at age ninety-eight. She was buried in Marlow on July 2, with our family friend, Rev. L. B. Saltzgiver, officiating. The obituaries were short and blunt. In the *El Reno Tribune:* "She was a longtime OKC resident and had lived in El Reno since 1980. She was a retired property manager. Survivors include a daughter, Mrs. Francis W. Hollingsworth of 1049 S. Ellison; and three grandchildren." Considering Lula's life story, the obituary was tightlipped.

The funeral prompted my second trip to Marlow. The first had been a quick and curious visit to Johnson's Hotel in the mid-1970s to check out the murder scene during the era of my mother's research. At the time of Lula's funeral, we grandchildren were in our late twenties and early thirties. Our family drove to Elmore City after the graveside services to visit "Aunt Mittie." She was ninety-two and recovering from two broken hips in a "rest home."

My sisters and I always struggled to remember how Aunt Mittie fit into the family picture. From our earliest days, we heard the names of Lula's sisters—Nettie, Fannie, Jessie—so "Mittie" slipped right in there phonetically. But Mittie was Lula's sister-in-law, not sister. Mittie had been married to Lula's only male sibling, Fred. After he died, Mittie lived out the next half-century as a widow.

Mittie had been too frail to attend the graveside services in Marlow. When we saw her later that afternoon, there was brightness in her sunken eyes, and she was very much aware of who we were, even though we had not seen her since we were small children. Aunt Mittie had been one of the many adults who frequented 1805 Northwest Twenty-Seventh on Sunday afternoons, that is, until Arrie Combs died in 1965.

Mittie spoke softly and calmly, her delicate features matching her gentle manner. Given that my sisters and I were all headed back to California, it did not escape my thoughts that this would be the last time for us to see her alive. Yet, Mittie lived another ten years, reaching the age of 102. She is buried in the Combs family plot in Elmore City with husband Fred, along with my great-grandparents, Arrie and William David Combs.

In reading the many letters found in the Hollingsworth attic (I don't think Lula ever threw out a letter), it's clear that the ones from Mittie dominated Lula's final years. In one letter, Mittie rejoices in getting to see Lula in person, and she thanks Almarian for making the effort to drive Lula to see her. She writes, "Tell Almarian how much she looks like her father. She really has his eyes and I'd never noticed it so much as when you were here. So sad he didn't get to live to see his daughter become an adult and the grandchildren."

Then, in a separate pile, I discovered a thank-you note from Aunt Mittie to my parents, written one week after our family had visited her in Elmore City after Lula's funeral: "It was so good for you to come by to see me last week. So good to see your children ... " Then I found a letter with the following:

> Almarian, your father was a fine man. We all loved him. He was trying to defend the colored hotel porter. The Ku Klux Klan was trying to run the black man out of town as Marlow had no Negroes at that time. Of course your mother had just lost Guy in an instant heart attack. He was a fine healthy-looking boy and his tragic death was a heart breaking blow for your mother. I kept you for so much of the time after this all happened.

Although I'd made the adjustment in pedigree for Aunt Mittie from sister to sister-in-law, the full impact did not occur until I read those words. *I kept you for so much of the time after this all happened.* Mittie had been there on the night of the murders in Marlow plus the aftermath. The little frail lady I had seen in the "rest home" in Elmore City in 1982 was the same "Mrs. Fred Combs" I was reading about from the 1920s.

Fred had been Lula's closest sibling, and he and Mittie—the only Combs family members living in Marlow at the time—arrived at the murder scene to comfort Lula that evening. They took Almarian home with them that night. And Mittie and Fred witnessed Lula's extraordinary flight from her husband's funeral, in protest of comments by the clergy.

By the time Mittie wrote the above letter commenting on Albert Berch, Almarian had already been researching her father's story for seven years, so it's not clear why Mittie waited until this late date to tell my mother something about her father. Nevertheless, while Mittie's

Mittie Combs (left) and Lula Berch Reynolds in the 1960s, some forty years after they were together the night of the murders

comments didn't add any information, I'm sure it was reassuring for my mother to read, "Your father was a fine man. We all loved him."

During Lula's life, Hell had been dishing itself out on the installment plan. Her obsession with the Klan and Albert's death ended in 1982 when she began her eternal rest. My mother then became heir to the family tragedy.

17

Almarian Berch—the Second Obsession

Almarian had no memory of her father's murder by the time she began Catholic boarding school at age five, a curious parallel to her father landing in a Catholic orphanage at age six. While sending her daughter away at such a tender age might seem callous on Lula's part, the exact nature of the exile has proved too slippery to capture. Aunt Helen's educational trust fund may have been the official rendering, but "wildcatting was no life for a little girl" held equal position. That said, at one point in her writings, Lula, a newlywed for the third time, admitted that the vibrant five-year-old "made Harry nervous." Of course, given what we now understand about Harry's untreated thyrotoxicosis, he was *always* nervous.

Almarian's letters home to her mother reveal a child wired for optimism, a trait more easily traced to Arrie than Lula. Lula kept these letters, often scribbling a notation on the envelope of how grateful she was to have such a loving daughter. From what we uncovered after Almarian's death, my guess is that Lula, to the end of her life, saved all of Almarian's letters.

Almarian seemed to enjoy her early years at boarding school. Harry and Lula, even in their nomadic extreme, were never more than a hundred miles away, and Almarian traveled home for the holidays and summers. Then in the caterpillar stage of becoming a social butterfly, Almarian loved the company of other kids. And she had an insatiable desire to learn all she could about everything. Her school notebooks and diaries reveal a Gatsbyesque character who strove to improve herself. She read compulsively, studied endlessly, and decided to become a physician— that is, once she moved beyond her age-five aspirations to become a telephone operator, where she could chat with the world.

So, given Almarian's precocious nature, it should be no surprise that she routinely read the newspaper while still a young girl. And at age thirteen, traveling on a bus from boarding school to Lula's home du jour, she read that Marvin Kincannon, the murderer of her father, had been paroled. Her reaction at the time remains unknown, but one can imagine a mixed bag of emotions, one of which was probably fear—for her mother and for herself.

Marvin had served eleven years in prison out of his twenty-five-year sentence. He returned to Marlow, worked in the oilfields, and, to anyone's knowledge, was never in trouble again. His wife, Ada Stotts, was long gone, not easily traced. Marvin never remarried. He died in 1972 at age seventy-one, buried in the Marlow cemetery. Almarian's research on her father began shortly after Kincannon's death, almost fifty years after the murders.

Almarian attended grades one through seven at St. Joseph Academy in Chickasha, Oklahoma, returning there again in the eleventh grade. For grades eight through ten, she attended Mount St. Mary's Academy in Oklahoma City, a school sponsored by Sisters of Mercy, where she boarded along with seventy-five other girls.

Almarian Berch, age fourteen (1936)

Grade twelve was Almarian's only year of public school. She graduated in 1938 from Capitol Hill High School in Oklahoma City. Lula and Almarian had sharply divided views on keeping promises to Aunt Helen. When I asked Almarian, late in her life, what motivated her to violate Aunt Helen's rules and her mother's wishes, she answered: "Boys, I guess." Aunt Helen died in 1926, less than three years after the murder of Albert Berch, leaving us to wonder whether or not she was truly able to call the shots from her grave.

By her teen years, Almarian had developed wide interests, from the classics to pop culture to science, while her ambitions for medical school were unusual for women at that time. Fully funded for college via Helen's trust, Almarian headed for the University of Oklahoma.

Two would-be suitors in Almarian's Chemistry I lab discovered a special connection. They were both premed students from Marlow, Oklahoma— Jack Gregston and J. T. Brooks. J. T. sat next to Almarian and agonized over hatching an opening line so smooth that it would break the thickest layers of ice and allow him to ask her for a date. Finally, he resorted to the old standard question about hometowns and announced his own as Marlow. Almarian's eyes lit up, with J. T. believing he had hit the jackpot until she replied, "Oh, my father was murdered in Marlow." After that, J. T. never had the nerve to proceed.

This vignette came from one of the young chemists, Dr. Jack L. Gregston, who returned to Marlow after medical school and spent his entire career in the area. Gregston consented to my interview when I began this project, as I was looking for anyone old enough who might have known something about the murders. Gregston was in his nineties when we met, so he would have been only a toddler in 1923. I was reminded that to have a helpful memory of the events, one would have to be over one hundred years old at the time of my interview.

Though too young to have any direct memory of the murders, Gregston heard various accounts while growing up in Marlow. And he recalled playing touch football with one of the culprits, Elza Gandy, after he was released from prison. The story from chemistry lab had been his greatest treasure: "I can't tell you anything you don't already know about the murders, but let me tell you about your mother and me and J. T. Brooks. . . . "

Almarian met Francis Hollingsworth while dissecting a shark in anatomy class, whereupon the most natural thing to follow, I suppose, was their marriage in 1943. Throughout their early marriage, including military service, Almarian sent a constant stream of letters home to Lula, who was growing increasingly anxious that Almarian might settle, permanently, somewhere other than central Oklahoma.

Almarian's desire to go to medical school was foiled by Francis and sublimated toward medical technology. To our knowledge, this battle over a "woman's role" was the last our father ever won. After graduating from the University of Oklahoma College of Medicine, Francis started his rotating internship at the Good Samaritan Hospital in Portland, Oregon. Almarian went to work at the same hospital in her new career, fresh out of training as a medical technologist.

After establishing roots in El Reno, Almarian, at the surface, adopted the role of the classic housewife of that era; yet inside, a motor was

Francis W. Hollingsworth and Almarian Berch on the University of Oklahoma campus, graduation day 1942. They would be married the next year.

humming while Gloria Steinem was still in diapers. Her 2011 obituary stated:

> Whenever she joined a club or an organization, it was likely she would end up in a leadership role, such as state president of the Jaycee Jaynes. She and husband Francis were early adopters of the newest trends in sports and hobbies, and the Hollingsworth family was a novelty on the slopes at Winter Park in the 1950s when children on skis were a rarity. She is fondly remembered for her 15 years as a Girl Scout Leader, a trainer of Leaders, Day Camp Director for 5 years, and a member of the Board of Directors and President of the Sooner Girl Scout Council. In addition, she organized fund-raising events over a 3-year period that eventually led to a bus trip for her Girl Scout Troop to Mexico City and Acapulco. While her children were in college at OU, she served as president of Sigma Chi Moms, as well as president of the OU Mom's association and a Board Member of the OU Alumni Association. After the nest was empty, she returned to OU where she earned a Masters' degree in journalism in 1976 and later taught creative writing at Redlands Community College. She and her husband were widely traveled, visiting 47 of the 50 states, as well as touring 40 countries. Their trip to the Amazon prompted a novel that was never really finished, but perhaps her most adventuresome step was putting one foot over the border into Afghanistan. Back in El Reno, she was a member of Athenaeum Study Club, P.E.O., Culture Club, and the Oklahoma City chapter of the D.A.R. In her later years, she devoted herself to supporting the First Presbyterian Church of El Reno where she served as an Elder. . . .

We forgot to mention in the obituary that our parents were named "Mr. and Mrs. Jaycee" for Oklahoma in 1956. Our father served as president of the local chapter, then became a national director, having once been a co-delegate to the convention with George Nigh, who would go on to become governor of Oklahoma. As governor, Nigh would be the one to appoint Justice Yvonne Kauger to the Oklahoma Supreme Court, only the second female to hold that position.

Almarian's interest in genealogy began in 1972, the year she became an empty-nester and, perhaps incidentally, the year Albert's killer died. While information on the Combs side flowed like a mountain spring, the Berch side was dammed. Efforts to burst through were hampered by Lula's unfamiliarity with Albert's family. Too, Albert Junior had been an only child, and there was very little contact with other family members, before or after the killings, with the exception of Albert Senior.

Several years into her research, Almarian took the plunge and returned to the University of Oklahoma to get her master's degree in journalism. She intended to publish a novel about her father's murder. One of the scraps of paper in her files, written to an unknown audience, says, "I want to write fiction. I want to write good fiction. I want to write good fiction that sells."

Her first step would be to have Lula write down every detail she could remember about the murders.

I discovered the resulting document after my mother's death, and unfortunately, the first five pages are missing. Nonetheless, excerpts from pages six through thirteen add new color, written by Lula in her late eighties, fifty years after the fact:

"While I was on my knees giving him water, they shot at me, they powder-burned my face, shot a hole in baby's gown sleeve. At that time in this terrible excitement I didn't know they was shooting at me. The negro was lying about 10 feet away writhing in pain pleading for someone to get a doctor. I screamed to the night clerk to get a doctor for the negro and my husband but no answer. I looked around to find myself and baby all alone in this great big lobby, not one soul could I see, then again I screamed and screamed for help. Finally, I decided there wasn't any help. I was frantic. I rushed to the telephone, I called the doctor (he was not at home) then called the drug store and he was there. I told him to come quick to the Hotel. There were 2 men dying from gunshot wounds. He was there in 5 minutes, gave me a sedative the first thing— then I called the police. No answer. Then I called the night watch whose son had killed the negro. At that time, I didn't know who had killed the negro. No answer from his office. He never did come. Then I called the deputy sheriff who came immediately, he in turn called the sheriff who lived 10 miles away. He also called my brother who lived 4 blocks away. He and his wife (Mittie) was there in a few minutes, they took my baby, then my brother called the ambulance for my husband's body. Until that time I couldn't realize my husband was dead. Seemed like 150 people in the lobby and dining room at the time this mob of killers stampeded the lobby of the Hotel . . .

"Bullets were embedded in the walls, in the floor, furniture, and night clerk's desk. . . . Everyone in both lobby and dining room had run for their lives. . . . The doctor, the sheriff, my brother and myself dragged and carried the negro into a downstairs bed room so the doctor could give him a sedative for his suffering, but all night long this semiconscious condition lasted and he kept repeating the same words our Savior prayed: *Forgive them Father they know not what they do. I never harmed anyone in my life. I have earned my living doing what the white man would not do. I hold no hate for anyone for before long I will meet my God. I can't meet him with hate in my heart, but why should I have to die and leave my family when I have done nothing to die for.* Then the sheriff asked him if he could identify the one who shot him. He said Yes and told him he had hit the boy who hit him with the iron pipe . . . the poor old negro died at sun up the following morning."

Lula goes on to explain how the first of the gang to be captured was Elza Gandy, who was found at home, in bed, wearing bloody clothes. Once in jail . . .

"he was very angry and decided they had all give him the dodge and intended for him to take the rap, so he told the sheriff and county attorney the names of all the men and boys. Also identified each one as the sheriff would arrest them and bring them in. The only thing he would not tell was who was back of the murder and it was not his idea or it was not the other boys idea but it was the idea of the business men who told them how to do it, and what part each one was to play, and to be careful not to kill anyone except the Hotel proprietor, wife and negro. This he said they told him would ruin the business at the Hotel and one of their members would take it from there. . . .

"Well the day of the funeral was at hand. I had to arrange for it with the help of my brother. I belonged to a Protestant Church in this town, so naturally I called my pastor who in all my grief had not visited me to console me with one word. But Al's death was such a shock, I had not even thought of it. I asked him if he would conduct the funeral services at the church and also at the cemetery. He said he would. An unusually large curious crowd gathered at the church. I was amazed they had to be pushed aside for our family to get in the church. The pastor of course had his bible. He must have had to search his bible for hours to find the passages that would suit his KKK members. A friend of mine jotted down verse by verse as he read and later gave them to me. They were as follows:

"When he be judged let him be condemned and let his prayer become sin (Psalm 109: 7-12) Let his days be few and let another take his office. Let his children be fatherless and his wife a widow. Let his children be continually vagabonds and beg. Let there be none to extend mercy unto him. Neither let there be any to favor his fatherless children.

"Don't know what the rest of the talk would have been. This was more than I could take. I arose from my seat, called to him to halt this KKK funeral from any further service to me. I told a singer of the choir to have the hearse take the body to the cemetery and sing only one song: 'Death Is Only a Dream.' This was my husband's favorite song. And as they left the church, hundreds of curiosity seekers followed to see what other excitement they could find now the funeral was over.

"I began to realize what had happened. I had to think of the next step to take. I became frantic. I had all my hired help at the Hotel, all drawing wages, and no money coming in since we hadn't had a guest at the hotel since the murder 3 days before. . . . So I called the help to come to my apartment. I told them I was ruined, my business all gone, so I would have to close the dining room and all other parts of the Hotel, but I would keep the cook and wife until I could dispose of it. They would live in the Hotel and I would stay in my apartment. Most of my bank account was in escrow for lawyers. . . . Little did I realize there was still the aftermath. . . .

"I was sitting at the desk in the lobby of the Hotel about 10 days after the murder. It was about 9 o'clock at night. Someone shot at me, striking the window casing, then shooting 2 more shots into the dining room, which was empty. Then I became panicky. They was still trying to kill me. Then I was afraid to stay at the Hotel at night, so I would go to my brother's about 4 blocks away at night. But one night I was a little late leaving the Hotel, it was nearly dark. I left the Hotel, baby in my arms, a shot was fired at me from a brick pillar of the Hotel porch. It struck the side of the Hotel and fell on the paving. I didn't see the person. I only saw the flash from the gun. I was terrified. I called our Governor and asked for help. I couldn't get help in our town or county as most officers were K.K.K. If they wasn't they were afraid to be against this organization.

"The Governor sent a detective to our Hotel and he stayed a month, and the second night the detective was there they shot 5 shots at the Hotel again, hitting the door once and the rest hit the side. This detective was following the cars on Main Street. He saw a flash from the gun and got the tag number, traced it and found it belonged to the man who was trying to buy the Hotel. My lawyer filed a twenty thousand [dollar] damage suit, but this county was so packed with K.K.K. that they proved he was out of town and didn't know who used his car. He said he never locked his garage and anyone could have used it. So the result, the court allowed me the measly sum of court cost and $1,000 in cash for mental suffering. . . .

"In about 3 months after the murders, the trial was set. No guests were staying at the Hotel. Only the people I had hired was there to look after the place until I could sell it. The newspapers kept a constant story of the K.K.K. parades that were still going on. There were crowds of 15 to 25 men and boys would go around the place with crosses bearing the words: *Don't be a witness at the trial . . . we warn you . . . you better beware . . . we mean what we say.* They scared my friends until all they would say at the trial was 'I didn't see a thing. I had to run for my life.' They had been warned and was afraid. . . .

"The court was called to order and the crowd was so great the sheriff had to deputize a lot of extras to keep order. The doors was closed when the court room was full, and the crowd was so disorderly in the halls on the outside that people on the witness stand was afraid to testify to the truth. . . . My lawyer asked the man who killed my husband, why did you ever do such a thing . . . didn't you know you would burn for murder? (premeditated). 'No,' he answered, 'I was told I would not have to stand trial. They told us to all go to shooting as soon as the negro was attacked, and not shoot anyone else except the negro, Berch and his wife. And that the confusion would be so great no one could identify us and to get out of the Hotel quick and every one to his own home and get in bed, and for no one to confess if arrested'. But the lawyer could never get him [Kincannon] to say who *they* were. He would always put the emphasis on *they*."

Lula then describes the trial of Marvin Kincannon, with the initial plea of self-defense and then insanity, an account that is identical to the newspapers. Her remembrance concludes with: "My best friends were afraid to testify in court since most of them had received telephone calls telling them the same thing would happen to them that happened to the Hotel proprietor and the negro. I couldn't insist because I was afraid for myself. Yet I testified because our Governor was waging a war on the K.K.K. at this time and congress had already impeached him, but he was still acting Governor."

That is where Lula's account ends, on the erroneous notion that Jack Walton was still king. In fact, Lt. Gov. Martin E. Trapp was in charge as acting governor and would go on to serve four years as Oklahoma's sixth governor.

From the account above, one particular item jumps from the page for my sisters and me: the "baby's gown." This is the fulcrum of our family folklore—that is, one of the bullets passed through our mother's gown, leaving her unharmed and assuring our place on the planet, my sisters and me. From a strict biological standpoint, we three siblings were half-present at the scene of the murders, each of us existing, in part, as an immature oocyte, resting comfortably in two-year-old ovaries that dodged the flying bullets.

As Almarian progressed through her courses in journalism, she eagerly anticipated the novel-writing class under the direction of Jack Bickham, noted Oklahoma author and teacher. During the semester, in Bickham's gristmill of learning, students would write their own novels. My mother would begin work on *One-Half Dream*, the story of her father's murder.

At the start of the semester, Bickham required each student to address the class and describe his or her project. Almarian stood facing her classmates and began with something like this: "I plan to write a novel that tells the story of my mother and her life as a hotel owner, oil wildcatter, and real-estate dealer, with the centerpiece of the story being the murder of her husband, my father, in Marlow, Oklahoma. My father was Albert Berch, and he was murdered by a mob that had been agitated by the K.K.K. . . . "

A throttled gasp came from the back of the room, prompting classmates to turn and stare as the noise softened to an agonal groan of disbelief. Bickham asked the woman covering her mouth with her hands if there was a problem.

In a stunning coincidence, the woman said, "My older brother was in that mob. At least he was with them the night before the murders when they tried to run the black man off."

Junetta Watson Davis went on from that classroom to become an emeritus professor of journalism at the University of Oklahoma. Her seminar course, Women in Media, received national recognition from the Women's Institute for Freedom of the Press.

Her 2008 obituary read: "Ms. Davis was born in Marlow, Oklahoma, June 7, 1925 to George Marshall Watson and Pearl Brooks Watson. She was their eighth child, with five sisters and two brothers as older siblings. She attended the first eight grades in Marlow Public Schools. The family moved to Texas in 1939. . . . "

After World War II, Junetta began work as a secretary, transitioning later into journalism. Covering stories mostly in Texas, she was part of the entourage that toured with then senator Lyndon B. Johnson in 1954.

She decided that formal credentials would help her career, prompting her to get her master's degree. And that's where she met Almarian Berch Hollingsworth in a most unusual circumstance.

Shortly after Almarian died and this story was in my lap, one of the first people I tried to contact was Junetta Davis. It was too late. She had died three years prior. However, as it turned out, budding journalist Almarian had already bled Junetta for everything she could, including information about that older brother, still alive at the time.

Although Junetta was not yet born in 1923, her much older brother Pete witnessed some of the intimidating actions before the final crime. Junetta readily offered her support to Almarian as the former had even toyed with writing the story herself. Two interviews follow. The first is a typed document from Junetta, who interviewed her sister Dorothy, and the second is an interview with her older, cantankerous brother Pete. The latter document is in my father's handwriting, and it appears that, always supportive of our mother's missions, he was making a copy from a recording. Neither document is dated, and my notations appear in brackets.

Junetta's interview with Dorothy begins, "I asked my sister to recall what she can about this incident in Marlow. . . . "

Almarian and F. W. Hollingsworth, MD, in 1988

Q: Dorothy, how did you happen to hear about this (Berch-Johnigan) murder? I mean when did you hear about it? The next morning?

A: Yes, the next morning. It was quite well-publicized by the next day.

Q: By word of mouth?

A: Yes, by word of mouth. Nothin' like that had ever happened before. Nobody had tried to bring a negro in and keep him overnight. See. That rule that Marlow had was not challenged until then. I had heard it when I was a small child. See, this happened when I was a junior in high school . . . these boys took advantage of the situation. And maybe some adult did urge them on but nobody ever knew who it was for sure. And I'm sure that if an adult had actually done that—(pause)—because Marvin Kincannon was mean enough to do that all by himself. He didn't need any help.

Q: He had a reputation for being mean and rowdy?

A: Yes, he'd already been in trouble a lot of times with the law.

Q: Oh, he had?

A: [Elza] Roy Gandy hadn't been in trouble but he was a pretty good follower. And in this case he became one of the leaders. I don't know who all the boys were.

Q: Now all my life I heard that our family was grateful that Pete was not involved.

A: Yes, because he was just that age and he would have followed. He would have gone right along with it.

[Junetta and her sister discuss how their brother Pete had frequent contact with many of the boys in the mob but did not feel welcome the night of the killings, as he was a few years younger.]

Q: What was the mood in Marlow? What did the people say after this?

A: Well, they were just talking about it . . . they really blamed the Kincannon boy more than anyone else because he was older, and he'd been in trouble before, so the main blame placed on him, rather than on Roy Gandy. . . .

Q: At this time in 1923 was this the period that the KKK was pretty active? I can remember mother said she was in church one night and the KKK came in and dragged someone out with their hoods on.

A: No, they didn't drag anyone out. They just came in and made a donation to the church.

Q: With their hoods on?

A: With their hoods on. Just marched in and you could have heard a pin drop. Honestly, it was something you would never forget. . . . See that was 1923 not too long after the war. . . . There was a man living on north second street who wouldn't take care of his family and the ku klux klan came in and took him out and whipped him. They were great moralizers. They made people do what they were supposed to do, they thought. Yes, then they discovered that there were men in the Klan that did much worse than what this man had done. . . .

Q: How many men came into the church that night?

A: Oh, there was a long string of them . . . maybe 20 or 25.

Q: They all had on white sheets?

A: All had on those white sheets and those hoods.

Q: At what point in the church service did they come in?

A: The man was preaching.

Q: And everything just stopped, huh?

A: Yes, and so there was a great deal of sentiment about the Klan during this period and that might have had some bearing on this case.

Q: Well I think Mrs. Hollingsworth thinks that the mood was such and she evidently has some more information. . . .

[The two sisters again talk about how fortunate it was that Pete was not with the boys that night. Moving on to Kincannon's conviction, Junetta points out that, given the mood of the time, a twenty-five-year sentence was "pretty hard."]

A: Well, he was a pretty bad character.

Q: Why didn't they give him life then? He killed a white man. But apparently the mood would have been 'well he deserved to be killed because he brought this negro in.' . . .

A: You see, they were shooting at the negro and hit the white man. They killed him accidentally.

Q: You think so? That's not the way she [Almarian] understands it. . . .

A: I was thinking they were shooting at the negro and hit the white man.

Q: That's how you remember it? You don't recall if people got pretty upset or pretty excited about it?

A: No not anything unusual.

Junetta and Dorothy interviewed their brother Pete Watson. Junetta asks, "Were you living in that house where I was born?" Pete says yes, and that they lived so close to Johnson's Hotel that he heard the gunshots.

Q: You were telling me the other night that you had been invited to go—

A: All the kids around the school, the boys, knew what was going to take place. He [Albert Berch] went out to Duncan and hired this n-----

for a porter at the hotel and some of the people didn't like it. And the boys all got together and went down there and they taken him [Robert Johnigan] down to the railroad track and told him to get out of town. He pulled out a razor and they left. So the next night they went down there and Roy Gandy give Marvin Kincannon a gun. [Note: This critical point could not be established in either of the two criminal trials.] And so when Mr. Berch started to get 'em out, the shootin' started and they killed Mr. Berch right then but the n----- lived till about 2 o'clock the next morning and they like to never found anybody to come get the n-----. And then I think they arrested Marvin first and they didn't get Roy until 3-4 days later [Pete has these arrests reversed].

Q: Was it Roy Gandy's gun?

A: Well, that was part of the problem. They never did prove that he did kill the n-----. They just gave him the 7 years.

Q: Did you talk to the boys before they went the second night?

A: It was all over the school ground that they were going down there that night.

Q: You were only 12 years old?

A: . . . [tape was garbled] they wasn't a whole lot older . . . boys I think was in on it but when the shootin' started they all left.

[Pete then describes an act of intimidation that occurred the night before the murders, which he personally witnessed and perhaps participated in. Junetta provided Almarian with this summary. The boys had wrapped Johnigan in oilcloth and doused him with gasoline while they stood around him in a circle lighting matches. It is not clear if this was the same event when Johnigan scared the boys off with a razor. Pete then returns to the murders.]

Q: Did you talk to these boys after this happened?

A: Oh, hell, everybody. You know you couldn't talk to Roy Gandy or Marvin Kincannon because—

Q: They were in jail?

A: No, they wasn't in jail, they were hiding. I think they found Roy Gandy at home. . . .

Q: Do you think adults put these kids up to this?

A: Frankly, I know they did. I wouldn't swear to it, but somebody put 'em up to it. They wouldn't just go down there on their own. That had to get organized and go down there. And there was a bunch of ruffians around in them days.

[They cover details of the murders that have already been presented, plus the fact that the phone booth stayed there through the 1930s, with a bullet hole still in it.]

Q: Do you remember how long Mr. Berch had been in town. Several years, hadn't he?

A: Yeah, he was a pretty good guy I thought and, uh, when he went and got that n-------why . . .

Q: Those boys hadn't been drinking had they?

A: No, they just some of the . . . I think the Gandys and Carters . . .

Q: What Carters?

A: George Carter. The Gandys and George Carter, he was that blind bastard up there. He tried to send me to jail but he didn't make it.

Q: Well you think . . . you mean the Gandys and George Carter incited them boys?

A: Why everybody in business around there incited 'em. They's goin' to get that n----- out of town one way or the other. And then they had a sign there . . . "N-----, don't let the sun set on you."

[Junetta, in spontaneously linking here George Carter and the Gandys, provides the only point-blank questioning known to exist that attempts to tie the two names to the murders, some fifty years after the fact. While tantalizingly close to a direct accusation, the evasive answer offered by Pete, as he retreats to "everybody in business," leaves us dangling. The interview continues with a recounting of the Berch-Johnigan murder scene.]

Q: Well if they were so intent on getting him (Robert Johnigan), why didn't they finish him off?

A: Well, I guess they ran out of ammunition. You know those damn pistols don't hold but about 6 shots. I don't know how many they put in Berch, but there's one in that old telephone booth, and put 2 or 3 in each one you don't have much of it left. (everybody talking). [Pete drifts off to another story about the Gandys, relating some sort of "row" when old man Gandy made his son, Elza Roy, issue punishment.] There was about 25 of those guys and he made Roy whip some of them guys and he held 'em off with his pistol one at a time and made Roy whip some of them.

Q: But that's not related to this story. . . . Do you think Gandy was a member of the KKK?

A: No. I don't think old man Gandy was although [several names offered] were. They all marched down the main street up there all the time. There was about 50 of them.

[They rehash the KKK scene at the church, with speculation that the preacher was courting a woman "that he shouldn't have been."]

Q: You were sitting there?

A: Yes, I was there when they marched in. But they just marched in gave some money and turned around and marched out

Q: Was there any reaction to them?

A: Well, everyone just sat there scared to death, I guess.

Q: Were you scared?

A: Yes, I was scared. I thought we was going to have something right there.

The novel, *One-Half Dream,* emerged from that semester in draft form. Almarian would work on revisions for a number of years as she queried agents and publishers. Then, our father was diagnosed with Parkinson's disease, and her work on the novel slowed and finally stopped. On several occasions, I offered to help "de-fictionalize" the story for her, but she would not consider it. She wanted to publish it as a novel. *Never* did she encourage me to write the story of her father's murder "after I'm gone."

In sifting through her exhaustive background files, I discovered her correspondence with a sociologist whose expertise focused on "sundown towns." I was surprised at how soon after our father's death the letters had been written (2004), long after I thought she had stopped working on her novel. With one of these letters from James W. Loewen at the Catholic University of America in Washington, D.C., he included a newspaper clipping from the *Pittsburgh Courier* about the 1923 murder of Almarian's father. Loewen stated, "Along with the *Chicago Defender*, the *Pittsburgh Courier* was the best African American newspaper at that time."

The date of the article is December 29, 1923, twelve days after the murders. The description of the crime offers a standard account of the day, though *Berch* is spelled *Birch* and *Johnigan* is spelled *Jernigen.*

Then, I made the connection between the *Pittsburgh Courier* and the misspelled names. I had found this information online eight years after this correspondence. Almarian had shown, once again, this time from the grave, how thorough her research could be. I had slacked my way to the information about James W. Loewen's book, *Sundown Towns,* online, while Almarian had been in correspondence years earlier with the author, before the book had even been published.

Dr. Loewen closes his letter to Almarian with: "I look forward to your material, including a copy of the passage on this tragic incident from your novel, if you are willing to send it. Do look for my book, *Sundown Towns*, next fall."

When Almarian was in her early eighties, I began to ask her questions, as I knew her time was limited and I intended to take a nonfiction approach to the saga "someday."

"What do we know about Albert's father?"

"Not much. Mother didn't like him."

"How are we related to Aunt Helen?"

"On the Berch side; one of Albert's people married into the family, or something like that, way back."

Either she was starting to get forgetful or she was stalling, not wanting to encourage me, even in the slightest way, to investigate the family lore. Her nebulous answers were the same ones I had heard in my youth. While it might seem as though she were intentionally concealing family skeletons, I tend to wonder if, in those final years, she had forgotten some of her own discoveries.

But one of her files remained empty to the end—her father's. More accurately stated, the file was full, but it was full of nothing. All letters bore the same bottom line: "No record of Albert Weldon Berch." There were no records of his birth, nothing about his youth in Southern California before age six, nothing about the years following the orphanage in Fargo, no specifics as to when he actually lived with the DeLendrecies—in short, not a trace of his existence between age six and when he showed up in Marlow in his late twenties as a new barber in town. Almarian's file on Albert Weldon Berch did not contain a single legal document bearing his name, nor any proof that the man ever existed.

18

One-Half Dream

Although autobiographies can be passports to self-deception, they still reflect how a person views oneself, valid or not. In the late 1970s, Almarian enrolled in a writing class where each student was first asked to jot down a mini-autobiography to explain his or her motivation for taking the course. Almarian's final paragraphs follow:

> About eight years ago, with my children self-sufficient, I decided to try writing. I knew nothing about it, and following my natural inclination toward formal instruction, I enrolled in a class at the week-end University of Oklahoma Center for Continuing Education, with Helen Reagan Smith, acquiring nine hours of journalism on my transcript. This counted for naught when I was accepted in the Graduate School at OU, where I received my Master's degree in journalism in May, 1976.
>
> Since that time, I have taken two courses in fiction and am now enrolled in this course on non-fiction. My fields of interest are so varied that I find it difficult to pinpoint one as the most significant . . . and I still read anything, from Peanuts to Saul Bellow. I wonder if I spend too much time reading and not enough writing. It is tempting when I receive a rejection slip to give up and concentrate solely on reading. But I have a desire to keep trying.

By the time Almarian had enrolled in this course, a fair number of literary agents and publishers had rejected her novel, *One-Half Dream*, a fate most writers know quite well. Her second novel, *The Green Canopy*, was drawn from her trip to the Amazon and was rejected as well. In the end, she never accomplished her dream of becoming a successful novelist.

The title of *One-Half Dream* was drawn from a quote she inserted after the cover page:

"O woman, you are not merely the handiwork of God, but also of men;

they are ever endowing you with beauty from their own hearts. You are one-half woman and one-half dream."

—Rabindranath Tagore

Almarian described the book as a tribute to her mother. When I first read it many years ago, I discovered that the murder of her father was a relatively minor component of the story, and it made me wonder why she had spent so much time researching his life and murder. As I have come to appreciate, Almarian's search for her father's roots, taking her to Los Angeles and Fargo, was an independent quest that she would have performed with or without having the book as her excuse. As for *One-Half Dream* being a tribute to her mother, I think it was more than that. It was, primarily, therapy. And it was a peace offering.

Growing up, what we saw of the Lula-Almarian relationship was perfect civility. There were no outward signs of affection or terms of endearment but no hint of friction either. Their pet names of "honey" and "darling" were long gone by the time we arrived on the scene, and Almarian always referred to Lula as "Mother."

So, imagine my surprise when, days after Lula's funeral, as Almarian said goodbye to me at the airport on my way back to California, she fell into my arms, weeping and asking, "What am I going to do now? What am I going to do?" I was caught completely off guard. I had never noticed a shred of emotional attachment between Almarian and Lula, until that moment after Lula was gone.

Lula's boxes of letters recovered in the El Reno attic held 500 envelopes by my rough count, well over half from Almarian. By reading them over time, I came to appreciate a relationship to which I had been oblivious. Granted, the letters were only those received by Lula, half of the full conversations, but one can draw enlightenment from half, much like listening to one side of a phone conversation.

A postcard from Almarian at boarding school (labeled "age 5" by Lula) says, "My dear mother, Joyous greetings for a Merry Christmas and Happy New Year. We may go home Friday the 23rd. Your little girl, Almarian." Thinking it unusual for Almarian to be writing in cursive form at age five, not to mention the precocious "joyous greetings," I checked the 1927 calendar, and December 23 fell on Friday that year. Almarian was indeed only five years old. Her excitement over "may go home Friday the 23rd" is somehow reminiscent of the effusive optimism of Tiny Tim, as though the twenty-third were a bonus day.

The letters continue through boarding school, and in the preteen years, they begin to sound more like shopping lists: "Send me this or that for the next event," and "Can I have the money to travel home to see Nelson Eddy when he comes to Oklahoma City?"

A letter dated August 27, 1941, is from Almarian while an undergraduate at OU. On the envelope, Lula wrote: "You will appreciate this letter when I am not here. Wish I had one from my mother." Note that Lula lived another forty-one years. Almarian had written, "I am beginning to get

Lula's handwriting can be seen at the top of this undated photo of Lula and Almarian, circa 1940. She used "Lula" and "Lulu" interchangeably but never her given name of Lucinda. Almarian Berch did not have a middle name.

lonesome for you, by the time the week is out I will probably sure be ready to get back."

We also have ample documentation from Almarian's side of the relationship. In addition to a daily diary that she kept her entire life, we found freestanding, free-associating notes, addressed to no one in particular, floating around our El Reno home. In one of these documents, writing at age forty-eight, Almarian reveals a major rift about which I knew nothing:

> I feel so guilty. I have just had an argument with Mother. She gets so wound up over these apartments and houses. I don't understand her love of these things. It may be because that's all I've heard—all my life. She has had no other interest except these low cost apartments and me. She has no friends—true friends. . . . But just let an idea for a deal come to her mind and she's off and running. I can't stop her. She has needed our money recently and our signature on notes. We want to use a lawyer for making contracts, etc., but she doesn't want to wait for one. She just goes right on. . . . I love her and I know that most of the work has been for me, not only for monetary reward but so that I would have respect for her. If I liked the real estate business, it would be different.

One curious feature of this document is the fact that Almarian edits herself, crossing out words and revising, as if the work were for publication. (And now, sure enough, it is.)

The simmering conflict was brought to a head with the "Mark Affair" (fictitious name), a young man who partnered with Lula and then sank tendrils of influence into her life. He could do no wrong in Lula's eyes. Almarian, right or wrong, gradually came to believe that Mark was taking advantage of Lula in their real-estate dealings wherein Almarian was a reluctant partner. In response, Lula was outraged at her daughter for interfering. In an undated letter, Lula wrote:

> This letter will explain more and better than I can talk with you since you are always in hurry. . . . Now about our partnership, as the old saying goes, no relatives ever get along in partnerships. We never had a cross word in our lives until this partnership arrangement came about. I never intended it as a partnership to start with. I only intended your name on the deed. . . . You know you didn't buy in as a partner. I let $2,000 in stock go into it to reduce the loan which I should have kept [two pages of mathematical computations]. . . . Let's see if we can be mother and

daughter again. . . . I don't know why all at once, you think I don't know how to handle my affairs. I have got a lot more out of my business with Mark than he has out of me. I am so glad he don't know how you feel [several pages of all that Mark has done for Lula]. . . . So don't fence me in. Let me get all these little equities sold and in something that I can get a comfortable life out of. I have worked like a slave all my life, no vacations, not even a lunch downtown without wondering if I could afford it. I am so lost since mother died. I never noticed being lonesome before. . . .

Lula continues, critical of the oppressive government regulations where, after a lifetime of flipping properties, suddenly, she must have a cosigner because she's over the age of sixty-five. Begrudgingly, she asked Almarian to cosign. Her daughter refused at first, proposing that her mother retire and move to El Reno. In another document, Lula responds (to herself):

> I can't live in her society. We live in 2 different worlds. I educated her to be a medical technologist, her husband is an MD surgeon. She has charm and grace. Her daughter is a medical technologist, her son is in medical school. So you can see I couldn't fit in. They know social life. I know working life. I am not against social life but I have never had time to study ediquette [sic] and I don't want to embarrass them, with my baked beans, corn bread and buttermilk manners. I have given her education so she wouldn't have to live in my world. I also tried to get my sister [Jessie] to give her daughter [Ben Marion Willingham] the same chance. . . . Her reply was, "You are educating her out of your life." That one remark has been 20 years ago, and it's real to me now. *That's just what I did.*

Contrast this to a letter Lula wrote *thirty years* earlier: "It will be still harder in your generation for one without special education. We are so proud of Francis and you and the more education you have the prouder Francis will be of you. With his disposition he could not endure a dumb-Dora, and neither can I."

The tension over "Mark" simmered to boiling over several years. Thirty miles away in El Reno, Almarian wrote in an essay to herself: "Have I been wrong? Have I misjudged a young boy trying to start out in life? I have made Mother, Mark, and myself unhappy. And if he was innocent, I've hurt someone unnecessarily. . . . "

The next page has two columns: 1) proof that Mark is innocent and 2) proof he is guilty. Indicators of innocence, such as "the bank account is in mother's name," are countered by indicators of guilt, such as "mother got rid of the people around her who were criticizing Mark."

Years later, Almarian wrote a short story recounting her life as the daughter of Lula Combs Garvin Berch Reynolds. She had just placed Lula in a nursing home to recover from a broken hip. As Almarian looked into Lula's room through a window, she recounts:

> Mother was talking constantly. First the nurse, then someone I didn't recognize. She never stopped. I knew she was discussing real estate—it was all she ever discussed. We were not even comfortably seated in her room until she started on some deal. This was not surprising. It had been her whole life. I had been secondary. Mother had never realized it or wouldn't admit it, but it was always obvious to me. . . .

Almarian never seemed to grasp that, long ago, Lula had replaced people with property.

Around this same time, Almarian completed her novel, *One-Half Dream*.

According to her files used to organize the book, the central character is "Loring Howard," based on Lula. Her primary goal is to possess gold coins (in recovery of the gold coins lost by Almarian's grandparents), while her secondary goal is to get an education, having been deprived of this as a young woman. The plot summary follows:

> Loring's first husband dies of the Spanish flu, then after acquiring a hotel, Loring encounters marriage proposals from men who are only interested in the hotel. Finally, she has a proper proposal from a well-educated, attractive man from California. First, she has to decide if she loves him and he loves her and also whether they could be happy with their very different backgrounds. She comes from pioneer stock, hard works and poor. He's a Catholic from wealthy parents in Los Angeles and has been educated at a well-known college in the east. He wins her heart. She trusts. Dramatic moments: tornado as a child, her sister's death, her husband killed by KKK, grandfather tries to get control of hotel and kidnap child . . .

Other than changing "Lula" to "Loring," and granting Albert Berch a Catholic background and East Coast education, where's the fiction? And given the mostly true-to-life outline, is the kidnapping intent by the grandfather fictional, or now that we know more about the shifty

"Doctor Berch," did this really happen? After all, Albert Berch, Sr., had to be aware that Almarian was attached to Aunt Helen's fortune in one way or another.

Almarian's plot summary continues: "Loring's daughter is a problem as there is no closeness, Loring fears storms and death, Loring gets her gold but has to give up gold coins to government in 1934, daughter marries well after rebellious years. . . . "

The story turns to a "young male renter who bonds with Loring through their common fear of storms, then fills the void left by the daughter's absence." More from Almarian's synopsis: "Loring goes into partnership with him and he cheats her out of most of her hard-earned money. Saved by the daughter. Daughter resents mother's business and the kind of people who she deals with . . . "

I rest my case. While *One-Half Dream* may have begun as a tribute to her mother and a search for her father's story, it ended up as a rationalization of Almarian's handling of the "Mark Affair," the most dispiriting mother-daughter duel they ever endured. Her notes describe how she would address that battle in her novel: "Daughter and mother have harsh words. Daughter checks mother's financial status behind her back. Makes mother mad. Big scene. Daughter accuses boy. Mother takes up for him. Daughter demands mother to break all relationships with boy. Mother says it's none of her business. Daughter threatens court action. (Haven't decided how to end it yet. Can either make the daughter realize that this is what makes her mother happy even if she loses all her money, or let mother lose all her money and has to admit daughter is right.) Finally, to admit times have changed and she is not as bright as early in life."

In the denouement of *One-Half Dream*, Loring realizes that gold is a symbol for the "satisfaction of knowing you can be useful to someone and being able to furnish understanding in their times of trouble." Almarian adds, "Loring realized that she had not been meant for material wealth but she had been blessed with unusually good health and a daughter for a friend. She was actually now a very rich woman."

To say that Almarian's work of fiction is thinly veiled reality gives too much thickness to the veil. Of course, a great deal of fiction springs from the pool of self-reflection.

The Hollingsworth attic yielded another surprise—a short story, not by Almarian but by Lula as a young woman, a singular example of trampled creativity. Written in pencil on financial ledger paper, brown and brittle, the penmanship is soft and innocent, like flowers in a row, long before the harsh calligraphy took over. In the story, Lula is clearly reliving a scene from the cotton patch where she and her father argued: "though she had rosy red cheeks, she also had red rough hands, which she hated as much as she hated the squalid surroundings of poverty she was being reared in . . . one day, while sitting on her cotton sack (which contained nearly 50 pounds of cotton picked in about one and a half hours or at the rate of 35 pounds per hour or 400 to 450 pounds in 12 hours). . . . "

The young girl grows irate with her father for dragging the family into grueling work that is completely detached from profit. The father then lowers the boom in return, pouncing on his daughter's lack of gratitude. Furthermore, he dampens her wild-eyed dreams and suggests she start paying more attention to the farmer next door, who is looking at her "with those big old calf eyes."

In the end, the cotton-picking protagonist learns that a new baby is on the way, a sister. And in a postscript, written years later in red ink and with the turbulent calligraphy in full bloom, Lula adds: "Really, mother was pregnant and in 4 months my last sister was borned and the whole family was thrilled. Everyone wanted to take care of her. I forgot all about not wanting another baby." Here is another true story, disguised as fiction.

Jessie, the final child of William and Arrie Combs, was born four years after the family's first tornado experience in Nocona, Texas. Jessie would have one child, a girl named Ben Marion, a first cousin to Almarian, though "sisters" would be more apropos. With telepathic eeriness, Ben Marion would die a few months after Almarian in 2011, both sister-cousins in their late eighties.

Shortly after the death of her third husband, Lula wrote a letter to her parents in Elmore City, asking them to join her for Christmas. Apparently she retrieved the saved letter after their deaths, as it was in her attic boxes. "I wish I were a little girl again," it begins, sadly, in a mood of regret and regression, by a woman of sixty-three. Lula describes in detail her very favorite Christmas, including her father dressed as Santa Claus. She recounts every type of homemade candy that year. Even her syntax is childlike. Then, she pleads for "Santa Claus" to join her in Oklahoma City for the upcoming holidays. Three husbands dead, two sons dead, two siblings dead: for Lula, everything was riding on Almarian, who had, in the same year as this 1947 letter, brought Lula's first grandchild into the world, my sister Susan.

In a letter written late in life, Lula acknowledges the common endpoint when personal dreams are left unfulfilled and all that remains is the pervasive hope that one's existence will have had a net gain on progeny. She writes to Almarian after receipt of an unnamed gift, "The older you get the more you appreciate being babied, but I could hardly keep back the tears. If it wasn't for you and your family, I wonder if I would care for life at all. Everything I do I am doing it for your benefit. After Alan left today, I began to live in the past (unusual for me). . . . " She then recounts vignettes about her three grandchildren.

Lula kept scrapbooks about our family that we knew nothing about, filled mostly with clippings from the *El Reno Tribune*. Our mother gave Lula a subscription to our town's newspaper that she received in the mail, and apparently she scoured it daily for some mention of one or more of the Hollingsworths. The scrapbook pages are filled with Almarian and the Girl Scouts, Francis as city councilman, both of them with the Jaycees, or any of the three kids doing almost anything, given that anything is potential news for the small-town paper. If one of my sisters served on the decoration committee for a pep rally, well, that article was enshrined in Lula's scrapbook. And in every story where a Hollingsworth appears, our names are underlined in red. In the end, we were, unwittingly, her raison d'être.

✮✮✮

Lula and Almarian, two very strong-willed women, shared a horrible bond, whether it was spoken or not. They had been together at the side of Albert Berch as he lay bleeding to death from a gunshot wound to the chest, and the cascade of events that followed the murder bore no resemblance to what would have been.

In spite of Almarian's wish in her youth that she not live to a ripe old age, she did—eighty-nine. She waited until her eighties to stop coloring her hair, but when she did, she began to resemble Lula. Her speech pattern devolved to her mother's as well, rapid-fire, tangential, and nonstop.

We promise ourselves we will not slide into the same abyss where our parents fell, and that we will not be a burden to our survivors, but apologizing in advance, we will.

Death becomes uniquely real when you walk into your mother's room and find her stiff with rigor mortis, eyes and mouth open, in a look of eternal astonishment, hopefully in awe of the celestial life beyond. Or as Lula would have said, "mortified." Life for earthly stragglers is altered, regardless of their age. At that moment, I understood why Almarian had wept at the airport in June 1982 after Lula's funeral, falling into my arms in a cloudburst of tears. It helped explain, too, why Lula became so lonely after the death of her mother, even though Arrie had been 102. After our parents are gone, the void is magnified knowing for whom the bell will toll next.

We'd found an aneurysm, a large one. The neurosurgeon said it was inoperable, and the nonsurgical approaches through interventional radiology carried a risk for stroke that was about the same as doing nothing. Nothing worked pretty well for two and a half years, though the constant thought of rupture loomed large in everything Almarian did.

Most of her friends had already passed on, but we heard common tributes after her death that declared her stature, such as "end of an era" or "grande dame" or "one of a kind." Perhaps a big fish in a small pond, but nevertheless, Almarian Berch Hollingsworth had risen well above the bizarre circumstances of her youth.

When Almarian began the research for *One-Half Dream,* she enticed her mother to return to Marlow, against Lula's fifty-year-old vow. Almarian was on a mission to find her father's grave, and she needed Lula's help. Given the timeframe of the mother-daughter crisis, perhaps the venture was an olive branch. Certainly, the search for Albert's gravesite prompted the unusual burial pact, incorporating the threesome who had been together at Johnson's Hotel.

Lula had not visited the grave of Albert Berch since the day of his funeral. In fact, she had not returned to Marlow after her move to Duncan in 1924. How sharp would her memory be? Almarian had procured records from the city that provided the grave's general location, but without a headstone, all remnants could easily be gone. The trip was deeply emotional for Almarian and, of course, she produced a manuscript detailing the event:

> I stood in the middle of the cemetery and stared at the bush. Surrounding it was a blank expanse of land, enough for many more graves.
>
> "It should be here somewhere." My mother was speaking to herself as well as to me.
>
> I scanned the area for some kind of marker. My skin battled the afternoon sun with defensive moisture, but there was no breeze for reinforcement.

I twisted a stem from the bush. "Mother, do you think this is wild or did someone plant it?"

If mother answered I didn't hear as I had uncovered a dull metal square object.

"Mother, look." I parted the bush. We both leaned over for a closer look. A dirty celluloid window with faded yellowed paper behind it gave no clue.

Mother rose up and read from a slip of paper. "This should be it according to the description the girl at city hall gave us."

I dusted some dirt from the metal. B-I-R-- "Mother, this is it!" It has BIRCH written in pencil. A caretaker must have written it because it's spelled wrong.

I don't know why my heart was pounding. I had not known my father. I was only two years old when it all happened. And it had been so long ago. Yet this was the closest I'd ever been to him. I didn't want mother to see the tears that I could feel hesitating on my eye rim. I blinked and they were gone.

Very quietly, mother said, "I waited too long to come back. I kept planning to move him. But when you marry again . . . well . . . "

I put my arm around her. "Mother, I think we are very fortunate to have found him so quickly."

"After 50 years?"

"I mean quickly after we started."

"I hated this place. I still do. Fifty years is a lifetime, but now it seems only like a few."

"Mother, I'm sorry to bring back painful memories. I didn't do this to be morbid. I have just reached a point in my life that it seemed important. One of those loose ends you are always going to tie up but never seem to get to. I wonder now if it was wise."

"I'm glad you made me come. I still hate the place. Come over here and I'll show you why."

She led the way across the road and down two rows. Four stones loomed.

"Here is Walter's grave. And our two sons. All of them dead. Glenn the baby went first, then their father. Guy's temperature was so high (from the Spanish flu) the day of Walter's funeral that I couldn't go." Her voice quivered.

"Shall we go? Now that we've found them?"

She didn't hear me.

"Next to them is your Aunt Fanny, my sister. She was only 31 when she died. There was no need—So young—"

"Let's go."

Either Almarian never finished the story, or the rest of the pages are missing. Or perhaps that was the end. Lula said, "Let's go," and that was it.

On the flipside of this document, Almarian was at work on a poem. The first of four stanzas reads:

> I stood there gazing at the lonely bush
> The lonely bush which marked your bed
> Around were stones neatly hewn
> While you had a living monument at your head. . . .

The poem seemed unfinished, at least the version I found. As one would expect with Almarian, she had made multiple corrections, placed accents, and divided syllables with slash marks in a system of scansion known only to poets. Somewhere, there's a finished version, even if it's only in Almarian's memory that she took to her grave. After all, death is only a dream.

Among the artifacts uncovered after Almarian died, I found a faded photo taken by my mother of that lonely bush on that unusual day. Almarian subsequently had the scraggly bush removed, its sentinel role no longer needed, and replaced it with a standard tombstone. *BERCH* is engraved on the side where Lula and Albert are buried, while *HOLLINGSWORTH* is on the flipside of the same stone, where Almarian Berch Hollingsworth and Francis Hollingsworth, MD are buried.

The four funerals, spanning eighty-eight years, took place in the four seasons: Albert in winter, Lula in summer, Francis in fall, and Almarian in spring. My sisters and I attended three of the four funerals.

As for us "kids" at the time, our mother's discovery of Albert's grave was revealed to us without any emotion on her part. It went something like this: "Mother and I found my father's grave. The marker was hidden beneath a bush."

While it sparked a modicum of interest for me at the time, nevertheless, it was still *their* story, Lula and her daughter.

19

Alan Berch (Hollingsworth)— the Third Obsession

For Proust in search of lost time, his main memory trigger may have been the aroma of a freshly baked madeleine. For me, it's a newly puttied window, or wet paint slopped onto a porch, or, most of all, the musty bouquet of a storm cave.

Lula's front-porch storm shelter was a kid's delight, especially if that kid's first magazine subscription was *Famous Monsters of Filmland*. Simply opening the cellar door allowed the darkness to spill out, overflowing the porch with puddles of gloom. Ominous cracks in the concrete walls seemed to ooze malevolent fumes, while glass jars of unrecognizable food on shelves mimicked scientific specimens in formaldehyde. Eons of wax wept over the sides of bottles used as candleholders in the gloom, completely engulfing the glass with multicolored tears, frozen as a tribute to the number of times the two women had scampered to their subterranean refuge whenever two or more clouds appeared in the sky. It was a fantastic cavern where the lighted candles teased us with a flickering glow, and where Lula and Arrie summoned electricity only as a last resort from a solitary, bare lightbulb hanging by its noose from the ceiling. Lula would be wringing her hands over the impending storm; Arrie not so much.

Where was my older sister Susan? Most of the time, when our parents were traveling, Susan would be assigned to our Grandmother Hollingsworth, newly widowed, though that was no concern of ours. The fact that Grandpa Hollingsworth had dropped dead of a heart attack at age sixty-one on Christmas morning would escape our understanding until we were adults. The widow Myrtle had two hobbies—one, collecting rare miniature bottles, and secondly, painting china plates. The boy was shipped to Lula and her rock-solid storm cave, while the girl was entrusted to Myrtle and her fragile collections.

Like Lula before her, Almarian handled all fiscal matters for our family and, in spite of her aversion to real estate, would close her own deals without an agent. Some of these pecuniary concerns flowed downstream. I recall sitting at my mother's knee as she taught me how to interpret an amortization schedule, even though I barely knew how to add and subtract at the time.

Notably distinct from Lula, however, Almarian was an animal lover to the extreme, such that we kids were never pet-less growing up. Lula, as a busy mother, would not let young Almarian have any pets, a source of ongoing grief for our mother. Almarian pined away, begging for a cat, even though she could not keep it with her at boarding school. Lula finally "gave in" one Christmas, presenting Almarian with a cat—that is, a ceramic one, glistening and cool to the touch.

Certainly, this was how the story of Albert Berch came to us as children: glistening and cool to the touch. "Murdered by the Ku Klux Klan" was a fabulous boast to grade-school friends and beyond, but without consideration for any possible impact of the tragedy on our mother or grandmother.

From my vantage point, Lula seemed remote from the events. After all, her last name was Reynolds, not Berch. Almarian's last name was Hollingsworth. Yet, we grew up with a constant reminder of the mysterious Albert Berch, given that Almarian kept portraits of her mother and father together in a dual frame, always near her favorite chair. To our knowledge, this was the one and only photograph of Albert Berch.

As a child, I had very little curiosity about the details of the Marlow murders. After Almarian began her midlife research, I recall being surprised to learn that the Johnson Hotel was still standing, but that prompted only modest interest even then.

In the early 1970s, I made my first trip to Marlow. I drove to the address Almarian provided, ending up on Main Street near the railroad tracks. The two-story building was a rooming house at the time, and the elderly couple who ran the place had moved to Marlow more than a decade after the murders. That said, they still knew the local folklore, and they pointed to the spot where the murders had happened, at least according to what they had been told. My grandfather had fallen near a staircase, and the black man (no one spoke his name) was attacked nearby. I still recall where this couple was sitting in the lobby as they described the scene to me, and just how the old man's arm levitated as he pointed first to Albert's death site, then to the site of Robert Johnigan's assault. There was no recognizable writing room, and the entry to the café had been walled off. The phone booth was long gone.

What is baffling to me now is that I left Johnson's Hotel that day satisfied. I had no questions. I had come to do something very simple, and I had done it. I never really considered exploring details any further, largely because Almarian was in the throes of her obsession, and the story was all hers. In short order, there was her discovery of Albert's grave, the fruitless trips to Fargo and Los Angeles, and then the memorable classroom gasp of Junetta Davis when she realized her brother had nearly been a part of the mob that had killed Almarian's father. The shockwave from the back of the room took place in the novel-writing course taught by Jack Bickham. So now, a vignette about Jack, a marker for the Third Obsession sprouting its roots. From here on, the story eases from true crime and its aftermath to a detective arriving at the scene of the crime decades after the fact.

Jack Bickham (1930-97) was the author of seventy-five novels, well known in Oklahoma writing circles even today, as many of his pupils remain. Two of his books were made into movies, the most recognized being Disney's *The Apple Dumpling Gang* in 1975.

"Jack wants to interview you and your father for a medical book he's writing," said my mother. "He's planning a father-son plotline where both are physicians." Almarian further explained that she was going to arrange a dinner date for our family with Bickham in May of 1977. But that wasn't the hook; this was: "That will give you the opportunity to run that plot by Jack that you've been talking about, for your own book."

The dinner in El Reno happened as planned, and Jack's interview of my father and me went off without a hitch. Then my mother said, "Alan, now tell Jack about your plot for a book and see what he thinks."

An hour later, I had exhausted the details of my plot for a medical thriller (a new genre at the time), and Jack had interrogated me up and down on how I planned to deal with the various angles. He completely abandoned further mention of his own book plans that night, concluding with: "There's a big leap between a powerful plot and a good book. Let me co-write that book with you."

And then, with the stupidity that can only be bestowed by youth, I replied, "No thanks." My stance was simple at the time: *If the plot is that great, I'm going to write it myself.* In a few months, I would be starting a one-year fellowship in pathology at UCLA, and I explained to Jack that I would have time to get the book drafted on my own. Jack replied, "Okay, then, do this. I'm the director of a short course on writing that starts in a few weeks, and I want you to come as my guest. Then, if you get the book written next year, I'll critique it for you."

I attended my first writers' conference in the weeks that followed, timed perfectly before my departure to Los Angeles, where I would spend one year before returning to Oklahoma to finish my residency in surgery. Six months later, still in California, I had finished my draft. And when I mailed it to Bickham, my mother cautioned, "Get ready. Jack's a tough critic, harsh at times, and he rarely dwells on the positives."

His critique came in letter form. "First of all, I don't know how in the hell you wrote such a nice novel the first time out. . . . In my opinion, you have a chance to find a publisher—an editor who might work with you on revision—right now as the manuscript stands." Sure, he went on to trash my writing for two more pages, but that opening line served to sustain me through decades of rejections.

Jack correctly predicted the book's potential, in that it was lifted from the slush pile of a major New York publisher and an editor worked with me for several years. But in the end, it was a bust. It was deemed "too much like *Coma,*" a story that had not yet been discovered when I began my book but was at its peak popularity and being filmed by the time I had finished. Through the next twenty-plus years of rejections, after shelving my medical-thriller manuscript in favor of writing nonmedical fiction, I would hang on to the words of Jack Bickham whenever I doubted myself. That remarkable phone call finally came in 2000—"We'd like to publish your novel."

It is not my intent to invoke the cascade here in claiming that Albert Berch died so that I could immortalize the antics of a bunch of high-school goofballs on the golf course. I mention it as an example of the "butterfly effect," where a seemingly simple event, too subtle to be noticed at the time, alters the illusory balance (a.k.a. chaos) in the universe. Every event in the cosmos has an antecedent, and for the purposes of this book, I use *cascade* to denote direct causation or aftermath, while the *butterfly effect* is meant as a minor tweak with a major impact, accomplished through countless, nearly invisible steps.

If I had not written that novel, then I would not have been in the southern part of Oklahoma doing a book signing in the city of Ardmore, and I would not have been traveling alone back to Oklahoma City on a Saturday morning in 2003 and, therefore, would not have been on hand for what is likely the most remarkable coincidence in my life, an event alluded to earlier in this book.

The I-35 corridor between Oklahoma City and the Dallas-Ft. Worth metroplex is well worn by Oklahomans, be it for football games or extended weekends. I began a long series of trips to and from Dallas after starting college in 1967, always feeling a twinge of guilt as I passed the exit sign for Elmore City. I recalled that Arrie Combs had been buried in that town in 1965 and that I had skipped her funeral, based on the flimsy excuse that Almarian had not pressed us. If Elmore City had been located immediately adjacent to I-35, it would have been different, I can claim, weakly, knowing I would have visited her grave to apologize postmortem for missing her funeral.

However, exiting at the Elmore City sign still means you have to travel another ten miles west to reach the town, plus the time spent there, then the time back to I-35—too much to ask family or friends to endure, I note flimsily. But on this Saturday morning, the fact that I was traveling alone after the book signing opened a door I had ignored for more than thirty-five years. I saw the exit sign to Elmore City, and in an act of rare impulsivity on my part, I turned the wheel toward Combs Central, where the family mercantile store had thrived.

The cemetery road was well marked, and it took only one excursion through the graveyard to see the name *COMBS* jump off a large tombstone located in a quaint family plot. Shade trees, a curb around the perimeter, and a concrete bench and planters all made for a pleasant ambiance. And there, among names barely familiar to me, was Arrie's marker.

Given that most small-town cemeteries are deserted, I took notice of one other car, parked at the opposite end of the graveyard. Although I'm not one to talk to tombstones, I paid my respects to Arrie, apologized for my absence from her funeral, and thanked her for a life of labor and sacrifice that benefitted her descendants.

Then, out of the corner of my eye, I noticed that the other car was no longer at the far end of the cemetery. It was headed my direction. Surely, it would make a turn and ease on out of the graveyard. But it didn't. It continued directly toward me. A confrontation was looming . . . in a cemetery, no less. The car parked directly behind mine. Was it trying to prevent my escape? Worse, was the driver crazed? Had I walked into my own horror movie?

A woman about my age, with no particular expression on her face, stepped out of the car and walked quietly toward me, without any hint as to what she was intending. I don't need to tell you I was spooked.

As she came within a few feet of my position in front of the Combs plot, she finally spoke. "Do you mind my asking—what are you doing here?"

I wondered, did she mean "here" as in this cemetery, or this spot, or this town?

Ready to apologize for nothing identifiable, I replied, "Well, I'm here to visit my great-grandmother's grave."

"Oh? Who's your great-grandmother?" she asked, her eyes riveted to mine.

"Arrie Combs," I said, pointing toward the grave.

Then, with heightened scrutiny, she uttered this unforgettable response:

"Arrie Combs is my great-grandmother, too. *Who are you?*"

And that's how, at age fifty-three, I met my cousin, Barbara Combs McKay.

20

The Cardboard Box

On that summer day in 2003, my second cousin had been at the opposite end of the Elmore City cemetery visiting gravesites for her husband's side of the family when she spotted a stranger standing in front of the Combs family plot, prompting her to investigate. She explained her relationship as the granddaughter of Lula's only brother, Fred, and his wife, Mittie, and the daughter of Fred's son, Doyle, and wife Charlotte. Eleven more years would pass before I would place Barbara's grandparents at the scene of the Marlow murders, making our chance encounter that much more bizarre.

Mittie had assumed care of the young Almarian that night, after the initial protective comfort of Bessie Benight, who ran the café. Assuming Mittie took Almarian to her home four blocks away on the night of the murders, Fred and their thirteen-year-old son, Doyle Combs, helped to babysit my mother. As an adult, I met Doyle once or twice, but no one indicated that he might have played a role in this story.

In my unusual introduction to cousin Barbara, my foggy knowledge of our genealogy was obvious, as I struggled to place her within the family tree. Barbara, sympathetic to my plight, later sent me copies of the genealogy files amassed by her parents. From these, I was able to draw a formal pedigree chart, an exercise I perform routinely for genetic counseling in my work but had never done for myself and my family. When I began work on this book over a decade later, I would use this chart as my core reference.

Turning back the clock from this coincidental meeting in 2003 to September 1979, while I was frantically trying to rewrite my first attempt at a novel and finish my surgery residency at the University of Oklahoma, Lula fell and broke her hip. She was ninety-five years old and had lived alone for the past fourteen years.

The incision from her hip surgery became infected and required dressing changes, at least twice daily, the morning change performed by a visiting nurse. For the evening change, I dropped by her duplex at 1805 Northwest Twenty-Seventh every night over the course of many weeks.

By this time in her life, Lula was no longer taciturn. She talked nonstop. She talked while I changed the dressing, she talked for thirty minutes thereafter, and she talked as I was walking out the door. I did not mind. I was collecting sticks for the nest that would nurture writing projects in the future. I kept a log of medical adventures and ordeals during my surgical training, and I simply added the information from Lula as she spoke it.

I pumped her about the murders, I asked her about wildcatting, I encouraged her to talk about Almarian in her youth, and so on. In keeping with the family tradition of hypergraphia, I wrote it all down. Sadly, when I finally got to the point in my life where I could begin writing seriously, I had lost the logbook during a prior move. Here I am, decades later, still lamenting.

What I do remember, however, is the long list of names Lula would recite during her account of the murders. And when I would ask her why certain characters in her story had behaved strangely, the answer was always the same: "He was Klan, don'tcha see?" Frankly, the pat answer seemed improbable.

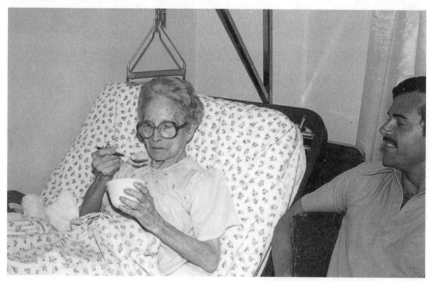

The author visits Lula during her recovery from a broken hip. Lula would live another two years after this photo was taken.

This was also when I asked that critical question in reference to the family folklore about the one stray bullet that had pierced Almarian's sleeve, only to learn that Lula had not saved the gown. One would think that this query would have prompted Lula to inform me that she had kept other items from the murders. For example: "No, I didn't save the gown, *but . . .* " Instead, her answer was a decisive "no," a global "no," almost as if the horror of the event was so overwhelming that she had been unable to keep anything that might resurrect the nightmare. I was left with the impression that there was absolutely nothing left on earth to corroborate her story.

Several years after Lula died, my father was diagnosed with Parkinson's disease, and both his and Almarian's lives knotted around this mast for more than a decade. Almarian remained in fairly good health through the ordeal, although exhausted from the years of intensive care she gave our father as he declined neurologically. He would die in his own bed, in his own home. For the first year or so afterward, she remained flat, and I encouraged her to start afresh with the story of her father. I signed her up with a subscription to one of the trade magazines for writers and offered to help her rewrite the story. She didn't respond, nor did she encourage me to write the story.

Her obsession with the topic of Albert Berch began to decline with her health. She fell repeatedly, after she lost one eye to macular degeneration and her balance worsened with age. Miraculously, she never broke a bone, though we dealt with lacerations, black eyes, and a bruised and battered face. The large brain aneurysm was then discovered. It had the decency to wait a few years before it ruptured. Almarian Berch Hollingsworth died on April 26, 2011.

Gold coins, or more specifically, *giving them away* had been the unconcealed metaphor for happiness in her novel, *One-Half Dream*. Most assuredly, she extracted this theme from her fascination with the buried gold coins in our Combs family lore. Perhaps the same folklore was responsible for Almarian's lifelong hobby (among many) of coin collecting. Maybe she took the concept of buried coins to its extreme when she planted bags of coins, some quite valuable, some not, throughout her house to make sure that, after her death, her progeny examined every drawer, closet, and box that filled the large home on Ellison Avenue in El Reno.

Her instructions, written over many years, made no bones about it. "Look everywhere" her notes told us, in reference to the coins, as if she had concocted one final game we could play as her children. The amazing thing is that, until her death, we did not even know these coins existed.

Although she could still compete with the best while watching *Jeopardy*, Almarian's first symptom of failing cognition was her forte— finance. Almost two years before her death, when it became evident that she was no longer tracking her checkbook balance, I took over her routine personal business. It took me a while to uncover all her accounts, but once accomplished, it was apparent that she might outlive her money. "Didn't you have a coin collection at one time?" I asked, looking for an ace in the hole, considering the longevity of her mother and grandmother. Her evasive answer was enough to satisfy me that the coins were long gone or of minimal importance. So there I was, liquidating her assets to pay her bills, trying to keep a promise to let her live and die at home, and all the time she was sitting on one final surprise for her children—buried treasure, hidden all over the house.

Like the archaeologic site at Oxyrhynchus near the Nile River, where diggers have been sifting through a trash heap for rare and valuable artifacts for more than a century, my sisters and I were overwhelmed by the three-story pile we faced upon Almarian's death. During her fifty-five years in that house, not one fragment of memorabilia had ever been tossed out. But it gets worse. Those attics and closets served, too, as multigenerational storehouses for both sides of the family, wherein ancestors of the same mold had willed their disintegrating cardboard boxes to posterity's resting place on Ellison Avenue in El Reno, Oklahoma. This meant that nothing could be thrown out during the El Reno excavation without closely examining the contents of every box, drawer, and file, which filled every nook, cranny, and corner.

As I awaited the arrival of my sisters to begin the dig, I stumbled on a pair of barber shears in a drawer, lying loose among rubble. I would have tossed them in the trash had it not been for a label attached to the finger loops:

"Almarian: According to Mother these shears were given to her by your father in 1921, after he got into the hotel business and retired from the barber profession. Mother has kept these all of this time, and ask me to give them to you."

Almarian had no living siblings, so "Mother" meant someone else. The notation was from her first cousin, Doyle Combs. Mittie, his mother, had helped Lula at the hotel with maid service, plus odds and ends, working alongside Albert Berch. These scissors supported the lore that Albert had been a barber.

I was astounded that we had physical proof of Albert's existence, and I

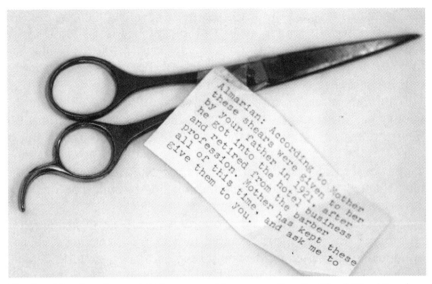

The first hint that there might be more evidence regarding the life of Albert Berch in the El Reno home came through the discovery of these barber shears, tagged for Almarian as belonging to "your father"

was holding it in my hand. Up until that moment, we only had the single photograph that Almarian proudly displayed along with the photo of her mother. Albert Berch was palpably coming alive through tempered steel. His fingers had presided over this instrument. But how could Almarian simply have tossed them in a drawer? I could only conclude that the barber shears represented the sum total of all known belongings of her father. Where else do you put a pair of scissors, tagged as once belonging to your murdered father?

The excavation was scheduled to last five long days over Memorial Day weekend, one month after Almarian's death. Our primary goal was to pluck keepsakes from the piles, saving detailed analysis for later, then leave the bulk for an estate sale. Before the arrival of my sisters, one from the West Coast and one from the East Coast, I knew there were tasks I could perform to make the process go smoother and quicker. First and foremost, I could help by emptying the large walk-in "attic" or closet, unpacking the sardined boxes so that we could have a good look at the contents spread out.

The closet was accessed through an upstairs bedroom door, camouflaged as part of a wood-paneled wall. Reminiscent of *Alice in Wonderland,* the door itself was so small that one had to stoop to enter.

Rather than a "room," the space was more of a long hallway, perhaps twenty-five feet in length, with a ceiling of odd angles, the inside reflection of the multifaceted roof and a dormer window. Thus, one side of the hallway had a ceiling six feet high, but the severe slope allowed only two feet of space on the other side.

Within, there was no space left unused, and I'm not referring to the floor alone. The room was stuffed to the ceiling. Decades of income-tax information, each year in a separate bag, teetered at the top of the stacks closest to the door. My strategy was dictated by the towers—boxes and bags nearest the door had to be removed so I could burrow through the long channel. There I was, a solo ant, looking to build my tunnel by removing one grain of sand at a time.

Once I cleared away the financial records, I found boxes of memorabilia, and this is where my sprint slowed to a crawl. Removing each box prompted a quick peek inside, and it soon became apparent that, of all the household contents, it would be the remaining treasure from this attic that would threaten our short five-day strategy.

I uncovered memorabilia from our parents' international travels, community activities, school scrapbooks, and so forth. But as I worked my way deeper into the tunnel, it became apparent that when *their* parents had died, as well as previous generations, similar scrap had also been entombed in cardboard boxes and stashed in the attic. In the deepest recess, the end zone, when I flipped open photo albums, the pages were filled with strangers.

One large box midway down the tunnel held a bounty of letters Lula had stored. But within this container, like a coffin within a sarcophagus, was a plain cardboard box, eighteen inches square and six inches deep, unsealed and unlabeled, submerged in envelopes. Small and unassuming, the box beckoned only by virtue of its antiquity. Alone in Wonderland, I flipped open the flaps that had likely been interlaced for nearly ninety years.

Within seconds, I knew that I had struck a rich vein of gold and that the barber shears had only been a speck of downstream dust panned from the water. Before my eyes shone photos never seen by my generation, mysterious letters, the homicide scrapbook with gold letters, notes by Lula scribbled during the murder trials, and a long bronze keychain denoting room number sixteen at Johnson's Hotel. But my fingers tore beyond these findings at first, lured to items of clothing: a leather belt, a wallet, a starched collar, a tie.

Recognizing the tie immediately, I pulled it from the box and

A belt, wallet, and keychain for room number sixteen at Johnson's Hotel in Marlow, Oklahoma, taken by Lula as remembrance of Albert Berch at the time of his death

crosschecked with the single photograph we had of Albert Berch. Yes, it was the very bowtie he was wearing in his only portrait. Attached was a note in Lula's handwriting: "This is the last tie your daddy ever wore." Was this the murder wardrobe?

I lifted the white collar from the box to look for bloodstains. There were none, but I felt my hands raising the collar to my own neck and I wondered how much of Albert Berch's DNA had found its way into mine. It was a bit snug around my neck, and I saw that the size on the adjustable device had been set on 15 1/2. Since I wear a size-16 collar, the mysticism of the moment diminished, until I remembered that Albert had been murdered at age thirty. I was sixty-one at the time, trying to fit into a young man's collar. At age thirty, I wore a 15 1/2.

Our physical resemblance had always been suggested, even when I was a child. Clearly, I favored the Berch side more than the Hollingsworths. I have delayed until now the mention of a question I posed to Lula many years ago during one of my nightly visits to her home for the dressing changes in 1979. As she was relating stories surrounding the murder of her husband, I interrupted her to ask if, in her mind's eye, I bore a

Greetings

From Our House to Your House...

The Hollingsworths

The Hollingsworth family Christmas card in 1956. Many of the key artifacts relating to this story were discovered in the attic of this home in 2011.

resemblance to my grandfather, Albert Berch. I recall her stopping her discourse. Pausing only a second to look me straight in the eye, then smiling subtly as though she had already considered the question, she answered, "Yes, Alan, you do favor him."

The items in the cardboard box added flesh to the dry bones of what had been only a name, a legend, a rumor. For me, the pulse of Albert Berch began beating. I resolved to write this story, no longer out of a self-imposed duty, but out of obsession. Almarian, resting in the Marlow cemetery, had yielded her authority over the saga.

The treasures in the cardboard box belied the small size of their container, several of the documents remaining undeciphered to this day. "Grandma," I wanted to ask thirty years too late, "who do you think wrote this anonymous death threat? Who wrote this letter of support from the Astoria Hotel in New York? Why did the Dutch embassy write you? How in the world did you get your hands on these letters written by one of the murderers?"

Later, I learned from the trial transcripts that Albert had removed his Sunday best and dressed in khakis only moments before his murder, thus explaining the absence of blood on the starched formal collar. But the abundance of murder material in the box cannot be overstated, from hotel logs to photographs. For the first time, I saw a photo of the hotel's interior, with Lula at the front desk, standing beside a clerk. In other photos, Lula was outside the hotel in various locations—photos that I would reenact ninety years later. The number-sixteen keychain likely was used for the Berch suite at the time of the murder. I suspect that Lula grabbed Albert's wallet, tie, belt, collar, and pocket contents in one fell swoop shortly after the murder.

I've thought about it from every angle. Did Almarian know about this box? I don't believe she did. For starters, she never mentioned it. If she *did* know about it, how could she *not* mention it? "After I'm gone, don't forget to look for Lula's cardboard box of things she kept after the murder." It would have been so easy. And if it were something Almarian wanted to keep secret, why would she store the box for future generations? The letters were bundled within, neatly in their envelopes, stacked according to size, with no evidence that anyone had rummaged through them (in contrast to their ruffled state today). Too, the box was resting in a larger box, both unlabeled. And I have yet to reveal all the contents of the letters and logs inside the box, providing so much information that it's inconceivable that none of this would have made its way into *One-Half Dream*, so thinly disguised as fiction.

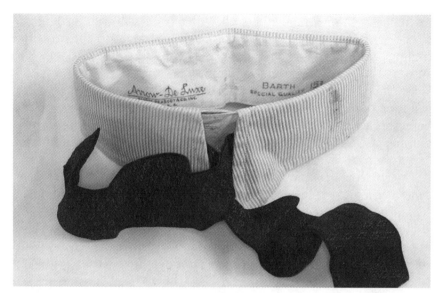

The collar and tie worn by Albert Berch in his studio portrait, as well as the night of his murder

Lula Berch in 1920, standing at the main entrance to Johnson's Hotel. Grandson and author, Alan Berch Hollingsworth, in 2011, in the same location.

If it seems improbable that Lula would not tell her daughter about such an important container of memories, recall that Lula never admitted her true age to Almarian until very late in life. Nor did she tell her daughter about the El Reno honeymoon until Almarian began to write *One-Half Dream*. And Lula *never* confessed the true age of Albert Berch. By the time of Lula's death in 1982, my mother may have been so grief-stricken (and guilt-stricken given their recent tiff) that she simply jammed all of Lula's boxes into the attic with the intent to sort through them "at a future date," a day that never came after Parkinson's disease wormed its way into our family.

Another bit of circumstantial evidence indicated that the box had been untouched—it was buried so deeply in the Wonderland tunnel that it had long been sealed away. The boxes of memorabilia sandwiched between ceiling and floor after Lula's death became impenetrable from a practical standpoint. Thirty years of "stuff," resting like bricks without mortar, blocked access until the day I struck pay dirt. While vertical strata are the key to chronology in archaeology, in this particular closet of memories, time was marked by horizontal strata. I had burrowed about twelve feet beyond the last bag of coins before I stumbled upon this true mother lode in the cardboard box.

21

Oxyrhynchus

Lula's cardboard box held the most concentrated source of riches. But in terms of sheer volume, by the time we had completed the El Reno excavation, I was contending with a dozen boxes of maternal-side memorabilia that I spirited to my home, where I sifted and probed for over a year. It was not unusual for me to spend many hours chasing down leads from my findings, only to discover later from a different box that Almarian had worked out the details thirty years earlier.

In total, Lula created ten scrapbooks still intact, most of the contents having served a previous life in a popular magazine or, in one case, a dissection manual for comparative anatomy. Some of the scrapbooks are filled with newspaper clippings of crimes and natural disasters that have no bearing on the story at hand, other than to demonstrate that Lula became increasingly consumed by thoughts of doom.

In her scrapbooks and the cardboard box, she saved editorials written about the Marlow murders, primarily in the Oklahoma City newspapers, the *Oklahoma City Times* and the *Daily Oklahoman*. In one editorial, "Restraining the Klan," the author rejoices over passage of the new state law hindering secret societies in general but clearly aimed at the Ku Klux Klan: "Oklahoma now has a law designed to regulate and restrain the Ku Klux Klan. It is not as fierce and sweeping as opponents of the invisible empire desired. It does not make the klan roster available for court action. But it does ban the mask in public. . . . It is far better than no anti-klan law at all, and the best that could be expected from a legislature including many klan sympathizers. . . . The power of the klan is not ended, but it is less likely to be abused than in the past."

This new state law did not come about easily. It was not in effect at the time of the murders in Marlow, but it was gaining support through a statewide petition.

Other letters are remarkable for Lula's notations on the envelopes rather than the contents. One letter is from a resourceful person who realized that the dead porter at the hotel meant a potential job opening. The query, written in beautiful cursive and formal English only three days after the murders, offers service as the new porter, his qualifications being that of a night clerk at a large hotel in Tulsa. More interesting, however, written in pencil by Lula on the back of the envelope, are the words of the minister at Albert Berch's funeral, the inflammatory citations that prompted her to jump up and leave in the middle of the service.

Editorials appeared in other newspapers as well, mostly regional, from the *Kansas City Star* to the *Dallas Morning News*. An editorial written by James Britton Buchanan Boone Cranfill, known as "J.B."— the colorful Texan doctor, scholar, minister, and journalist—castigated the evil deeds at Marlow like no other, with hyperbole taking him all the way to the Turk-Armenian genocide in progress at the time. Lula clipped the editorial for her scrapbook, but she didn't stop there. She contacted J.B. and asked him to write a book about the murders, an exposé. The following is his polite regret, thus starting the rejection process one generation earlier than *One-Half Dream:*

> From J. B. Cranfill, 631 Wilson Bldg., Dallas, Texas, March 3, 1924; To Mrs. Lula Berch, Marlowe [*sic*], Okla. c/o Johnson Hotel:
> I have your kind letter of the 28th and have been very much interested in your statements. I have expressed my own convictions concerning this outrageous crime in The News which article you have doubtless read. Concerning the book, I regret to say that my talents do not run in the direction of writing scenarios or things of that kind. I had newspaper training and was in newspaper work for nearly a quarter of a century, but I have never done anything in the matter of scenario work. . . . I think if you would write to the American Magazine or to Hearst's Magazine, in New York City, you might find some on of their staff that could take this matter up and function it most happily. . . . Please be assured of my tender sympathies for you and your orphan children, who are the victims of one of the most diabolical murders in the annals of crime. With every kind wish, I am,
> Very truly yours, J. B. Cranfill

Whether or not Lula ever contacted the magazines in New York, we do not know. However, we do have a mysterious letter written from the Hotel Astor in New York City to Lula, with a signature that used only a single letter *S* followed by a dash. The letter is dated June 1, 1924, about six months after the murders:

"My Dear Mrs. Berch, Just a line from The East from one who is indeed interested in the splendid battle you have waged as well as the real courage you have developed in your fight. I have mailed several cards and one additional letter I hope you have received them. I expect to be in Oklahoma in a few days and I will call you by long distance. . . . Will say good by and good luck. Hoping to have the pleasure of talking in person to you very soon from one who is [illegible adverb] interested. S—"

Condolences came within a day of the murders from one of Al Berch's friends, perhaps a business partner, J. A. Bermingham, oil operator, sent from the First National Bank Building in Ft. Worth, Texas:

> Dear Mrs. Berch:
> I have just heard of the awful tragedy and my heart goes out to you and little Al Marion [sic]. It is beyond all conception of human understanding how anyone could deliberately shoot down an innocent man like Al. Nothing that I can say will bring him back to his wife and baby and his friends but I feel very deeply. . . . Poor little woman you certainly have had your share of trouble and to think that Al, as fine a fellow as ever lived, was cut off right in the start of his life. Al had a wonderful personality and was a man of great business ability and know that he was on the eve of making a big success in the business world. . . .
> Assuring you of my heartfelt sympathy in your great loss, I beg to remain, Very sincerely yours, J. A. Bermingham.

Once again, we have attestation as to the remarkable Albert Berch. From jury trials to Aunt Mittie's endorsement, we have nothing but praise. Granted, the men behind the murders might have had a different reckoning, but even with that considered, Albert Berch seems to have been a man who waltzed into Marlow with a magic touch that went well beyond cutting hair.

In another letter dated February 4, 1924 (about one month after the murders), Lula was contacted by the newly formed American Civil Liberties Union. Field Secretary Lucille B. Milner at 100 Fifth Avenue, New York City, Chelsea 0340 ("Chelsea" being one of the early phone exchanges), wrote:

> My dear Mrs. Birch [sic]:
> We are writing you requesting certain information regarding the tragic killing of your husband, and trust that you will not consider this letter an intrusion.
> The American Civil Liberties Union is a non-partisan organization

composed of citizens throughout the country devoted to the maintenance of civil liberties as the only sure process of orderly progress. The enclosed leaflet states fully our aims.

We are planning in the near future to issue a pamphlet on the Ku Klux Klan and are anxious to obtain all possible evidence regarding criminal acts committed by the Klan throughout the country. In this connection we are writing you in order to ask whether or not in your opinion the Marlow Klan was implicated in the murder of your husband. We feel sure that you will understand our motives in requesting this information of you and hope that you will be willing to cooperate with us in this connection.

Enclosed is a stamped self-addressed envelope to facilitate your reply.

Thanking you in advance for your cooperation, I am

Sincerely yours, signed Lucille B. Milner, Field Secretary

The officers listed on the letterhead are a who's who if one knows the history of the ACLU, but the only name that was familiar to me on the left sidebar of National Committee members was Helen Keller.

We do not have Lula's response, but I suspect they received an earful, or handful, in the form of newspaper clippings and her handwritten story. Perhaps overwhelmed, the ACLU wrote back nine days after their original query, noting that the murders were "an outrageous case of mob violence and we trust that the leaders will be brought to justice in April." The ACLU continued, "A letter which we had from the Mayor of Marlow assured us that the authorities are making every effort toward this end. Please keep in touch with us and if we can be of any service do not hesitate to call upon us."

Again, the letter was signed by the national field secretary, obviously impressed with the high-minded motives of Marlow's mayor.

Ranking near the top of the bombshells in the cardboard box are two letters written from prison by Marvin Kincannon to Ada Kincannon. Since some sources claim that Marvin Kincannon was single his entire life, it took some effort to put the relationships together, but Ada Stotts Kincannon was his young wife. And as has been revealed already, one of the men initially arrested for the murders was Ada's father, Fred.

Fred Stotts was a Marlow farmer who had six children, one of them Ada, born in 1904. She was nineteen at the time of the murders. Three daughters were listed in Fred's obituary, all by their married names using their husbands' initials, so it is not clear which one might have been Ada. She apparently divorced Marvin, remarried, and moved on with her life.

The question, of course, is how in the world did Lula get her hands on these letters from Marvin to his wife? And why? Did Lula and Ada forge a kinship while Marvin was in prison? Did Lula befriend Ada and guide the young woman to a life without Marvin? Did Lula scheme to procure these letters, hoping to discover the "mastermind" behind the murders, a quest always on her agenda? Did one of Walton's detectives seize the letters? Whatever the story, it must have been a doozy.

The two letters from Marvin Kincannon are written in barely legible pencil, on Oklahoma State Penitentiary stationery. *William S. Key, Warden,* is printed at the top, with "Rules for Writing and Receiving Letters" as part of the stationery. Ada's address is 508 1/2 North Broadway in Oklahoma City, today an empty lot just north of a popular steakhouse. Here is one letter, with cautious punctuation added for readability (Marvin did not believe in commas or periods):

> Mrs. Ada Kincannon,
> Dearest loved one, will answer your letter of 26 and 27th. Was surprised to hear from you, the last letter I got from you was Nov 5th[?] and I ans it and wrote home twice and to sister Ruby. I haven't received an answer from her yet. . . .
> I was expecting to hear from that lawyer through you but I haven't heard a thing so far. I had better put you wise Ada, that lawyer is Mrs. Berch's and all they want is to pull country people for money and don't think for a minute that they want to see me get out. I knew that before that lawyer ever come about here. I want you to see him and ask him why he didn't do as he promised, and if he is going to, and ask him any more questions that happen to come to your mind at the time and write and tell me all he says.
> Say sweetheart if you had a boring Xmas just think of the one I had . . . could have been there if it would have made anyone happy. I know I would be for I am always happy when I am with you.
> Ada dear I might suggest something that would make you feel better, just save up and buy a one way ticket to that part of the world where your mom is, but no honey that would be leaving all of your friends.
> Say honey, I have been thinking of that card game and I sure would like to have that now. It is sure going to be good with just you and me, just think of the time we have lost honey, well darling one, here is hoping I eat the next Xmas dinner with you.
> With lots of love, Kinny.

The second letter to Ada, two weeks later, is dated January 15, 1926.

Similar passages fill the pages, but this paragraph is notable for its mention of his coconspirator:

> I didn't know that Gandy had told anything, what did he know and who did he tell, let me know all about it and anything also that has a bearing on my case. Say honey did you see that lawyer and ask him what I told you to. When I ask you to do something I wish you would do it as quick as you can for it just slows things up when you don't. . . .
>
> I will close with lots of love. Kinny. I would sure like to play some cards tonight with you
>
> P.S. Tell Ruby and Snooks that they can write to me if it does not greeve [*sic*] them and Dovie to.

Of course, the most chilling letter in Lula's cardboard box is from the Deep Throat informer at the Doss Hotel in McAlester that implicates Albert Berch, Sr., in trickery to get the hotel and perhaps the baby, Almarian, away from "that woman." As noted earlier in this book, pronoun confusion and syntax ambiguity keep us from confirming that Lula's father-in-law was the person who aimed a gun at her in contemplation of murder, holding back only "because of the child looking up at him so appealingly."

The cardboard box also contained odds and ends that defy explanation as to why Lula would save them. For instance, there is a whimsical draft from the Guaranteed State Bank in Marlow, a check dated July 3, 1926 (two and a half years after the murders), from A. W. Berch (Albert Senior) to Lulu Berch for $1 million. As twisted as this joke is, given what we know about her father-in-law, it is an important clue as to the whereabouts of Albert Senior after the murders. He was still in Oklahoma in 1926, about the time that Aunt Helen was dying of cancer at her home in California. In fact, she died on July 22, 1926, three weeks after the "million-dollar check," so it raises the question: was Albert Senior salivating about his upcoming inheritance?

Almarian, in her active research days, secured a copy of Aunt Helen's wills, the version before the murders and the version after. While we don't know the exact amount that Albert Senior inherited, it was only one-thirty-third of the DeLendrecie estate. Still, it was apparently enough money to propel Albert out of Oklahoma to attend to his dying aunt. We have no record of him being in Oklahoma after his pseudomagnanimous gesture of $1 million for Lula, a sharp contrast to the Doss letter where he is possibly implicated as aiming to kill.

✯✯✯

Some of the documents in the cardboard box made little sense until I had learned more about the murders. Lula was terribly frustrated by the fact that people were afraid to tell the truth. But for the few who were willing to put their lives on the line, she somehow convinced them to give sworn statements before a notary, or at least make comments, often in their own handwriting. As a result, we have information from Lula's personal quest that is not found in any other source.

Lula wrote on a scrap of paper, "George Orr says he answered telephone when call came from Hotel. He says it was a woman's voice, very much excited. Saying there has been 2 men killed at Hotel. Send the law. . . . "

A major issue for Lula was determining the exact point in time when the police were notified, in order to document their delay. For her, this was a road to discovery.

More troubling is another scribbling by Lula, as if she is taking dictation from someone:

> I was in front of Siever's when the mob began to form and Leslie Armstrong called the Gandy boy off and talked. Then Gandy come back to the boys and said Berch will pay the "Well boys let's go. Leslie Armstrong says if Berch won't pay off he will. That he will stand back of us. Let's get busy" then we went down the street. I followed behind. I stopped at window at about the time Mr. Berch fell, or as they shot at the negro, Mr. Gandy come up to the window where I was and looked in [this is H. R. Gandy, night policeman and father of Elza Gandy, and the only account that has H. R. at the scene]. Then I looked around and he was gone. I thought I would go in there I decided.

The writing ends there. The first reference to Berch, crossed out then restated, appears to have intended: "Berch will pay the price." But when restated, "if Berch won't pay off he will," it raises the question if this is two Berch men or one. Certainly, "about the time Mr. Berch fell" is referring to Albert Junior.

The "one Berch" interpretation takes some twisting and torturing of the word "pay" to make this work. But one way to reconcile the odd syntax is if we are reading about two separate Berch men, father and son. This narrative fits nicely if Berch Senior is backing up the boys in the mob, with similar motivation as Leslie Armstrong—"Leslie Armstrong says *if Berch won't pay off he will. That he will stand back of us.*"

Improbable as it sounds, once again, Albert Senior could have been a Klan sympathizer in league with the mastermind, as was implied in the "Carter affair" after the murders in the Doss letter. Was he working with Klan supporters from the get-go to rile the mob in an effort to run Robert Johnigan out of town? Perhaps he was acting as protector of his son, who seemed oblivious to the danger Johnigan presented. This proposed motivation can be adopted with some ease, remembering that Kincannon may have overstepped his directives when he killed Albert Berch in addition to Johnigan. Surprised, perhaps, that his son had been murdered along with Johnigan, Albert Senior, not particularly close to his son anyway, adapted to the new situation with malevolence. He realized that the baby, Almarian, held a ticket to Los Angeles and the key to a Fort Knox guarded by Aunt Helen DeLendrecie.

Keep in mind that this particular testimony is written in Lula's hand, as if taking dictation, but it is not one of the notarized statements she procured. In fact, there is no attribution—we don't know who is allegedly telling Lula their story.

Albert Berch, Senior, was a resident of Johnson's Hotel at the time of the murders. Oddly, there is no explanation as to why he was never put on the witness stand in the preliminary hearing or the two trials. Even more perplexing is the fact that in spite of multiple accounts of the events leading up to the murders, Dr. Albert Berch is not mentioned anywhere, in any context, except in the note above. Where was he on the night of December 17, 1923? And why does he not appear on the scene until a few days later, when he provides the needed information to the coroner for the death certificate?

A sworn affidavit in Stephens County, notarized by Mary E. Shields, reads: "I, Pete Magnusen, of lawful age and being first duly sworn on oath for himself deposes and says . . . That on the 17th Day of December 1923 as I was going up the street, Mr. Wesley Armstrong called to me and asked, 'Is that Negro still at the hotel?' I said yes. He said, 'I ought to get a crowd of boys together and run him out tonight.' Said in the presence of Marvin Armstrong. Further Affiant Sayeth Not. Signed, Pete Magnusen."

Pete was the night clerk at the hotel, who served as a witness in the trials, but nothing about the Armstrongs was ever brought out in trial testimony. In fact, adult involvement, in general, was not covered at the trials. In Lula's notes, however, it is clear in several locations that she considered the Armstrongs to be among the many rabble-rousers.

The possible connection of Albert Senior to the Armstrongs remains unsettling, but further clarity was not to be found.

I previously offered a glimpse from one of Lula's logbooks that provided her sparse description of Johnson's Hotel and its contents. Lula also has many lists in this logbook. However, I intentionally left out one list until now, avoiding an early spoiler—the list of Johnson's Hotel employees. Of the fifteen employees recorded along with their duties, three are named as porters. One of the three is Marvin Kincannon, the future killer.

I had never heard this from Lula, Almarian, or any other source, including newspaper accounts. And yet, there it was, written in Lula's hand, with no special notation, no asterisk, nothing in parentheses, nothing. He was just another employee. For six months or so, this was all I had—Marvin Kincannon's name on a list. But once I got the transcripts from the trials, it was clear that this fact did not go unnoticed in 1924. Here is the testimony I withheld earlier, with hotel employee Bessie Benight on the stand in the Gandy trial:

Q: You knew the Kincannon boy pretty well?

A: Yes sir.

Q: Do you know whether or not he and Mr. Berch had had any trouble prior to this?

A: They had a little difficulty.

Q: Tell the jury how it arose.

A: Well, it seems the Kincannon boy had a way of coming in the lobby and playing cards in Berch's absence and he came in and caught him and told the boy he didn't want to catch him in there again. Of course the Kincannon boy left and he was pretty mad on account of getting the bawling out. Several days passed and he came in again and Mr. Berch told him again to leave and he said the next time he caught him there he would give him a licking. The Kincannon boy came to our place and he was real mad and he made the remark that he had bawled him out again and one of these days his time would come.

Mr. Bond [for the State]: How is that?

A: When he bawled him out the second time, the Kincannon boy said he wasn't going to take another bawling out and some day his time would come.

Q: Some day his time would come?

A: Yes sir.

Q: That was prior to the killing?

A: Quite a while.

Q: Estimate the length of time.

A: Oh my goodness, maybe eight months or a year.

Mr. Bond: I will ask you if the trouble was that he was playing at these tables that were reserved for the traveling men to do their writing at?

A: Yes sir.

Q: That is all.

Remarkably little was made of this subtle threat by the bellboy Kincannon in subsequent testimony or by anyone thereafter. He was no longer employed by Berch when Robert Johnigan was hired as a porter, so it seems as though this earlier tiff was treated as "old history." Today, attorneys would have jumped all over the prior relationship between Berch and Kincannon. Perhaps, in modernity, we appreciate that a good, strong grudge can last a lifetime.

Without getting too conspiratorial, however, it has to be considered that *if* a mastermind were behind the murders, someone who wanted to keep their hands clean, it would make sense to enlist a stoolie with a built-in vendetta. And recall how Marvin Kincannon was not really part of the mob. Marvin appeared on the scene as a lone wolf, joining the group from across the street tangentially as they marched from Siever's drugstore to Johnson's Hotel. Perhaps Lula was correct when she said that the murder was not about Albert Berch "getting in the way," as had been proposed in most accounts. She minced no words in describing the bullet to her husband as an "assassination."

One more list stands out from Lula's cardboard box, because it is typewritten. I do not know if Lula knew how to type or not. Certainly, she did not like to, and I don't recall a typewriter in her home. I have several real-estate contracts that she drew up using legal jargon, all handwritten. That said, I have to wonder if this list was compiled by someone else, trying to assist Lula in her (dangerous) accusations of adult influence. The list includes each of the original seven defendants, and beneath each name are four to six others. In reflecting on these names, such as the Armstrongs, one is inclined to think that these are the adults who allegedly held influence over the boys who had entered the lobby of the hotel.

Because the list is so large, with some names appearing under several of the boys, it is beyond comprehension that this many adults could have been involved without someone ratting them out. Recall that Marvin Kincannon said from prison to Walton's detective that one man had engineered the event (whatever that was worth). Regardless, I have chosen not to print the entire list as most of the names appear nowhere else in any of my research. I have mentioned surnames in this book only when there is more than one source, trying to minimize the bruising of descendants. Realize, too, that both sides of this story have ancestors wallowing in dirty laundry.

Besides the Armstrongs, the other name that keeps popping up is Carter—George Carter specifically—the blind businessman and father of Oklahoma icon, aviatrix Pearl Carter Scott. George Carter's name arose during the interview with the older brother of Junetta Davis. She did not prompt her brother in any way when he blurted out the names of George Carter and H. R. Gandy during that interview. But Junetta jumped on the statement, asking her brother point blank if these were the men responsible for the murders. Her cantankerous brother then evaded the question and moved on, pointing out that the "blind bastard" had once tried to send him to jail.

On the typewritten list, we have the name of George W. Carter listed under defendant Byron Wright, while the name of George's brother Arthur T. Carter is under the name of Ellis Spence. This was too intriguing to pass up, especially when added to the "Carter affair" in the Doss letter. So I bought a copy of the biography of George's daughter, Pearl Carter Scott, where associations are forthcoming.

As this story unfolds, one has to consider the possibility that Albert Junior was an opportunist, someone who wooed Lula where others had failed. Lula freely admitted that she had many suitors (for her and/or her hotel) after the death of her first husband. What made Albert different? And given his very young age compared to Lula, do we have yet another red flag?

I can only respond with a heartening letter from the cardboard box, from Albert to Lula, a private communication now made public, and the only letter like it in all of Oxyrhynchus:

My dear Sweetheart,
You know I love you dearer than my own life and would do anything in the world for you.
Sweetheart I am lonesome for you, your hugs and kisses. I long to hold you in my arms until you cry, "I love you! I love you!"
Girl of my heart I love you,
Your sweet "daddy."

There is no date on this note written on Johnson's Hotel stationery.

Attached to the letter is a phony bank draft, just like Albert Senior's million-dollar tease a few years later. Only in this case, Albert Junior wrote on the blank check from the National Bank of Marlow, dated March 30, 1920:

> Pay to: Lulu Berch. Love and Kisses/Forever
> Signed: A. Weldon Berch

This "check" was dated two weeks after their marriage, and two years before the birth of our mother. The love letter to which the check was attached, however, was likely written a few years later, given that his signature as "daddy" was how Lula referenced Albert from the birth of our mother on. Perhaps Albert was trying out the new nickname for size, placing it in quotes. Perhaps Lula had recently informed him that she was pregnant. Perhaps, perhaps . . . regardless, we cling to this single scrap of paper as an indicator of Albert's genuine love for Lula among the many suitors who envisioned themselves as hoteliers.

Not all revelations came from Lula's cardboard box. The entire heap in El Reno's Oxyrhynchus was three stories tall, and we found wonders throughout. The concluding document in this chapter was recovered from its decades-long resting place beneath a double bed. I found it along with copies of Jack Walton's newspaper early in the excavation, and the latter's startling headlines and multiple stories about the murders drew my attention. I let the companion document, devoid of headlines, slip by without scrutiny for nearly a year. The yellowed paper was scroll-like, long and narrow, with such tiny print that one is not inspired to scan it. Little did I know that smoke was teasing its way out of the gun barrel in the smallest of fonts.

I have noted already that when Gov. Jack Walton was removed from office two months before the murders, M. E. Trapp was appointed acting governor, this becoming official on October 23, 1923. Trapp, outspoken as "anti-Klan," endorsed the movement to introduce a state question that would outlaw secret societies, obviously targeting the Ku Klux Klan.

In order for a proposed state question to make it on the ballot, there would need to be signatures on petitions from across the state. Whether or not this took place coincidentally while Albert Berch was bringing a black man to Marlow, or if this statewide movement was the *reason* Berch broke the sundown rules to make a point, I do not know. But the document found beneath the double bed in El Reno is a petition, copy #83, to bring State Question 123 to a vote, circulating in the town of Marlow *three days* prior to the murders of Albert Berch and Robert Johnigan. All twenty spaces are filled by signatures.

The first name on the list is Albert Berch. The second is Lula Berch.

The petition was never notarized or turned in to the state, kept by Lula instead. She stated that Albert Berch was solely responsible for

Initiative Petition for State Question 123, addressed to the acting governor of Oklahoma, M. E. Trapp and circulated by Albert Berch in Marlow mid-December 1923. The signature page was not yet notarized, and the document was never submitted.

driving the petition and was murdered before it could be submitted. Although State Question 123 was successfully passed by the legislature and entered as law, it did so without Initiative Petition #83. Near the bottom of the twenty signatures, one can make out "Fred Combs," Lula's brother, whose granddaughter I would meet graveside, at the Combs family plot in Elmore City, Oklahoma, quite by coincidence.

Thirteen years after our graveside encounter, I notified Barbara that my book about the killing of Albert Berch was going to be published, as I wanted to mention the story of our meeting. And since her father had likely helped babysit Almarian on the night of the murders, while her grandparents cared for Lula, I wanted to discover any additional insight about the murders she might have from growing up in the Combs family. Confirming the tightlipped tradition of our immediate ancestors, however, Barbara's reply was the same I'd heard from second cousin Roger Collins when I told him about the murders.

Who is Albert Berch? Aunt Lula was married to someone before Mr. Reynolds? And this Berch husband was murdered? No one in my family ever talked about this!

22

Loose Ends and Dead Ends

I had seen the picture as a photocopy in the Marlow town museum, prefacing the scrapbook of newspaper articles dedicated to the Berch-Johnigan murders at Johnson's Hotel. This memorabilia exists thanks to the persistent work of Debbe Ridley at the Marlow Chamber of Commerce. The photocopy was a group shot of a trial scene, with the identification, "Duncan's earliest attorneys," and a listing of the names of the lawyers seated in the foreground. There was no explanation about the occasion that prompted the photo, and I made the mistake of dismissing it as a mood-setter for the scrapbook. The names of the attorneys meant nothing to me at the time, and even when I viewed the picture on a subsequent trip, recognizing a few of the names by then, I still believed the photo to be window dressing.

However, in one of my research trips to Duncan, I stopped by the Stephens County Historical Museum on the long shot that they might have something pertaining to the Marlow murders. The museum was surprisingly large and well stocked with photographs. Around the perimeter of the interior were historical displays of a one-room schoolhouse, a doctor's office, a dentist's office, a small church, and a lawyer's office, as well as exhibits of home life for the Oklahoma pioneers. Each showcase was stocked with antiques from the time. A good part of the history was devoted to oil giant Halliburton, which was founded in Duncan.

The museum director at the time, Pee Wee Carey, greeted me as I entered, bringing the grand total of people in the museum to two. Pee Wee, who appeared to be pushing eighty (or more), was eager to give me a tour. I explained why I was there, and we began circling the displays of the old-time lawyer's office, the doctor's, and so forth. Pee Wee told me he had been the company photographer for Halliburton, as well as the *Duncan Banner* newspaper, and had contributed to a number of books.

Pee Wee had a photographic memory, of sorts. That is, he remembered nearly all the photographs in the facility, including thousands mounted in racks. As he guided me through these photo slabs, it became apparent that the museum was mostly about Duncan, with only sparse information about the other towns in Stephens County.

Then Pee Wee apologized and asked the critical question: "Tell me again what it is you're looking for?"

"The double murder in Marlow, 1923, at the Johnson Hotel."

"Oh, well, yes, I have a photograph of that trial."

I couldn't believe I heard him correctly. Or, perhaps, he misunderstood me.

We left the racks of photographs and headed back to the old-time lawyer's office, where a framed picture sat on the desk as a prop. It was the original photograph of the copy I'd seen in the Marlow scrapbook.

Pee Wee took the picture from its frame. A misleading date (December 23, 1923) was written on the back, but close enough, as the photograph was labeled as the courtroom scene from the preliminary hearing on the Berch-Johnigan murders, the actual date being January 4, 1924.

Looking at the original for the first time, I focused on, amidst the crowded courtroom, a row of young men lined up behind the attorneys. These were the defendants, preserved in time by the only known photograph to exist of the proceedings. I could not identify them since I had no reference photos, but the young men are there in a row, just as the *Duncan Banner* had described: "the defendants were brought down and seated in a row in front of the jury box." Of course, there was no jury for the preliminary hearing, so the box was full of spectators.

One defendant jumped out of the photo, even though I had never seen his face before: Marvin Kincannon. In every newspaper account, the journalists focused on one feature of Kincannon and his cocky response to it all–placing one hand over the lower portion of his face and smiling through his fingers. And there he was in the photo, exactly as the reporters had described. The eyes of the other defendants are turned toward Marvin, as if to plead, "What in the hell did you get us into?" Seated next to him is an older defendant, very likely Fred Stotts, Marvin's father-in-law. Eventually, a photograph of Marvin in middle age confirmed my identification. I cannot confirm which one of the defendants is Elza Gandy, even though a Gandy mugshot was found later on. Perhaps his face is partially obscured by one of the attorneys.

Then, my heart skipped, or stopped completely, when I recognized my grandmother sitting directly behind the defendants in the jury box. Her face is so small that I would never have identified her if it weren't for the newspaper photograph of Lula, taken the same week, wearing the same style hat.

Just as Albert's wallet, belt, tie, and collar had made his tragedy so real, the photograph of my grandmother as a young woman having to suffer through this trauma was particularly sobering. The discovery of this photo, and especially seeing Lula's face frozen in tragedy, was one of the most compelling events in my research, well worth the nearly one thousand words I've used here to describe it.

★★★

Elza Gandy, sometimes spelled *Elzy* or *Elzey,* and often called "Roy," was born November 26, 1902, thus turning twenty-one a few weeks before the murders. He died in July 1971, in Hobart, Oklahoma, around the same time that Almarian was in the first phase of her research. However, she had no files on either Gandy or Kincannon, and we have no evidence that she ever made an attempt to find them.

The Oklahoma Department of Corrections could not locate Elza's records initially, as the crime was too ancient to have been placed online. However, after a manual search for which I am grateful, the staff was able to find the Gandy file.

As noted previously, Elza's appeal was denied. His seven-year sentence began on June 8, 1926, and he was released on December 21, 1929, having served half. Almarian would have been seven years old at the time. Lula raged for the rest of her life at the light sentences handed down to both Gandy and Kincannon, as well as the dropped charges for the others in the mob.

By all accounts, Elza was never in trouble again, dying at the age of sixty-eight. Here is his obituary, headlined, "E. Roy Gandy Dies Tuesday":

E. Roy Gandy, son of the late Mr. and Mrs. H.R. Gandy, Sr. died in Hobart, Okla., July 6 at the age of 68.

Gandy was born in Bailey, Indian Territory, November 26, 1902. He attended Marlow High School but lived for a number of years in Hobart where he was a stockman. He was a member of the First United Methodist Church.

Survivors include his wife Hazel of the home, one daughter . . . seven sisters . . . two brothers . . . five grandchildren and two great-grandchildren. . . .

Burial was in Marlow Cemetery under the direction of Callaway-Smith-Cobb Funeral Home.

Preliminary hearing, Stephens County Courthouse in Duncan, Oklahoma, January 4, 1924

Seated around the table:
Jesse Barnes, back to camera—court clerk
Joe Foster, pencil in hand—role unknown
Ben Saye—defense attorney (next two faces are defendants, slightly behind their attorneys)
George Womack—defense attorney for Ellis Spence only
Joe E. Wilkinson—defense attorney
Paul Sullivan, back to table—county attorney
Ed Bond, Sr.—assisting Paul Sullivan
Jess Long—assisting Paul Sullivan

The Duncan Banner *reported that "the defendants were brought down and seated in a row in front of the jury box." Marvin Kincannon was described in the article as covering the lower part of his face with his hand, while smiling between his fingers. So Kincannon is most likely seated slightly behind two defense attorneys, and to his immediate right is his father-in-law, Fred Stotts, the oldest defendant. The remaining defendants (in unknown order) were Elza "Roy" Gandy, Byron White, Ollie Lloyd, Homer Thompson, and Ellis Spence, seated in a row behind the attorneys; however, we do not have confirmation to match names and faces. Newly widowed Lula Berch can be seen sitting in the jury box (arrow), her face partially obscured by one of the defendants.* (Courtesy of Stephens County Historical Museum)

Marvin Kincannon died the next year, 1972, and was also laid to rest in the Marlow cemetery. His obituary was quite brief:

> M. M. Kincannon, Life Long Marlow Resident Dies
> Marvin M. Kincannon, 71, died at 11:00 p.m. Friday in a Marlow hospital after a long illness. He was born July 14, 1901 in Marlow, a life long resident of the area. He was a retired oil field worker. Survivors include one brother, Dee Ellis Kincannon, Enid. Funeral services were held in the Callaway-Smith-Cobb Chapel at 2:00 p.m. Saturday, July 22, 1972, conducted by Rev. Gene Nease.

Marvin's survivors are understated here. Maybe there was only one living brother, but Marvin had four brothers and five sisters, so today's relatives are myriad, even though there are no direct descendants. Two of his sisters, mentioned previously, were highly regarded teachers in the Marlow school system.

If there had been a mastermind behind the Berch-Johnigan murders, then Marvin took that secret to the grave. It is easy to imagine how a character like Marvin would have taunted Walton's detective with a "mastermind" ideation, adding to his own importance as the "chosen" one.

As with Elza Gandy's file, the Oklahoma Department of Corrections had to perform a manual search to find the scant prison records for Marvin Kincannon. In his intake interview, when questioned as to the "cause of your downfall," Marvin replied, "Self-defense." Other questions and answers include: Married? Yes. Children? No. Number of years in school? Eight. Drink? No. Chew? No. Occupation: None. Working when arrested? No. How long before, if not working? "Never did work." Previous terms in other prisons? "Pauls Valley."

The city of Pauls Valley, Oklahoma has been home to an institution with many colorful transitions. At the time of the events of this story, it was the State Training School for Boys ("Boys" is sometimes delineated as "White Boys"), a reformatory for delinquent and incorrigible males aged ten to seventeen. The McAlester prison record does not explain how Marvin got a ticket to that facility.

Marvin must have been a model prisoner at McAlester, though. His minimum term was to have been through March 29, 1936, yet he was released in October 1935. And as often occurs, he was granted a pardon upon release, restoring citizenship rights, such as voting. This does not expunge the record, and is bestowed only if prisoners display evidence of a reasonable return to society.

Marvin's twenty-five-year sentence began on June 11, 1924, and he was discharged on October 5, 1935, having served eleven years for shooting my grandfather at point-blank range. Albeit with shaky forensics, and without trial, he likely killed Robert Johnigan as well. His time served may seem short, but it should be understood that, given the zeitgeist in 1923, it was possible Marvin could have walked away from the murders scot-free.

Apparently, Marvin was never in trouble again. Unfortunately, his prison records do not include a photograph. The Department of Corrections has no explanation for this, given that mugshots were already standard at the time.

Nevertheless, a 1958 photograph of Marvin Kincannon would appear in the *Marlow Review* March 29, 1997, which proved to be another stupefying discovery in my research. This time, he is posed with Oklahoma icon, his good friend, Pearl Carter Scott and her husband, Lewis Scott, while the accompanying article provides a short summary of the nearly forgotten Berch-Johnigan murders. Marvin was long dead at the time of this 1997 story, but Pearl was not.

At the risk of upsetting another group of descendants, I am left with explaining this mindboggling photograph of Kincannon and the Scotts, with the "down-home" caption describing Marvin's visit to their home in Colorado Springs in 1958. The fuzzy picture of the scrawny fifty-seven-year-old Marvin is taken from too great a distance to allow much detail, but the lean face matches the one partially covered by a hand in the crowded 1924 courtroom.

In the article, Pearl says, "Marvin was a small man. He was quiet and soft-spoken. I liked him." Her husband at the time had been an oilfield roughneck, so one explanation could be that their friendship emerged from the oilfields. Lewis became a pipefitter, and for a while, the Scotts lived in a mobile home, traveling from job to job. Lambert's biography of Pearl implies that she and Lewis were residing in Colorado Springs during the building of the Air Force Academy, as part of the nomadic life of a pipefitter for industry and defense. This would have been the time of Marvin's visit.

Pearl Carter was a native of Marlow, and she achieved her fame, as noted earlier, when Wiley Post landed his plane in a pasture owned by her father, George. Post was not yet a world-famous aviator. Not yet. He was still learning to fly. In fact, this was Wiley's first solo flight—the unknown Wiley Post of 1927 who had been paroled from the prison at Granite, Oklahoma, sentenced to ten years for stealing cars.

One of the many remarkable photos in Pearl's biography is the prison mugshot of young Wiley Post with two good eyes. Later, he would lose one eye in an oilfield accident, making his skills at piloting airplanes even more extraordinary. Post had been sent to prison two years before the Berch-Johnigan murders in Marlow but was likely paroled before Elza Gandy showed up in the same prison for killing Robert Johnigan.

Given George Carter's blindness, Pearl was his cane, so to speak, as he never used the iconic walking stick of the blind. Even his horse knew how to get George to the office and back, according to Pearl's biographer. Carter was able to appreciate the advantages of air travel immediately since he was involved heavily in real estate and leases, prompting him to buy a plane to be piloted by his daughter. Pearl learned to fly at age twelve and was regarded then as the youngest person in the United States to fly solo.

Soon, Pearl was barnstorming and performing in an air circus, with a commercial pilot's license by age fourteen. As a high-school cheerleader, she would fly her private plane to out-of-town games to cheer, then fly back to Marlow.

In attempting to match names, places, and times, the tough question is whether or not Pearl Carter Scott knew Marvin Kincannon for reasons other than the oilfield. She would have been eight years old at the time of the Johnson's Hotel murders, but Marvin was released from prison in 1935, when Pearl was twenty and he was thirty-five. Pearl married Lewis Scott in 1931, so if their friendship later rose from her husband's association with Marvin in the oilfields, the chronology is a nice fit.

However, George Carter was still alive at this point, his death coming in 1936. So if there had been a connection between him and Marvin, there would have been a year or so for George to greet Marvin upon his release from prison, allowing an introduction of Marvin to Pearl and the Carter family. Always devoted to the downtrodden, Pearl might have seen Marvin as a lost puppy, sparking their friendship.

In the movie *Pearl,* the story begins in 1927, the year she became an aviatrix at age twelve, and extends through the end of her flying career in 1934. She was still a teenager, though now feeling the responsibility of a young mother. George Carter assumes a major role in the movie, sympathetically played by Andrew Sensenig, a Tom Hanks look-alike, act-alike, and speak-alike as well as a George look-alike.

George Carter's only moral lapse in the movie comes when he falsifies his daughter's age on an application as being sixteen, allowing her to get a pilot's license. Mother Lucy fumes. In the movie's most endearing scene, after a father-daughter falling out (over Pearl's subsequent elopement), they reunite near their church's front pew after the Sunday service. Pearl interlocks her little finger with her blind father's pinkie, letting him know that all is well. It's a teary moment, given their unique and touching relationship, and I nearly forgot that, in fact, the minister at that service was a Klan sympathizer (at least), that George Carter was suspected of being the "mastermind," and that my grandmother was sitting on the front pew when she bolted from the real version of this church after hearing the condemning comments about her dead husband that rolled from the tongue of Rev. N. U. Stout.

Although Pearl's life took many bumps throughout the years, she was recognized as a living treasure before her death and inducted into the Oklahoma Aviation and Space Hall of Fame, as well as the Chickasaw Nation Hall of Fame. George Carter was white, but he first married a Chickasaw woman named Sarah Brown, who died before having children. No details about her death are provided in Pearl's biography. However, George Carter inherited the land that had been his wife's allotment. He then married another full-blood Native American, Lucinda "Lucy" Gibson, who was half-Chickasaw and half-Choctaw, this being Pearl's mother. George was twenty-five; Lucy was fifteen. The Carter kids were "raised white," but George was highly respectful of Native Americans and their culture.

George Carter was born in 1886 in Booneville, Arkansas, moving to Marlow in 1906 (the same year Lula and husband Walter Garvin arrived in Marlow from Texas). George built an empire for himself and his family in Marlow, mostly through real-estate holdings and "working farms with his major crop being broomcorn." Pearl claimed in the DVD extras that her father had owned more than 350 properties by the time of his death.

However, George's primary business had originally been a livery stable that he prudently switched to an automobile business when the time came. This stable, later his office, was located at 115 1/2 West Main Street in Marlow, placing it very close to Johnson's Hotel at 103 West Main, on the same side of the street. In spite of this proximity, in Lula's long list of townspeople who ate at the café, there is no mention of George Carter, his brothers, or any members of their family.

To quote from Pearl's biography, her father, even though blind, became "highly influential in community affairs in Marlow, serving for a time as justice of the peace, playing a major role in getting one of his best friends elected sheriff, helping his brother-in-law Bill Bayliss get elected mayor, and assisting in the selection of the town's law enforcement officers."

George Carter was viewed by all as a key town leader, though his activities were primarily financial and behind the scenes. His name only rarely appears in the social and community pages of the *Marlow Review*.

Pearl's biography also reveals that "over the years, both Gladys and Lelia [*sic*—Leila] Gandy worked as his secretary at different times." No other secretaries are mentioned as assisting the blind business tycoon.

Gladys and Leila Gandy were the daughters of H. R. Gandy, the night-watch policeman who may or may not have shown up at Johnson's Hotel the night of the Berch-Johnigan murders. They were the sisters of Elza Gandy, convicted of killing Robert Johnigan. Gladys Allen (1900-84) of Hobart, Oklahoma was formerly Gladys Gandy, while Leila Martin (1904-95) of Marlow was Leila Gandy. Both women are now buried—where else—in the Marlow cemetery.

As for Horace Ramsey Gandy, Sr., he lived until 1944, when his obituary appeared in the *Marlow Review* on September 14:

H. R. Gandy Dies While On Duty—
Veteran Peace Officer of City 18 Years
H. R. Gandy, resident of this community since 1903, died suddenly about 11 o'clock Tuesday night from a heart attack. Mr. Gandy was acting as a special police at the district fair grounds in the ball park. . . . An ambulance was called but Mr. Gandy had died before he reached the hospital. This was the second heart attack Mr. Gandy had suffered in recent months. Mrs. Gandy and other members of the family were at the fair grounds when Mr. Gandy died.

Horace R. Gandy was born in Meridian in Bosque County, Texas, November 22, 1871. He was 72 years old at the time of his death. He was married to Martha Elizabeth Phipps, November 15, 1895 in Texas. . . .

Mr. Gandy served as deputy sheriff in Grady county six years while he farmed at Bailey. He moved to Marlow in 1913 and became a member of the city police force where he served for 18 years. Since his retirement from the regular police force in 1930, Mr. Gandy has been relief man on the force and died while on duty as officer. . . .

Mr. Gandy joined the Methodist church at the age of 13 and affiliated with the local Methodist church when he came to Marlow in 1913. . . .

Burial was in the Marlow cemetery.

In the 1920 census, H. R. Gandy listed his occupation as "night watch." In 1923, at the time of the murders, son Elza Roy Gandy was twenty-one, older sister Gladys was twenty-two, and younger sister Leila was eighteen. Had they begun their employment yet as secretaries for George Carter? We don't know. Gladys married George A. Allen of Enid in 1924, the year after the murders. The exact date of Leila's marriage to Roy Martin is unclear, but they are listed in the 1930 census as married and living in Marlow.

Returning to George Carter, by all accounts, he and his family were God-fearing, with his wife Lucy making sure that the family was in church every Sunday and usually every Wednesday as well, with Pearl playing in the orchestra. This was the First Methodist Church where the Klanophilic reverend N. U. Stout served as pastor to both the Gandy and Carter families, and where the funeral of Albert Berch was held.

Pearl's biography points out her fear of and disgust with the Ku Klux Klan. She once sided with a young boy being tormented by classmates after Klan members whipped his father for drinking and beating his wife. (This event was filmed for the movie *Pearl*, although the Klan was never mentioned, and the scene was deleted from the final version.) The boy was ever grateful, thanking Pearl for her support in an interesting encounter thirty-eight years after the fact. Pearl also mentioned the wording of the notorious sign as "N----- do not let the sun set on you in Marlow" and specifically mentions two signs, at the north and south boundaries of the main thoroughfare into town (presumably Highway 81).

Could George Carter have compartmentalized sympathy or complicity with the Klan, such that family members were clueless? Given that Pearl was his "living cane," a young girl who "worshipped" her father, it seems unlikely. In contrast to today, however, where everyone's life is an open book, we have seen the tightlipped standard of the day, and there's more to follow. Of course, George Carter's dealings at work would have been under the watchful eyes not of his daughter but his secretaries, the Gandy sisters, trusted links to the world outside. All the while, their father, H. R. Gandy, appears to have been the "muscle" for George Carter.

As with so many characters, we have a saint-sinner combination in Carter. Testimonials abound with George Carter as a lenient landlord and loving father and grandfather, with one man telling Pearl that her father was "the greatest man I ever knew." At the same time, when George was running for the Oklahoma House of Representatives, during a "pie supper" a female heckler yelled that George "would steal a penny off a dead man's eyes," whereupon Lucy gave the woman a beating. And then we have the opinion of the brother of Junetta Davis who, in his late years, called George Carter "that blind bastard."

Lula was convinced that there was a "mastermind," but she never spoke a name. Was she afraid to? She believed that the drive-by shootings at the hotel after the murders could be traced to the man who had orchestrated the "massacre," but again, no names.

Nevertheless, the anonymous author of the Doss Hotel letter, be it one of Walton's detectives or another informant, describes the "Carter affair" after the murders that impelled me to explore all avenues. The far-reaching power of George Carter at the time, his development of downtown Marlow with the notable exception of Johnson's Hotel, the proximity of his office to that hotel yet his apparent absence from its very popular café (recalling, too, that Lula wrote that the Klan had boycotted her hotel), his name on the typewritten list of "behind-the-scenes" adults under the names of the defendants, the Gandy girls as his secretaries, his appointment of law-enforcement officials and the mayor, and the blurting out of his name along with H. R. Gandy by the brother of Junetta Davis raise an obvious question—was George Carter the mastermind?

George taught his children "it's a sin to laugh at someone who could not help what or how they were," "be friends with everyone," and "it's what's inside that counts," so we would be looking at an exaggerated example of compartmentalizing. Still, those who have studied racial hatred point out how easily this can be accomplished.

As I read Pearl's biography, I wanted to discover at least one person who appeared on Lula's customer list from her café. There were none. Was Lula an outcast long before the death of Albert Berch?

Her 1918 purchase of the hotel came a few years after George Carter's livery stable transitioned to his business office. She was a woman, owning a profitable hotel, just steps away. She married a (presumed) Catholic, a Marlow outsider. They refused to sell the hotel and hired a "crippled negro" who lived there. They circulated a petition to outlaw the KKK. It is easy to imagine how the Berches could have raised Carter's ire.

In Pearl's biography, one reads that she enjoyed taking trips in her youth to visit Uncle Jim Lominick in Iuka, Mississippi, where other Lominicks and Carters lived as well. Jim was a Confederate veteran who had served as a cavalryman under Gen. Nathan Bedford Forrest. "Lominick loved to wear his cavalryman's hat and tell stories of the action he saw in the war, mesmerizing children and adults in the process. He then taught the children to sing 'Dixie' while he accompanied them on the fiddle."

Other trips to visit George's relatives were to Alabama, Tennessee, and Georgia. Lambert, continues, "George's mother, Amanda Lominick Carter, was from a southern family with roots in Alabama and Georgia, as was his father, James Madison Carter. Several ancestors of James Carter fought for the Confederate States of America during the Civil War."

Uncle Jim's tenure under Forrest is intriguing, given Forrest's history as one of the most colorful of all Civil War characters. He had the distinction of enlisting as a private, as one of the richest men in the South, and rising to brigadier general. Along the way, he was accused of war crimes in the mass extinction of Negroes fighting for the Union as well as white Union soldiers, while at the same time a brilliant tactician. And after the Civil War, recall that Forrest was one of the organizers of the original version of the Ku Klux Klan and served as its first Grand Wizard.

Given George Carter's origins and ancestors from the Deep South, it need not be a stretch to believe that he approved of the signs at the city limits and everything else that went with them. As for his strong attraction to Native Americans and their culture, recall that many members of the "Five Civilized Tribes" were slave owners.

A less-incriminating version of George Carter's possible role as the "mastermind" would be a parallel to King Henry II of England and his alleged pronouncement: "Will no one rid me of this meddlesome priest?" This culminated, perhaps unwittingly, in the assassination of archbishop of Canterbury, Thomas Becket. Perhaps George Carter simply announced to the dark room where his blindness kept him wherever he went: "Will no one rid me of this meddlesome hotelier, his uppity wife, and his African lackey?" And from that, the muscle took over.

George Carter died in 1936 after a rather sudden illness (kidney failure), and if he had been the mastermind, there was no evidence of it on the day of his funeral. The stores in Marlow were closed. The county courthouse in Duncan was closed in honor of one of Marlow's greatest citizens. Dignitaries and celebrities flooded Marlow, including none other than ex-governor Jack Walton, the embodiment of anti-Klan sentiment. The answer regarding a "mastermind" has been lost to history.

Pearl Carter Scott died in 2005 and was buried in the Marlow cemetery, joining a host of characters from this story.

After the murders, Albert Berch, Sr., landed in Holdenville, Oklahoma, as we have seen from the anonymous Doss Hotel letter. Then he's gone: no record, nothing. At last I discovered a tiny clue, a "Dr. Albert Berch" listed in the *Los Angeles Times* as having died on December 29, 1928. This was a fine-print notice under a lengthy column of "Deaths," as one sees for unclaimed bodies or those unwilling, or unable, to pay the price of a written obituary. The only information provided was that services were by the Huppe (*sic*—Ruppe) Mortuary, at 950 West Washington Street. If this address meant Washington Boulevard, then we have a location that is two blocks south of Wilshire, between Normandy and Western, only a short hop from the home of Aunt Helen DeLendrecie. As one can already guess, Albert Senior had smelled the money and circled his way back to Aunt Helen when her 1926 death drew near, only to meet his own death two years afterward.

While I had no other information to go on at the time, my working premise was that the 1928 death notice in the *Los Angeles Times* was a brief record of my great-grandfather. Months later, I found his death certificate in Almarian's files, once again realizing that I should have exhausted all boxes of memorabilia before beginning my own research. The informant for the death certificate was the last person to see him alive, Dr. Edward E. Basye, Aunt Helen's brother. Lula had referred to him as "Uncle Ned," so this was the first time I had seen him designated as a doctor. The mystery deepened as to why the men in this family were becoming doctors, and relatively late in life.

An autopsy was performed, and the cause of death was determined to be cirrhosis of the liver, nicely confirming Lula's assessment all along. Albert Senior was turned to ashes at the Los Angeles Crematory, and we assume his remains stayed put. The Los Angeles County Crematorium Cemetery (a.k.a. "Los Angeles Crematory"), located in Boyle Heights in East Los Angeles, is used for burials of unclaimed remains and has been active dating back to 1922, at least. These unclaimed remains are stored individually for several years and then buried in a common grave by yearly groupings. Albert Senior's remains are long lost.

In trying to connect Albert Senior to Aunt Helen and her family, I had a single hint—a written note from Lula to my mother, in response to Almarian's request, noting that Aunt Helen's maiden name was Basye, and "Uncle Ned" was also a Basye. It was clear that Almarian was in hot pursuit of the relationship in the 1970s.

I made little progress in my search for our family's relationship to Helen DeLendrecie. Operating with the Basye clue from Lula, I hit a dead end at first with the online ancestry services. A trip to the "private" genealogy pages is where I found a long list of Basyes mixed in with spousal names. Not only did I discover an A. W. Berch but also a Jesse Lisbon Berch married to Mary Ann Basye. Jesse was already on my short list of possible fathers to Albert Senior. And when I came across the fact that "Mary Ann" preferred to go by "Marian," I had the possible origin of the second half of Almarian's name, clinched simultaneously with the discovery that Marian was Aunt Helen's sister.

In today's parlance, it was a double-OMG moment. "Al + Marian" was named for her father and her paternal grandmother, and this grandmother was a sister to Josephine Helen (Basye) DeLendrecie, a.k.a. Aunt Helen.

While Helen married into wealth and became the grande dame of Fargo, North Dakota, sister Marian married Jesse Berch, a Union soldier and incidental hero. Remarkably, he may have carved the destinies for both Albert Senior and Albert Junior, a theory to be explored shortly.

So, Aunt Helen was not an in-law, step-, or half-; she was Albert Senior's maternal aunt. She was Albert Weldon Berch's great-aunt, and great-great-aunt to Almarian. To my sisters and me, Aunt Helen is our three-times great-aunt. We are the direct descendants of Helen's sister. This helps to explain the intensity with which Aunt Helen devoted her resources to baby Almarian, her great-grandniece and her sister's progeny.

One of the last sensational items I uncovered, not in the cardboard box but free floating in one of the ten boxes I swept away to my home, was a letter from Aunt Helen to her grandnephew Albert and his wife, Lula. It is dated May 14, 1922, the occasion being the birth of my mother. The letter said, "I hope the beautiful little girl will grow up under the Benediction of your grandmother, the saintliest woman I ever knew and for whom I christened her Almarian."

A third OMG—Aunt Helen was the one who named the baby Almarian. It seems that everyone, including Lula, deferred to this towering figure. Helen goes on to describe declining health and problems for which "I cannot meet with my accustomed bravery, the presence of things that cause me unhappiness and anxiety."

And then, she switches topics:

> Grandaddy Berch would like to open an office outside the hotel, as he thought he would do better than to treat in the hotel and asked me to finance his fixing up of a couple of rooms. I wrote in reply that it would be impossible for me to do it before fall and maybe not even then because I had given to you the full extent of my bank account to tide you over. [She describes multiple cash outlays for other family members she supports who have cancer, etc., including Albert Senior's sister.] I cannot understand why A. W. B. Senior should object to your loaning him the necessary furniture for an office (he does not need elaborate furnishings) . . . so it seems unreasonable to press me for more funds at this time. Another thing, while I would think it quite the right method to ask cash payments for each treatment (*as a rule*), I still think that in exceptional cases, and particularly such cases as he was sure of relieving, he ought to give services (free), and feel in his soul that he was receiving full compensation even if he received no money for the same.
>
> I said *exceptional* cases. He cannot afford to work without pay, neither can he afford to turn a cold shoulder to suffering fellow creatures whom he thinks he can relieve. There is a happy medium to follow in all lines of life and a quick relief to a suffering man or woman is a better advertisement than a paid bill sometimes. If he had a large paying practice, it would not be advisable for him to use up his strength and vitality, but if he has strength to spare at all, I *think results* would be a better advertisement than paid newspaper ads.
>
> I believe love is the one enduring lesson of life, and that *service* is its highest expression. Life is what we *are* and *do*.
>
> I am merely suggesting, not laying down a rule for him to follow. I know that he was a most capable operator and would be so glad to see him maintain his position, and demonstrate his ability.
>
> With love to all, Aunt Helen.

The oddity here, of course, is that the letter is not so much about the new baby as it is about Albert Berch, Sr. From other sources, we know that the renovations to Johnson's Hotel were largely financed by Aunt Helen. The total cost approached $50,000, though we do not know how much of this was from Helen and how much through bank loans.

A second letter from Aunt Helen is written in an entirely different vein. Dated June 5, but without the year noted, it is addressed to Lula alone—no Albert—composed after the murders. In this letter, Aunt Helen is frantic, given that a letter from Lula took two months to arrive at Helen's home, and she worries that Lula's many letters are being scrutinized and censored in the outbox from Marlow or Duncan. Helen writes:

> Your letters may fall into other hands—I do not know. I am certainly most anxious to do all *right* things, by all who belong to me. I am daily expecting a letter from you, in answer to one I wrote you a few days ago. Write to me every week whether you hear from me or not. I surely will be true to every obligation that I feel belongs to me.
>
> Always the same, Aunt Helen.
>
> P.S. I have not heard from Albert's father for some time.

23

A Prequel

I chose to tell this story in lurches, pressing on the gas pedal, braking, even moving in reverse, yet attempting to present the revelations as discovered over the course of three lifetimes rather than according to the calendar. Now, I'm switching to reverse. I intend to summarize what I learned toward the end of a three-year research effort, when I scanned all available microfilm copies of the *Marlow Review* newspaper from 1912 through 1925.

Most of the newspaper accounts presented so far were taken from the Duncan and Oklahoma City newspapers. The *Marlow Review*, on the other hand, nearly opted out of reporting the killings, with only a paragraph on jury selections here, or a sentence on guilty verdicts there, but *no major headlines after the murders*.

Had I performed this 1912-25 review at the beginning of my research, it would have filled in some of the blanks sooner, but it would have been nothing like the time-traveling experience that placed the cherry on top of the soda. By the time I began this final journey through microfilm, Marlow had become a spectral hometown, and there wasn't a single issue of the newspaper wherein I wasn't familiar with many of the people making news.

I followed the careers and social lives of many of the town's residents through those fourteen years, especially those whose lives intertwined with the story at hand. I watched as T. T. Eason, owner of a hardware store in Marlow, struck it rich with one oil well after another, selling his early holdings to Sinclair and Standard and finally emerging as president of his own company. Had I read about this up front, the name would have meant nothing. However, Lula listed Eason, his wife, and son as "regulars" at the Johnson's Hotel's café. Furthermore, Eason befriended Albert Berch upon his arrival to Marlow and was among the few who attended his funeral, serving as one of only two pallbearers. Eason's wife even delivered a eulogy. At the time of the funeral, the Easons were in the

Marlow, Oklahoma circa 1910, prior to the construction of Johnson's Hotel (Courtesy of Marlow Chamber of Commerce)

process of moving their oil company and their lives to Enid, Oklahoma, where their former home is now listed in the National Register of Historic Places.

H. R. Gandy was busy during these years as the night-watch policeman and constable of Wall Township. He made headlines every time he "busted up a crap game," usually under a popular cottonwood tree north of town—"ten in one raid and eleven in another." In December 1921, he was part of the law-enforcement team that broke up a gambling party at Johnson's Hotel, issuing eight arrests. The proprietors of the hotel (my grandparents) were not among those arrested, and this incident does not surface again, even during the later murder trials.

H. R. Gandy's daughter Gladys made the local news in 1921 when she became the first enrollee in a new stenographic school, dazzling everyone with 75 words of shorthand a minute and typing 105 words per minute. She and her sister Leila went on to serve as long-term secretaries to blind businessman George Carter. Their brother, Elza Gandy, of course, left his mark on Robert Johnigan, then received a blow from Albert Berch, finally spending due time in the state penitentiary at Granite.

I've included many of these last-minute research discoveries in the story already. However, the closer I got to the 1923 murders, with endless pages of dimly lit newsprint zipping by on clattering reels, the more it seemed that my bleary eyes could paradoxically rise to the occasion and extract one-liners in microfont even without a headline. Here's more.

Albert Berch's father, Dr. Albert Berch, did not come to Marlow with his son. Albert Senior showed up, without his second wife, in January 1922, one month before the birth of my mother. The paragraph announcing his arrival from his former residence in Minneapolis states, "He will make his home at the Johnson Hotel with his son Al Berch and wife, and will open an Osteopath office in the hotel building some time this spring. Dr. Berch will probably go to Oklahoma City next month to stand an examination for a license in this state."

"Probably" is a curious word for a doctor in need of a license. In fact, "Doctor" Berch never made it to Oklahoma City for licensure, so I'll leave the quotes in place as we have no proof that he completed his training. Established by the Oklahoma Osteopathic Medicine Act in 1921, the State Board of Osteopathic Examiners has kept meticulous records of those who successfully completed the examination for licensure, as I learned in my visit there. The executive director, Deborah Bruce, took it upon herself to scrutinize the licenses from the era dating back to License #1. There was nothing on record for "Doctor" Albert Berch, a huge disappointment as I had hopes that a photograph would accompany his application, allowing the first good look at my shadowy great-grandfather.

Granted, credentialing and licensure was a relatively new concept at the time, and it may have been acceptable in the day to rely on licensure obtained in another state. Still, it is clear that he knew to check in at the new headquarters in Oklahoma City, but never managed to comply.

Dr. Berch "for the present will maintain offices in the Johnson Hotel where he will be pleased to meet all those interested in Osteopathy and its results," notes the February 9 edition of the *Marlow Review*. "Special attention given to treatment of the eyes. Dr. Berch was one of the first Osteopaths to practice in Wisconsin and for many years maintained an office in Milwaukee."

The father-son dynamics here are unknown, but I suspect that tension reigned. On May 18, four months after his arrival in Marlow, Dr. Berch announced he was relocating his office to the second story of the First National Bank Building, where he practiced until the death of his son nineteen months later. He took out a standing ad in the "Business and Professional Directory" of the *Marlow Review*. This ad ran in every edition until the time of the murders, with only slight variations, sometimes noting "free examinations" and sometimes "glasses removed," as if his treatments would obviate the need for corrective lenses.

His reception by the established doctors in town is unknown, but an educated guess can be made that he was shunned. Traditional MDs had fought the legalization of osteopathy with virulence, and the fight wasn't really over. Not that "traditional medicine" held much sophistication of its own. When the Marlow hospital was opened, obviating the need for patients to travel to Duncan, the "traditional" doctors held a gala affair where they removed tonsils for free. The newspaper proudly announced that twenty-two such operations had been performed, and since the demand was high, they would continue for a few more days, with the Duncan physicians joining in the fun.

Just prior to Christmas in 1922, Dr. Berch violated the advertising taboo. It was okay to have a listing in the newspaper's directory, but a large display ad wishing everyone a Merry Christmas from Dr. Albert Berch was met with an apology from the newspaper the next week, admitting they had forgotten to mention that Dr. Berch was actually an osteopath. There's a story there, and I doubt that it's one of acceptance into the traditional medical community.

Dr. Berch's odd behavior shortly after the murders, first with his comments to the press about his son having been fairly warned, then with his apparent efforts to wrestle away the hotel and perhaps the meal-ticket baby, has already been addressed. But as for the *Marlow Review*, there was no more Dr. Berch after the murders.

This March 9, 1922, headline, shortly after Almarian's birth and nearly two years before the Berch-Johnigan murders, caught my attention: "Officer Gandy At Liberty on Bond."

H. R. Gandy, city night watch and constable of Wall Township, that stickler for peace and quiet and law and order, was charged in the shooting death of Corbett Watson. Gandy claimed to have shot the man in self-defense during an altercation at the City Café (not the Johnson's Hotel café) in Marlow, "during which he [Gandy] was remonstrating with Watson about his demeanor in that eating place."

The team of Saye and Wilkerson (who would later defend the killers in the Berch-Johnigan trials) were able to get the murder charge reduced to manslaughter. Friends of the deceased paid for Edward Bond and Eugene Morris to help County Attorney Paul Sullivan prosecute Gandy (the same team that would prosecute the killers in the Berch-Johnigan trials), a remarkable prelude that hints at a town divided.

As testimony revealed, Gandy was peacefully eating his meal when Watson entered the front door of the café "intoxicated and hollering" and headed straight for him. Gandy stood and admonished the man, telling him to be quiet and that there was "no use in acting that way." They tussled, and upon freeing themselves, Gandy pulled out a gun and began shooting, first into the air, then other random shots, then perhaps three or so into Watson.

The deceased left a widow and small son, while Gandy "was accompanied to the trial by numerous friends and members of his family." The trial took place the next month, and witnesses for the state, against Gandy, included the widow and one Clyde Stanton. A key part of their testimony was the simple recognition that the victim was unarmed.

Stanton was one of Marlow's leading citizens of the era, owner of the Ford, Fordson tractors, and Lincoln dealerships, with his showroom near Johnson's Hotel, and a frequent patron of its café. He and his wife were active in all civic and cultural events in Marlow, their names appearing in virtually every issue of the *Marlow Review*. One other item of interest—Mr. and Mrs. Stanton were among the handful of Marlow citizens who sent flowers to the funeral of Albert Berch. It begs the question once again. When Albert Berch received the okay to hire Robert Johnigan from the town leaders, were there two different sets of leadership, a fatal error for Berch?

The speedy trial was followed by swift justice—it took the jury fifteen minutes to render a "not guilty" verdict. Four months later, H. R. Gandy was reelected constable of Wall Township, one of nine townships in Stephens County, by a vote of 370 to 313 over J. R. Mason.

During the same time as the H. R. Gandy trial, articles began to surface in the *Marlow Review* regarding the Ku Klux Klan. The major newspapers of the day were locked in debate, with pros and cons of the KKK being tossed about almost daily in editorials. But in Marlow, the stories were personal and intense. On March 30, 1922, this article appeared on the front page:

Ku Klux Klan Gives Warning

"The following notice was found on the editor's desk this morning: Marlow, Okla., March 28, 1922. Editor Marlow Review. Dear Sir:—Please print the following on the front page of the Marlow Review this week.

BE WARNED

The citizenship of Marlow has been outraged recently by members of low skulks peeping into homes at night. Thieves, gamblers, liars and pilferers of all kinds are honorable compared to a whelp who will stoop to such as this. There are 100 members of the Ku Klux Klan in Marlow composed of the very best citizens in all walks of life who know you and will get you. BE WARNED.

Signed: Exalted Cyclops, Marlow Klan No. 95 Realm of Okla. (Seal.)

In general, Klaverns based in and around a city tended to operate independently, focusing on issues in their particular locale. For the KKK in Marlow, all recorded events and statements that I unearthed dealt with their demands for Victorian standards, while their carrot for obedience was actually a club. Until Robert Johnigan came to town, the Marlow Klan had never needed to address the race proviso.

Although there are few footprints in the *Marlow Review*, it is clear that many residents intensely disliked the Klan. And if you wanted to hurl an insulting epithet, you could accuse someone of being a Klan member. Citizens, to protect their reputation or livelihood, would sometimes place articles in the paper denying their membership in the Klan, as well as including the name of a notary who had cosigned a sworn statement to this effect.

Even the owner and editor of the *Marlow Review* was not immune. When a disgruntled employee claimed he was fired for refusing to join the Klan at Jim Nance's insistence, the editor published this scathing reply on the front page:

EDITOR NOT A KLANSMAN

It has never been the policy of the editor of this newspaper to answer his critics but in this particular instance I am going to deviate from the rule long enough to brand one L. P. Seitz as just a slanderous liar. This man is said to be making the statement for the purpose of gaining sympathy that I discharged him from my employ because he did not belong to the Ku Klux Klan. The fact is, that I discharged this man for petty thievery.

For the information of all concerned, I hereby unequivocally deny that I am a Klansman.

Editor Jim Nance owned and operated several newspapers before launching a career in the Oklahoma legislature as an elected representative from Stephens County in 1920, eventually becoming Speaker of the House of Representatives and also President Pro Tempore of the Senate. Nance was the patriarch of a well-known Oklahoma family.

And as noted earlier, he was a frequent diner at the Johnson's Hotel café and a friend to Lula.

A related coincidence would follow over forty years later, when Jim Nance's granddaughter (Nance Langdon) would be assigned as roommate to Lula Berch's granddaughter (Susan Hollingsworth, my sister) during 1965 Rush Week at the University of Oklahoma. This tidbit was revealed only when my sister read the first draft of this manuscript. In 1994, Nance Langdon Diamond would run as the Democratic candidate for lieutenant governor of Oklahoma, losing to Mary Fallin, who would later become the state's first female governor.

Consider the deep chasm that separated opinions about the KKK. At the same time that some considered accusations of Klan membership to be insults to integrity, others, even when not card-carriers or hood-wearers, were conferring collective sainthood upon the Klan. According to the August 31, 1922, edition of the Marlow newspaper, the Klan visited two revivals, presenting ten dollars to the evangelist one at Oak Lawn and twenty-five dollars to a Presbyterian revival later on, both with assurances of total Klan support for the churchmen. The ministers could not contain themselves in their fawning accolades for the wonderful work of the Klan. As for Klan whippings and their use of tar and feathers to make a point, throughout all my readings of the *Marlow Review*, I could not find a single incident targeting a black man or his family—understanding that there were no such residents in Marlow.

Backing up to December 1921, it is time to revisit Rev. N. U. Stout of the Methodist church, who also served as secretary of the Ministerial Alliance. It was Reverend Stout who accepted the donation from the Marlow Klan designated for the "poor children" of the city, described earlier. The money was delivered first to the newspaper's editor, Jim Nance, with instructions on how to pay it forward to the Ministerial Alliance.

In the next edition of the *Marlow Review*, a large display ad jumps off the page: "1922 and Ku Klux Klan—Reverend N. U. Stout will preach Next Sunday on the subject 'Nineteen Twenty-two and the Ku Klux Klan.' Sunday Morning: 'Things They Believe,' Sunday Night: 'Things they propose to do and Things they propose to un-do.'"

While the pronoun "they" might be regarded as a cushion between

Church and Klan, here is the story that followed one week later describing Reverend Stout's New Year's Eve sermon: "The Methodist Church was crowded almost to its seating capacity at both services Sunday when the pastor, Reverend N. U. Stout delivered sermons on the Ku Klux Klan. The morning sermon was given over to a detailed and enlightened explanation or description of the organization which, according to Brother Stout, 'if thoroughly observed in all their significance by the members renders the organization worthy of the utmost respect and consideration.' The subject at the evening service was 'what they propose to do and to undo.'"

Since there are no membership records for the Klan, the question will never be settled as to who actually kept a white robe and hood in the closet at home. But it's not critical to our story. Extremist groups always have silent sympathizers, and Reverend Stout was not silent about the Klan. He was, at a minimum, a vocal sympathizer. Thus, Lula's record of Albert's funeral service being under the direction of "N. U. Stout, Ku Klux Klan" does not seem so farfetched.

One question that persists is Lula's choice to have the funeral at the Methodist church where Reverend Stout was so public in his beliefs. However, Lula and her brother, Fred, were members of that church. She was quite addled after the murders, but she stated in her memoirs that both she and Fred made the arrangements. That Lula was okay with the Methodist church as the funeral site, knowing Stout's position, speaks to the fact that being a member or sympathizer of the Klan was so common as to be acceptable. Surely, Klan rhetoric would not emerge during a funeral service. Or so she thought.

On July 26, 1923, headlines announce "Plans of New Church Shown," as N. U. Stout will lead the campaign for a new Methodist church. On the list of committee members planning the church is Judge M. W. Pugh, who, months later, will recuse himself in the murder trial of Marvin Kincannon for killing Albert Berch. Judge Pugh will also rule against Lula and Cruce Oil in a decision some years away, an act that "blindsided" Lula. In her writings about the case, she refers to the judge as "Klan," but remember that this was a moniker she applied liberally. On the other hand, Judge Pugh was also on the bench in the suit brought forth by Lizzie Johnigan against Lincoln Health and Life for her $1,000, unpaid. In this instance, the judgment was in Lizzie's favor, against the insurance company, not consistent with a Klan bias.

One week after the coverage of the Methodist church campaign, a short article notes that Albert and Lula Berch have returned from an oil-drilling sabbatical in Stephens County and an extended vacation in Los Angeles, having leased out the hotel in their absence. Berch "has a crew of carpenters busy this week, remodeling the dining room of the hotel," according to the piece. "A hardwood floor is also being laid which will enable the hotel to offer this spacious room for dancing parties." At this point, Albert has about four months to live.

In the September 13, 1923, issue of the *Marlow Review*, a headline notes that the "Comanche Parade Is Called Off," that town being located south of Duncan. The subhead explains: "Grand Dragon of Ku Klux Klan Cancels Parades and Masked Gatherings Following Order of Governor Walton."

And then I find a researcher's trifecta—on a single front page, September 20, 1923, three stories of interest: 1) "Martial Law Reigns Over Entire State," 2) "The Proposed Home of the First Methodist Church" (including the first artistic rendering), and 3) "New Grocery Store to Open." Okay, so number three doesn't seem spectacular, but it explains where Fred Combs has been the past three years after selling out his part of Combs & Son, with his father returning to Elmore City. Fred had been out of the grocery business, working in a department store. Now, he's back in, and the food from his store near Johnson's Hotel will come in handy the night of the murders.

As for martial law, it seems to have been a ho-hum deal in rural Marlow, where an accompanying article asks this question: "What Does Living Under Martial Law Mean for You?" At this time, of course, Governor Walton was embroiled in the fight of his life.

In the October 4, 1923, issue of the *Marlow Review*, a new name appears along with Jim Nance in the masthead—Curtis M. Anthony—and the two are called "Editors and Owners." I introduce this now to make note of the fact that Lula eventually slings some mud at her friend Jim Nance, but I believe she was in such a state that she didn't realize the paper changed hands in the days immediately following the murders.

On October 18, the cornerstone for the new Methodist church was laid, along with pomp and circumstance under the direction of N. U. Stout. The new building was under way.

With Albert and Lula Berch back at the helm of Johnson's Hotel, no further mention is made of the couple until the day of the murders. Not surprisingly, there is not a word about the hiring of Robert Johnigan. In the Christmas edition of the town newspaper, December 13, four days before the murders, it is business as usual in Marlow. An article titled "Birthday Party" states: "Mrs. George Carter gave a delightful child's party Friday afternoon in celebration of the birthday anniversary (8th) of her daughter Eula Pearl. A number of games were played and refreshments served the guests who presented the honoree with many dainty remembrances of the occasion."

Reading this December 13 issue of the *Marlow Review*, I couldn't help but react as one does when watching a favorite movie for the umpteenth time, when immediately prior to the death of a favorite character, something tugs inside, saying, "Maybe it will be different this time." For me, I wanted to shout at the words on microfilm, "Wake up, folks! Stop this thing before it happens."

In this same edition, remarkably, it is reported that Aldrich Blake came to town to address the citizens of Marlow. He was Governor Walton's right-hand man who engineered his career and, as we have seen from one viewpoint, steered Walton to his political death by convincing him to adopt the anti-Klan agenda. At the time of his visit to Marlow, Blake had already been fired, and Walton had already been ousted.

The article reads, "Aldrich Blake of Oklahoma City, delivered an address on 'The Philosophy of Government' at the City Hall Tuesday night. . . . Mr. Blake described some of the recent Klan incidents and the various activities of the organization. However, the Klan question was a minor point in his talk. A large number of local people were present to hear Mr. Blake's address in spite of the inclement weather."

This same issue reports, "Dr. and Mrs. J. A. Mullins are traveling with daughter." Whether for his medical practice, community activities, selling prized hogs, or traveling with his wife and daughter, Dr. Mullins was *always* in the paper. It is noteworthy in this story for several reasons. First, shortly after Berch and Johnigan were shot, the call went out initially for Dr. Mullins, who was, as one might expect, out of town with his wife—in this case, to pick up their daughter from Christian College in Columbia, Missouri for the holidays at home. Secondly, Dr. Mullins signed the death certificate on Albert Berch, wherein Albert Senior was the source (oddly scratching out the false age of his son and writing the correct age and birthdate). And lastly, the "Mullins mystery" holds a place in the Marlow historic annals nearly equal to the story at hand.

In 1930, Dr. Mullins, or at least a bundle of bones, was found in his burning car after he set out to make a house call. Primitive forensics at the time questioned the cremated remains as an oddity, given the nature of the fire, but Mullins was counted as officially dead. Reportedly,

Dr. Mullins' nurse left town a few days after his "death," and an alleged sighting of the two of them together in California led to wild speculation at the time, as well as a permanent niche in the Marlow town museum. The mystery remains unsolved.

Also in this Christmas edition is a listing of thirty-eight new residences built in Marlow; "nearly all are modern and occupied by owners." One of the most expensive homes was built by George Carter ($8,000), while other homes of interest were built by H. R. Gandy ($3,000) and Judge Pugh ($3,000).

"Wake up, folks! Stop this thing before it happens," I wanted to say again as I cranked the microfilm reels to the next issue of the *Marlow Review*. But it was to no avail. A bold headline proclaimed: "Hotel Proprietor and Negro Porter Shot to Death." After that, the headlines in the *Marlow Review* end for Albert Berch and Robert Johnigan. Only small print would follow, with no more than a few minor stories over the ensuing months, while the *Duncan Banner* is loaded with information.

Effective January 1, 1924, three days prior to the preliminary hearing on the Berch-Johnigan murders, Jim Nance sold his one-half interest in the *Marlow Review* to Dr. R. L. Montgomery, a prominent citizen of Marlow whose name had graced its pages as often as Dr. Mullins'. Montgomery had been one of the most active oilmen in town, partnering at the right place and right time, such that his reason for being in the news was usually oil, not medicine.

R. L. "Dolph" Montgomery, MD, is a living memory today, with prominent Marlow citizen D. B. Green having taken his role in a historic reenactment where descendants and actors stand by the tombstones of their characters in the Marlow cemetery, delivering oral histories. In my interview with Green, I learned that "Dolph" became an instant legend in Marlow while simply passing through town, a veritable "Doc Hollywood" when he was called from his hotel room and casually performed a miracle.

A horse at the livery stable had kicked a young girl in the head, crushing her skull. All the practicing doctors in Marlow pronounced the situation as hopeless, with death imminent. Dr. Montgomery, roused from his repose to deliver an additional opinion, calmly walked to the town blacksmith, requested that a metal plate be fashioned to the proper shape and dimensions, then applied it to the crater in the girl's head. Since this is an oral history, we do not know for sure whether the frontier surgeon slipped the plate under the scalp or whether it was worn as an external prosthesis. Nevertheless, the girl recovered and lived to an old age. Dolph never left the city, where he was forever revered. In fact, his medical skills were in such demand that he had to summon his brother, Dr. David Montgomery, to relocate to Marlow in order to handle the load.

With R. L. Montgomery serving as a prominent figure and later a chief Marlow historian, it is worth mentioning that the doctor was an active member of N. U. Stout's Methodist church and was on the campaign committee for the new church, along with Judge Pugh. On the day of the cornerstone ceremony, Montgomery delivered the opening address, "The City and the Churches."

If the name of Dr. Montgomery sounds familiar, we first met him when he was one of the attending doctors who pronounced Guy Garvin dead, Lula's fifteen-year-old son who collapsed on the athletic field. Then, we met Montgomery again as a witness for the defense in the murder trial of Marvin Kincannon, testifying that Marvin's mental status was "subnormal." When cross-examination pointed out that Marvin had passed a rigorous mental and physical exam for the army, Montgomery modified his testimony, noting that the subnormal condition was "intermittent."

And one other point—in the weeks following the murders, recall that the newly formed American Civil Liberties Union offered their support in tracing possible Klan activities that could be related to the killings. However, the ACLU wrote Lula a second time, backing off after receiving a letter from the mayor of Marlow assuring them that the situation was under control. The mayor at the time was, in fact, Dr. R. L. "Dolph" Montgomery.

Although it is indirect evidence, perhaps even a stretch, Lula wrote that the "Klan boycotted the hotel and café from the beginning." In the long list of customers that Lula recorded as regulars at the Johnson's café, none of this cadre from N. U. Stout's Methodist church appears.

Other prominent citizens ate there regularly, and it raises the question again, only now with names: did Albert Berch get permission to hire Robert Johnigan from the wrong set of town leaders? Was it Clyde Stanton and T. T. Eason, prominent men who attended Albert's funeral, who said it would be okay? If so, perhaps they were naïve themselves as to the reach of secretive Klan sympathizers among their friends. After all, the downtown building that held Stanton's Ford dealership was constructed by George Carter. If Stanton and Eason were aware of the Klannish influence that had taken hold of many of their contemporaries, they likely underestimated its power.

Lula listed Jim Nance, "newspaperman," as a regular customer at the café. In addition to selling his remaining interest in the *Marlow Review*, Nance resigned his position in the Oklahoma legislature and moved to Lubbock, Texas to take on a newspaper venture there. He would be back, though, and with the honorary title of a "Legislator's Legislator" and induction to the Oklahoma Hall of Fame. He lived a long life, full of tribute, dying in 1984, sixty years after the murders in Marlow.

Subsequent to the Johnson's Hotel killings, the *Marlow Review* did not hold back when announcing a change in management at the café. In fact, greater exposure is given to the Benights leaving the café at Johnson's Hotel than any of the legal proceedings against Marvin Kincannon or the Gang of Seven. After the murders and her role as an eyewitness, Mrs. Pete Benight, the first to comfort the crying toddler at the scene, left Marlow with her husband and headed for Ft. Worth.

In a previous chapter, I covered the anti-Klan newspaper launched by ex-governor Jack Walton, with its overt attacks on the Klan after the murders and its depiction of Marlow as a Klan haven. On January 10, 1924, the *Marlow Review* fought back, with a lengthy front-page article headlined, "Walton's Paper Hits Us." This excerpt covers the gist: "When a nondescript sheet like ex-governor Jack Walton's paper goes so far as to cast reflections on the good names and reputations of some of the best people in Marlow, and also says in effect that our city officials are making no effort to enforce the law, it is high time that such a paper be answered with the truth. The good people of Marlow regret that one of their substantial business men was murdered [no mention of Robert Johnigan], in his place of business, and they are standing squarely behind the courts to see that proper punishment is inflicted upon the perpetrators of the crime." The article is written by Curtis M. Anthony, editor, while the new co-owner of the newspaper by then was Dr. R. L. "Dolph" Montgomery.

In Walton's paper, Lula indicts Jim Nance and the *Marlow Review* for his coverage of the murders (or lack thereof), but she was obviously unaware that ownership had changed hands shortly after the murders. Indeed, when Nance returned to Oklahoma after his venture in Lubbock, he was labeled as a "Walton Apologist" for his early support of Mayor Walton in the gubernatorial election, and his continued support for

Walton that lasted longer than most. This was in sharp contrast to the *Daily Oklahoman* and associated Gaylord newspapers of the day, which hounded Walton from the get-go. If anything, Nance would have been in Lula's underdog corner.

Finally, we come full circle. On April 19, 1924, Mr. and Mrs. W. A. Johnson of Oklahoma City returned to Marlow to take over Johnson's Hotel. The *Marlow Review* made no mention of Albert Berch, Lula Berch, "baby," or the murders. The article states, "Both he [W. A.] and Mrs. Johnson are well known in the city and we are glad to have them with us again." Although the tiny-font headline says "Johnson Buys Hotel," Lula maintained that Johnson only leased the contents, with the building lease going to J. B. Klein of Oklahoma City. It's a pretty safe bet that Lula was correct on this account, as I have her lease documents in my files.

This article about the hotel in the *Marlow Review*, under new management, is notable for two reasons. First, most real-estate transactions prompted bold type and a large font. Even headlines such as, "Large Turnips on Exhibition," capture top billing, as with any small-town newspaper. Yet, this business-transaction blurb is barely noticeable. Secondly, these commercial exchanges were quite common, with both buyers and sellers given credit for their role, as well as for their contribution to the town of Marlow. With a tiny blurb that did not mention Lula Berch as the seller, it is clear that by the time she left Marlow for Duncan, she was persona non grata, in spite of the fact that she had lived there for eighteen years, the first twelve married to a prominent Garvin, the last six in a highly visible role as a hotelier. Albert and Lula often appeared in the paper prior to the murders, but now the newspaper wanted nothing to do with the surviving members of the Berch family.

In the end, the prequel answered many questions, yet still revealed next to nothing about Albert Weldon Berch, the stranger who came to town. Where did he come from? When did he arrive in Marlow? What was he doing during the missing years? A half-century later, Almarian would exhaust all available sources in her search for her father's story. As I scrolled through the microfilm of the *Marlow Review* during the years of the Great War, I read the many lists of hometown men who were called to service or rejected, served, injured, or coming home, and there was no Albert Berch to be found. I had the uncanny feeling that Almarian had been there before me, staring blankly at miles of microfilm that led nowhere.

24

The Zinger

A 1990 letter from Catholic Family Service to Almarian states, "The records for the orphanage were destroyed by fire in January 1907." She had been actively looking for her father's missing years for two decades. Yet, remove the letters of disappointment in her "Albert Berch" file, and it is empty.

When I accepted the torch, I encountered the same. Even with online searching, it was a dead end. Compounding the problem were the multiple options for the spelling of Berch, not to mention that Albert was such a common name at the time.

Yet, one nagging question persisted—where was Albert Berch during the Great War, later known as World War I? When Congress passed the Selective Service Act on May 18, 1917, authorizing the draft, the registration process was all inclusive. Only a minority were drafted, but few escaped registration, including visitors to the U.S. and the disabled.

Indeed, the WWI draft registration process proved to be the ticket to my search. One year after Almarian's death, when online genealogy sites began offering WWI registration cards, I unraveled the mystery of the missing years.

During the course of my research, I had clicked on so many links for Albert Berch, Al Berch, A. W. Berch, Albert Weldon Berch, Birch, Burch, and Birtch, Burtch that I held little hope for finding anything new. But when one more click opened the magic door to the detailed image of a WWI draft card, it was clear I had found the link to my grandfather's past. How was I sure it was him? Oddly enough, I had settled on what I believed to be his true birth date, and now there it was, written in his own hand, an exact match—October 5, 1893. Middle name? Weldon. Birthplace? Los Angeles. It was him.

An exhilarating breeze seemed to circulate through the keys of my computer. Although the information on the card was limited, I now had key facts to open the remaining doors. His address? Lansing, Kansas. No wonder we couldn't find out anything about his years prior to Marlow. Nothing in the Berch family history ever drew attention to Kansas, so Almarian had not scoured the public records there as she had in other states. On the card, he described himself as a single Caucasian male of medium height and medium build, with light blue eyes and dark brown hair. He was employed by the state of Kansas as a minet, working for the Kansas State Penitentiary.

But what's a "minet"? Knowing that Albert had been a barber before moving to Marlow, I had a theory. A "minet" must be a term used in those days for a prison barber. Albert's handwriting was surprisingly good, bordering on ornamental. But there was a slight hesitation mark on the *t* of minet, sending me to the dictionary as well as online, searching all the possibilities.

After several hours, I gave up. I could find nothing that clarified the word "minet." Frustrated, I decided to check out the history of the Kansas penal system, to see if I could perhaps stumble on an explanation for the term.

Quoting from the online history: "The need to keep inmates occupied caused the state to sink a coal shaft in 1881. The coal supplied not only the prison, but all other state institutions. . . . The prison mine employed several hundred convicts and the mine produced as much as 10,000 bushels of coal a day. . . . "

The word wasn't "minet"—it was "miner." Albert Berch wasn't "employed by" the state of Kansas; *he was a prisoner!*

The discovery sucked the air from my lungs. Our romanticized notion of Albert Weldon Berch evaporated. No, worse than that: the idealized image of the progressive hero from Los Angeles reversed itself 180 degrees, and I was staring at a blank wall where the portrait of my noble grandfather once hung. Furthermore, I was well into writing this book, so where could my story go now? Then, I remembered a promise I made at the beginning, long before I had a clue what I would uncover about the characters I was researching:

"Whether or not my grandfather died as part of an honorable act is a central issue in the differing versions of the murder. I do not seek blue blood. Hasn't history already taught us that blue blood tends to run downhill? If my research indicates an ancestor to be a scalawag, then so be it."

So, I made the decision to continue as I had all along—researching every detail to the fullest. I would allow the story to take the lead now, and I would simply follow.

I found an online photograph from the time, with Kansas prisoners sitting in a semicircle having their lunch together. Black men sat with whites, yet all the men shared a bond deep inside the earth, with faces homogenized by soot.

My sisters, also trying to catch their breath after this revelation, suggested that Albert Berch met Robert Johnigan while in prison, thus explaining the extraordinary employment of a black man in all-white Marlow. That is a nice fit for a movie, perhaps, but does not appear to be the case. Defense attorneys scrutinized Johnigan's history, and in the end, he came out with a perfectly clean record. That said, so did Albert Berch.

Using convicts in the mines was a controversial experiment, even though the penal authorities promised that the coal would not be sold on the open market. The working conditions were dangerous, with the average vein only twenty-two to twenty-four inches wide. Riots were common. One such uprising occurred in 1927, with 347 convicts barricading themselves in the mine at the 729-foot level, taking eleven hostages, and threatening to destroy the mine. Fortunately, their demands were met.

In the *Images of America* volume devoted to the Lansing Correctional Facility (Laura Phillippi, Arcadia, 2014), a caption reveals that in 1927, a prisoner was required to mine ten tons of coal each day, the quota "to earn his keep." On the bright side, for every ton of coal mined beyond the basic ten, the prisoner earned $1.50 (rendering new appreciation for the old song "Sixteen Tons").

I didn't submit completely at first to the notion that my grandfather had been a Kansas convict. Wouldn't the men in these coal dungeons need supervisors? Wouldn't there be experienced miners directing the operations? Why else would he list himself as a "miner," rather than a prisoner? This would explain why he was "employed by" the state of Kansas, as the draft registration indicated.

After contacting the Kansas Department of Corrections, I learned that prison records from the early 1900s had been transferred to the Kansas Historical Society. Emails led to phone calls, and the search began. Nothing could be found for Albert Weldon Berch, and I don't mind admitting my relief. My theory of Albert as a mining supervisor was holding its own. But when the staff member told me, "We have nothing," I fought the temptation to say, "Thank you very much," and hang up.

"Would you please check under *B-i-r-c-h?*" I asked. "Sometimes the last name is spelled differently."

Moments passed on the phone while I waited.

"No, nothing under Birch, either."

Yes, that's it, I thought with relief. Albert was a supervisor, a mining expert, though a far cry from a barber. Or maybe he was simply a prison guard assigned to the mines. Once again, I was ready to hang up the phone, but . . .

"Try one more spelling, please. On occasion, I've seen it spelled as *B-u-r-c-h.*"

Moments passed.

"Oh, yes, here it is. Under Burch, but it's been misfiled. It's correct on the paperwork; someone simply filed it wrong. Oh, my, he was a handsome devil. We don't have many pictures of the criminals that look like that."

I requested a copy of the complete prison records of Albert Weldon Berch. That's Berch, with an *e.*

25

Out of Kansas

While it is tempting to claim that Almarian's motive for fictionalizing her father's story in *One-Half Dream* was to conceal the fact that he had been a convict, I don't believe that's the case. I don't think she knew. Her efforts, exhaustive in every detail (pre-Internet), to uncover his "missing years" are reflected in the footprints of her files. I believe she fictionalized the story first because she wanted to be a novelist and secondly because she was fully aware that some of the principal culprits were still alive in the 1970s. Regardless, I am glad that I kept my hands off this story until she had passed.

The tougher question is this: did Lula know? Recall that this was an era when a man could walk across the border of one state into another and start life anew. Out of Kansas came Albert Weldon Berch, at a time when there was no standardized form of personal identification—no driver's licenses in Oklahoma yet, no Social Security, no nothing. Birth certificates were standard, but there was no requirement to possess or display one's proof of birth. Even marriage licenses allowed people to put down anything they wanted, as no corroborating identification was required. We have in our family archives all three marriage licenses for Lula, and she didn't put down her true age on any of them, railing in her diary that if we didn't know our own ages, we'd live thirty years longer.

And why should Albert Berch tell *anyone* of his past?

Albert Weldon Berch lost his mother when he was not yet two years old. Given what we have learned about Albert Senior, anything is possible. Senior seems to have dumped his son into the lap of Aunt Helen at this point, and as mentioned earlier, Albert Junior was raised partly in the DeLendrecie home in Los Angeles and partly in the orphanage at Fargo.

Albert Junior's attachment to Aunt Helen as a mother (and father) figure became clear to me after I obtained the copy of my grandfather's prison records. He struck through the word "father" and replaced it with Aunt Helen's name and address, even though his father was living at the time.

"Daddy & Almarian," with Albert Berch's face mostly hidden in this family photo taken a short while before the murders

Albert Berch, Sr., remarried, and eleven-year-old Albert Junior lived with him and his stepmother. Prison records tell us more than census records, however, and all was not well in the Berch household. Albert Junior managed to get through the eighth grade, but he ran away from home at age twelve and was "on the road" thereafter until he landed in a Kansas reformatory. He became a teenage bum, cutting off contact with his father. And this would be his life, the "missing years," until he showed up in Marlow with wounds so fresh it is unimaginable that he could transform himself into a "leading citizen."

Albert Weldon Berch was sentenced initially to the Kansas State Industrial Reformatory on March 13, 1916, for second-degree burglary and larceny. For stealing twenty dollars from a pool hall, he received the maximum sentence of fifteen years. He was twenty-two years old, and the reformatory was reserved for men under the age of twenty-five. Before considering the punishment too harsh, any comparison to Jean Valjean should be withheld, as one comes up empty-handed in trying to put a noble spin on the story. According to a Consumer Price Index calculator, twenty dollars in 1916 would be over four hundred dollars today. Here is the summary from the admission records to the reformatory:

> Nothing is known here of Albert Berch except such information as he has furnished himself. He had been in this vicinity since last December only. During his stay here he worked at some common labor, but spent most of his time loafing at pool halls. By his own statements it would appear that he was somewhat of a gambler and frequenter of resorts of ill fame. His father is said to live in St. Paul, Minn., but this boy claims he has heard nothing from him for seven or eight years.
>
> He and another young fellow were convicted of burglary and larceny. The facts of the crime are: Berch entered a window of a pool hall in the night-time (while his companion kept watch) and stole from a cash register something like $18 or $20. The two then boarded a freight train and rode to Dodge City. From there they made their way to Kingsley and finally to Hutchinson, where they were arrested and returned here. They pleaded guilty to the charge.

Albert had a history of rabblerousing across the country, with multiple short-term jail times for drunkenness, vagrancy, and disturbing the peace. His most significant crime involved displaying a deadly weapon in a public place, landing him in jail for forty-nine days in San Diego at the age of twenty.

Given his March 1916 sentencing, more than a year prior to the U.S. entry into WWI, it is unlikely Albert pulled this stunt to avoid the draft. First of all, there was no draft in 1916, and secondly, his track record for this type of behavior goes back to age twelve at least, the pattern well established long before European hostilities began.

After one year in the reformatory, Albert Berch was transferred to the Kansas State Penitentiary, and not because of his age (still under twenty-five). It is recorded that Albert did not understand the reason for his transfer, his best guess being: "might be on account of my fighting record or refusing to work cutting rocks." The reason from the prison's standpoint is not stated. As an aside, the Kansas State Penitentiary would, a half-century later, become famous as the execution site for Richard

Hickock and Perry Smith, as told in Truman Capote's *In Cold Blood.*

Upon transfer to the penitentiary and life as a coal miner, Albert is listed as being 5 feet 10 1/4 inches tall and weighing 145 pounds, with dark brown hair and eyes noted as "hazel," a word I first heard as a child when my mother described the color of her own eyes. Other identifying features were "clean, nose broken, large eyes."

The transfer records then outline detailed information about his "Bertillon Class," taking measurements of head length and width, as well as of the cheek, ear, left foot, fingers, and so forth. The Bertillon Class was a scientific approach to criminal identification. Fingerprinting was new at the time, with the science still under study, so Alphonse Bertillon (1853-1914), a French police officer and "biometrics" researcher, created the popular system of its day. His other contribution was much more lasting—he originated the idea of the now-famous two-angle "mugshot." Indeed, the prison records from Kansas also contained the classic mugshot of Albert Weldon Berch, not quite the favorable pose in his portrait on my wall, but thanks to Bertillon, I could positively ID the suspect.

In the transfer records, Albert offers the following responses to questions. Married? *No.* Occupation? *Barber.* Number of months employed in the last year? *Four months.* Drink? *Yes.* Smoke? *Yes.* Gamble? *Yes.* Use dope? *No.* Chew? *No.* Lewd associations? *(Left blank.)* Ever tramped? *No.* Cause of downfall? *Bad associates.* Church? *No.* Do parents and friends know you are here? *Yes.*

Then, in responding to questions about his father, Albert notes the following: Occupation? *Physician in St. Paul.* Religion? *Methodist.* Temperate? *No.* Ever arrested? *No.* Financial condition? *Not good.* As for Albert Senior's mother—*died twenty-two years ago.*

Returning to Albert Junior, the questions continue. Whereabouts for the past twenty years? *Bellefield, Wisconsin, St. Thomas, St. Paul, New York for preparatory school, San Diego and other points in California.*

Albert mentions that his eventual destination was St. Paul, Minnesota to see his father when he was nabbed in Kansas for the pool-hall incident. There is no further information about the preparatory school in New York, a seeming outlier, though Lula noted that Albert had been educated at a "military school."

Albert's prison record includes a log of all letters sent and received. He did not receive a single letter from his father, nor did he send one. Number one on the list, outgoing and incoming, is, of course, Aunt Helen.

The log is fascinating, including many names not found in any other line of research. And there are four letters addressed to the governor of Kansas and one from him. Although the log notes all these letters, we do not have the actual correspondence.

The list also records mail to and from the O. E. Library League in Washington, D.C. It would be simple to describe this organization in 1917 as a prison reform movement, dedicated to the rehabilitation of the criminal. However, the O. E. (Oriental Esoteric) Library had already been through so many mystical reincarnations, accompanied by leadership peccadillos, that today's soap operas would pale in comparison.

It was founded in 1905 for the dissemination of esoteric theosophy (philosophy of the divine), and one of its leaders, Dr. H. N. Stokes, a chemist, occultist, and librarian, encountered some entanglements with the Liberal Catholic Church. By 1917, Stokes popularized a unifying chant, "Back to Blavatsky," one of the founding lights for the Theosophical Society in New York City, an organization that later moved to Bombay as the Adyar Theosophical Society. The Blavatsky name is not as esoteric as her organization might suggest, as today's New Agers consider her a primary thought leader.

Stay with me now—shortly after the formation of the O. E. Library League as a network of pen pals with like minds in theosophy, many prisoners nationwide jumped at the chance for communication with the outside world. By the time Albert Berch began corresponding with them, the league boasted 8,000 members, with two-thirds being prisoners. Whether or not he experienced some form of spiritual revitalization through the O. E. Library League is unknown, but I'll place my bet on the direct influence of Aunt Helen.

As it turns out, Helen was no stranger to the unorthodox. In 1918, at the same time Lula was buying Johnson's Hotel in Marlow, Helen DeLendrecie from Los Angeles was listed as one of several hundred dues-paying members of the American Society for Psychical Research, an organization that was more international than its name would suggest. "Prof. Sigmund Freud" and "Prof. C. G. Jung" are listed as honorary members in this society, which was founded in 1885. One of the founders was preeminent Harvard psychologist William James. The organization is still in existence, with a focus on all aspects of what we term today as "metaphysics." In 1918, its purpose was listed in the organization's journal as "the investigation of alleged telepathy, visions and apparitions, clairvoyance including dowsing or finding water or minerals by supernormal means, premonitions, coincidental dreams, all kinds of mediumistic phenomena, and, in fact, everything of a supernormal character occurring in this field."

Although there are many blanks left to fill, I don't think Helen DeLendrecie was your average Catholic. Her influence over Albert Berch is a consistent feature in everything we know, and she was very likely his *only* influence until he married Lula. Albert's mother died when he was a child, his grandmother (Helen's sister) died young, his grandfather died young, he had no siblings, and he was in perpetual conflict with his father. Aunt Helen's influence ran deep.

Albert's prison sentence was commuted to two to seven years with gubernatorial signature on a certificate dated September 26, 1918, with the earliest possible release date of December 30, 1918. Yet, a few weeks before this "earliest" date, on December 5, Berch was paroled, with a handwritten note at the top of the page, *"Out at once,"* signed by J. K. Codding, secretary of the Board of Administration. His total time served was two years, nine months.

While we have no documentation of correspondence between Aunt Helen and the governor of Kansas, I think it likely occurred. We do know that Helen had networked with Kansans during her suffragette days in the 1880s and 1890s and that she also had ties to abolitionists in that state, but whether or not these connections played a role is conjecture.

Albert later received a "citizenship pardon" on July 9, 1921, from Kansas governor Henry J. Allen. This did not negate the crime or its consequences but restored full citizenship, assuming good behavior while on parole. On August 5, 1921, nearly three years after his prison release, Albert's final discharge papers from the Kansas State Penitentiary were sent to 697 South Kingsley Drive in Los Angeles, the home of Helen and O. J. DeLendrecie.

But Albert was not living in Los Angeles in 1921. He was married and living as a hotel proprietor in Marlow, Oklahoma, a "prominent business man" by all accounts. Even those attorneys who would later defend Albert's killer could not find a skeleton in the Berch closet.

Conceivably, Lula never saw those discharge papers that had been sent to California. Did she know? I suspect she did. After all, Lula had few equals when it came to keeping secrets. If she could keep her own daughter from knowing her and Albert's true ages, then what went on in Kansas likely stayed in Kansas.

26

Osteopathy Meets the Underground Railroad
(Basye and Berch)

While the origin of so-called traditional medicine is steeped in the comfortable ambiguity of the ages, the foundation of osteopathy, in relative terms, was laid overnight. In sharp contrast to conventional MDs, who honor their heroes dating back to the pyramids, osteopathy attributes its birth to a single man—Andrew Taylor Still, MD, DO.

Still's MD degree appears to have been more de facto than sheepskin, though he did attend a short course in medicine at the new College of Physicians and Surgeons in Kansas City, Missouri in 1870. Prior to that, he had served as an apprentice under his physician father, as well as a hospital steward during the Civil War, where one could readily launch a career in medicine, first as an orderly or part-time pharmacist, then climbing the ranks to surgeon.

Disillusioned with traditional medicine, which at the time was teeming with poisons and potions and seemingly random surgical procedures, A. T. Still sought a different way, namely in a new science where bones (thus, "osteo") served as the framework for all bodily pathology. This iconoclastic bent is easier to understand when one considers that Dr. Still lost three of his own children to an epidemic of meningitis, in spite of the standard nostrums.

In 1874, Still took on the status of prophet, both with adoring disciples and bloodthirsty enemies, when he coined the term "osteopathy" as a newly minted approach to healing. In 1892, he founded the American School of Osteopathy, now called the A. T. Still University of the Health Sciences in Kirksville, Missouri, with a second campus in Mesa, Arizona.

Pausing to recall the whereabouts of Albert Senior, future osteopath, at the time of the establishment of the first osteopathic school, he would have been a twenty-six-year-old single rancher near San Diego, one year away from marrying his teenage bride.

Still, a dedicated abolitionist and close ally of John Brown, served five years in the Kansas legislature. His fervor for equal rights spilled into actual practice where, in contrast to the leadership in traditional medicine, Still encouraged women and minorities to enter his school to train in osteopathy.

In its earliest form, osteopathy seems to have drawn from preexisting "homeopathy," adding a tincture of what we call today "holistic medicine," in harnessing the body's power to heal itself. To that, Still added the innovative ingredient of gentle manipulations of the musculoskeletal system to promote cures. This final twist, claiming that the skeleton held underutilized keys to health, if not perhaps the only key, was hijacked by another solo visionary, D. D. Palmer, who founded the first school of chiropractic fifteen years after Still's school launched osteopathy.

Today, osteopathy has merged with traditional medicine, with graduates of both categories of schools moving into the same residencies for specialty training. For the current generation, the distinction between DO and MD has been lost. As I understand it, some older holdouts secretly harbor a quiet reverence for the courageous Still and, perhaps, some manual therapy as well.

Albert Berch, Sr.'s sudden career switch at the same time that osteopathy was born was a lure in my research. Especially enticing was the fact that the first satellite college for osteopathy outside of Missouri was cofounded by Aubrey C. Moore, DO, one of Still's first graduates in Kirksville who then moved to Southern California. In Anaheim, Moore and Dr. B. W. Scheurer (a traditional MD) founded the Pacific Sanitarium and School of Osteopathic Medicine in 1896. Today's iteration of that college is the highly respected University of California, Irvine School of Medicine.

Approximately one year prior to the founding of this college of osteopathy, Albert Senior, living nearby, would have been newly widowed and strapped with a toddler son, so perhaps he seized the moment to change occupations. Lula asserted that he gave his son over to Aunt Helen at this point, forming the Los Angeles part of the family story.

Did Albert Senior enroll in the new osteopathic college in California? And why would he take such an extreme leap from ranching to osteopathy? These questions were driving my research, but the trail ran cold. I had to ask myself, as I'd done a dozen times already, "Is this information critical to advance the story?" I judged that it was not. I would move on. After all, I was very pleased to have discovered census records that listed Albert's occupation as "osteopathy." Prior to that, even Almarian never learned why people referred to him as "Doctor Berch," given Lula's take on the man.

Later on, while searching through Aunt Helen's footprints online, hoping for serendipity, I found a newspaper clipping that revved my research. Among her many causes and exploits, she cofounded a college of osteopathy in 1897 with her brother, Dr. Edward E. Basye, who, it turns out, was also an osteopath (referred to as "Uncle Ned" in Lula's writings). This was simply too bizarre. Two members of the family were osteopaths while Helen established a school for osteopathy?

Didn't Helen have enough to do as mother hen to a full house of nieces and nephews? Weren't her Catholic charities enough? What about the many demands placed on the grande dame of Fargo, such as her passionate work on the Board of Education, where she was the top vote-getter on the ballot and the first woman elected to a citywide office? What about her role as president of both the Civic Improvement League and the Political Equality Club of Fargo? And wasn't her regular column in the *Daily Commonwealth* newspaper a time sponge? Wasn't she bogged down by the ongoing disappointments as a suffragette leader? And yet, in her spare time, she started a college of osteopathy. Why? Was she simply the money behind the machine?

Even though Aunt Helen had been popping up as a common denominator in my research, it would never have occurred to me to search online for "Helen DeLendrecie and osteopathy." Nevertheless, when I finally typed those words into the search engine, I landed in a virtual tour of the Museum of Osteopathic Medicine at A. T. Still University in Kirksville, Missouri, where my findings would astonish.

First, one has to consider that Andrew Taylor Still, founder of osteopathy, was demonized by the leaders of traditional medicine, some even seeking his imprisonment. Then, consider how, even today, we seek celebrity endorsements to validate everything from soap and beauty creams to fundraising for the malady of the month. Enter Helen Basye DeLendrecie, newly diagnosed with—of all things, considering my narrowly focused profession—breast cancer, her second round, now on the opposite side. The first round had prompted a mastectomy, and Aunt Helen was in no mood to undergo this procedure again on the opposite side.

The story was recorded by Alice Smith "Patty" Patterson, a member of the first graduating class of the American School of Osteopathy under Still's tutelage and one of his original seventeen disciples. From her memoirs:

The Fourth Osteopathic School was established in North Dakota upon a cure of a noted case, by Osteopathy, which had been diagnosed as a surgical case. The case was that of Mrs. Helen DeLendrecie.

The year before coming to Kirksville she had had a growth, diagnosed as cancer, in her breast which caused the surgical removal of the entire breast. Later an exactly similar growth came in the other breast. It was also diagnosed as unavoidably surgical. In the meantime she had heard of Dr. Still and came for his opinion. She had been sent to my room. After examining her carefully, Dr. Still said, "We can cure that without surgery." Mrs. DeLendrecie half-jokingly said—"If you can cure this without an operation I will go home to North Dakota and see that a bill is passed in our legislature this winter legalizing and recognizing Osteopathy in our State." Dr. Still replied—"If you do that I will bring two or three of my best students and we will start you a school." Dr. Still then turned to me and said, "Patty, cure this case" and he left the room.

In exactly five weeks, Mrs. DeLendrecie was cured and ready to go home. That winter the bill in legislature was an accomplished fact! Mrs. DeLendrecie being a prominent woman and a lawyer, asked the privilege of the floor to present the bill herself and it went through without a hitch.

This was the second state in the Union to legalize and recognize the practice of Osteopathy. . . .

This memoir was recorded three decades after the events described. In fact, Helen's own account was included in the 1897 *Journal of Osteopathy* and reprinted in the 2011 book *The Feminine Touch: Women in Osteopathic Medicine,* by Thomas A. Quinn (Kirksville, MO: Truman State University Press). Helen tells the same story but with her personal touch, adding, "It was a great shock [the removal of her breast] to my nervous system, and I had not recovered from it, when the same trouble appeared in my left breast. I had heard meantime of osteopathy and resolved to try it before again submitting to the knife."

Other embellishments exist, some claiming that Helen became a DO; then in the Patterson account above we saw that Helen was "a prominent woman and a *lawyer.*" No evidence supports Helen as either a DO or lawyer. Very likely, her charisma and skills as an orator gave rise to these rumors.

Multiple sources comment on Helen's ability to mesmerize an audience. A prominent newspaper editor wrote that she had a "hypnotic effect" when she addressed the legislature of North Dakota, winning the passage of the bill to legalize osteopathy in spite of harsh protest by the traditional medical community.

A. L. Conger recorded the following in "The Growth of Osteopathy" in the June 1897 *Journal of Osteopathy*: "Next came the now famous fight of the able, brave and courageous Mrs. Helen de Lendrecie of Fargo, N.D., for the recognition of Osteopathy in that state. Through personal experience recounted elsewhere in this journal, she had become convinced that Osteopathy was a science which the people of her state ought to have, and upon her return home from a visit to Kirksville she began the campaign single-handed and alone. Delegations of doctors from the larger towns in North Dakota were at the capital when the legislature convened to fight the admission of the new science, but, as she expressed it, 'one woman and might [*sic*] truth won the day.'"

With a copy of her "now famous" speech in my files, I would submit that her writing skills were as critical as her delivery. Using the hyperbole of the day, such as comparing the medical establishment to the Standard Oil monopoly, she took her gloves off and leveled one resounding blow after another.

Helen's nonsurgical breast-cancer "cure" was in 1896, and she established the Northwestern College of Osteopathy in Fargo in 1897 (with O. J. purchasing the First Methodist Church in Fargo and having it moved to Eighth Street South, where it began its new life). In 1902, the college was consolidated with the Dr. S. S. Still (nephew of A. T.) College and Infirmary of Osteopathy and Surgery, which after many name and location changes is the current Des Moines University.

Helen didn't restrict her pro-osteopathy activities to North Dakota. Her speeches and poems of adulation for A. T. Still (bordering on infatuation) were published in the *Journal of Osteopathy*. Another intriguing article in the journal (March 1897), published with Still as one of nine "co-authors," contains her speech when Missouri governor Lawrence Vest Stephens signed the bill legalizing osteopathy in that state. Helen hit the campaign trail arm in arm with Still for the acceptance and legalization of osteopathy.

✳✳✳

William Stewart Halsted published his first paper on the radical mastectomy in 1894, about a year before Helen's surgery, though he popularized the technique in an article about wound healing a few years earlier. Given his dominating influence in the surgical world at the time, it is quite likely that Aunt Helen had undergone a classic Halsted radical mastectomy, or worse, the first time around. Halsted was not the only surgeon who had launched innovative assaults on the disease.

The intrigue of Helen's story is the "melting away" of her second cancer through osteopathy. Diagnosing breast cancer through physical exam alone was notoriously unreliable. Only the most advanced cases were clear-cut. A host of breast abnormalities can mimic cancer so closely as to make benign versus malignant indistinguishable. In fact, the mimicry can last all the way to the microscope, where, even today, benign "complex sclerosing lesions" can tax the best minds in pathology.

But in 1895, breast pathology was still in its infancy, with the gray zone a mile wild. One of Halsted's disciples, Dr. Joseph C. Bloodgood, writing in *JAMA* in 1916, was still bemoaning the lack of distinction between benign and malignant pathology: "The radical operation for a benign lesion will occur in from 10 to 20 per cent of the cases. This is a mistake that must be made until we have developed a method of more exact diagnosis. I am quite certain that when women understand the situation, they will prefer the slightly mutilating operation to the danger of an incomplete removal of a malignant tumor."

Indeed, breast pathology was so ambiguous that Halsted and his followers did not require confirmatory biopsy at all, proclaiming the need for mastectomy on the basis of clinical judgment alone. This practice was so thoroughly established that Halsted rejected the introduction of the frozen section. Seventy years later, women fought to put an end to the one-stage frozen section followed by mastectomy under a single anesthesia, but the standard of care prior to that was even worse—mastectomy without confirmatory biopsy at all!

It is very unlikely that Aunt Helen had breast cancer the second time around, and one has to question whether or not she had cancer the *first* time around. Indeed, one account of Helen's medical adventure into osteopathy attributes her primary symptom, chest pain, to a broken rib rather than breast cancer.

One other point, and I write now as a scientist—breast cancer large enough to be felt on examination does not melt away without chemotherapy or hormonal manipulation. Yes, there is ample media coverage of "overdiagnosis" and "cancers that don't kill." This phenomenon is referencing some of the early cancers that are identified through mammographic screening, where it is acknowledged that this occurs, though sharp controversy persists as to how often and which ones. But by the time cancer becomes a large, palpable mass, it is well on its way to killing the host, unless treatment intervenes or the woman dies first of something else.

Aunt Helen's remarkable cure, driving her to zealotry, was most likely spawned by a misdiagnosis, a rather common scenario known to be a primary source for validating nostrums, miracles, or both. When a deadly cancer "melts away" as a true spontaneous regression (an extremely rare occurrence, though it has been documented), some physicians regard this as a yet-to-be-understood immunologic phenomenon, other physicians call it a miracle, and some straddle the fence, pronouncing both at work.

Helen wasn't simply the financial backing for her brother's chosen field. She was the source, the originator, the driving influence. She "converted" her own brother and her shiftless nephew, and she led a crusade to validate a highly unpopular movement at the time. The first board of directors for the new osteopathic college in Fargo had only three members, Helen (president), her brother Dr. Basye, and one Ernest P. Smith. The college was organized on a for-profit basis, an approach that plagued early medical schools, with a capital outlay of $50,000, sold in shares of $100 each. In spite of these details, I never learned whether Albert Senior launched his new career from the osteopathic school in North Dakota or in California.

But one late discovery came when I tried to chase down rumors that Helen had become a DO herself. It made no sense that she could be president and student at the same school she had founded, not to mention taking on the challenge of the twenty months of training that were standard at the time for a DO degree. Osteopathy was virtually identical to chiropractic in those days, though the curriculum was shorter for the latter and there was no early emphasis on licensure after obtaining the DC degree. Thus, DOs snubbed DCs from the get-go. Too, there seemed to be more of an element of mysticism with chiropractic. Its founder, D. D. Palmer, had been a "magnetic healer" prior to his conversion to chiropractic, a therapeutic strategy that he "received from the other world," i.e., necromancy with a dead physician by the name of Jim Atkinson. (Others note that Palmer very likely designed chiropractic after an encounter with the new field of osteopathy, if not from Andrew Still directly.)

A metaphysicist in her own right, in addition to her alleged Catholicism, Helen would have loved the blending of science and spiritualism. So I made the decision to enter the search words, "Helen DeLendrecie and chiropractic." And there it was in a link for the "National Institute of Chiropractic Research," in an article about Palmer written by Joseph C. Keating, Jr., PhD. Helen was the fourth graduate of the first school of chiropractic, founded by Palmer in Davenport, Iowa. The first two graduates of "The Chiropractic School and Cure" in 1898 had been MDs, expanding their horizons. Then, in 1899, Helen received her DC degree in a graduating class of five students, though she never formally established a medical practice or called herself "doctor," at least not to my knowledge. Though Aunt Helen has been dead for nearly a century, I still have trouble keeping up with her.

Josephine Helen (Basye) DeLendrecie was the daughter of Jane Barkley and Samuel Basye, who raised their family in Racine, Wisconsin. Helen was one of eight children, three of whom appear in this book. Besides Helen and her osteopath brother, sister Mary Ann (called Marian) married Jesse L. Berch, great-great-grandparents to my sisters and me.

I have already explained the good fortune of Josephine Helen (sometimes Ellen) Basye, who became Helen DeLendrecie and a lot more.

Helen Basye DeLendrecie, sister-in-law to Jesse L. Berch

Jesse L. Berch, grandfather of Albert Weldon Berch and married to Helen's sister, Marian Basye (Courtesy of Marc and Beth Storch Collection)

It's not too much of a leap from Racine to Fargo or back to Racine, where she wed O. J. in 1879, so their union is easy to attribute to geography. Fargo, due to its convenient location on the Red River of the North, was once a boomtown called "The Gateway to the West." If the Basye family took the train to Dakota Territory, as was common in the day, Helen might have caught the eye of the "best known citizen of Fargo," as O. J. is described in a document from Almarian's files, titled without source as "History of North Dakota."

Within two years after Albert Berch's murder in Marlow, both O. J. and Helen changed their wills, and not a day too soon. O. J.'s final will that established a trust for Almarian was executed on September 5, 1924, nine months after the murder and the same year of his own death from "pyonephrosis," a kidney infection. Aunt Helen's will was finalized on August 21, 1925, again defining the trust, less than a year before her death from uterine cancer.

While details surrounding Helen's formal introduction to French Canadian O. J. DeLendrecie are foggy, it's not hard to imagine how her sister, Marian Basye, met Jesse L. Berch. They were first cousins, both living in Racine, Wisconsin.

✲✲✲

Jesse L. Berch was born circa 1840 to Harrison Berch and Elizabeth Basye Berch, and his dates extend only to August 23, 1887. His death at age forty-seven and wife Marian's one year later left Albert Senior without parents by age twenty-two. Thus, Albert's lifelong attachment to Helen, his maternal aunt, makes more sense, not to mention the similar attachment of the motherless Albert Junior. Jesse and Marian are buried together with a single monument in Racine County Mound Cemetery.

Jesse Berch fought for the Union in the Civil War, and if one looks at his war record alone, it is undistinguished. He enlisted in Company A, Wisconsin Twenty-Second Infantry Regiment, on August 2, 1862, and was promoted to full quartermaster on June 5, 1863. He was mustered out on June 12, 1865, at Washington, D.C. In spite of no legendary feats on the battlefield, Jesse was one of those unique individuals who find themselves written into the pages of history through a single heroic act.

In the summer of 1862, President Lincoln called for 300,000 additional volunteers to the Union cause, and Wisconsin's Twenty-Second was one of the many regiments that formed as a result. But this particular regiment had a peculiar twist, prompting its nickname—the "Abolition Regiment."

William Fliss told the story of this regiment in the 2002-3 winter edition of the *Wisconsin Magazine of History*. The full-page photo that introduces the article shows three individuals, including my great-great-grandfather Jesse L. Berch in a bizarre pose, his pistol held across his chest and aimed directly at the head of a young black woman, seated in her Sunday best, unfazed. This is the iconic photograph I mentioned early in the book that I saw in a PBS documentary the night before I traced Albert Senior's life as a rancher near San Diego.

The caption in the *Wisconsin Magazine of History* notes: "Despite the impression that the angle of the gun held by Sergeant Jesse Berch (left) might give, the unnamed woman in this 1862 daguerreotype was far from being a hostage."

The third person, Frank M. Rockwell, is standing on the other side of the girl's chair, his pistol held at the same angle as Jesse Berch's, adding nice symmetry and helping to neutralize the impression that Jesse is about to kill the young woman. The photograph is a staged studio portrait documenting the completion of the threesome's heroic trip along the Underground Railroad.

Col. William L. Utley was commander of the Abolition Regiment, a man who was long on abolitionist beliefs and short on military experience. Union supporters were mostly concerned with preservation of the Union, while some were true abolitionists and others simply loved to fight. Utley's motivations are not entirely clear, but his recruitment zone was an area of Wisconsin heavily populated by transplanted New Englanders. Their regional mantra of abolition was expressed as early as 1857, when the four counties that filled the regiment voted in favor of a referendum extending suffrage for free blacks, even though the measure was defeated statewide.

The Abolition Regiment was called into service promptly after its formation, to counter a Confederate invasion of Kentucky. The state of Kentucky was an intense battleground in the war, and its relationship to slavery was tricky. Because Lincoln's Emancipation Proclamation pertained only to those states in the Confederacy, Kentucky as a "border state" was unaffected, and slavery continued. When the Union forces arrived in Kentucky, the slaves perceived them as liberators. Given Colonel Utley's abolitionist beliefs, he quickly accepted his role as liberator as well, long before any shots were fired.

Brig. Gen. Quincy Gillmore issued an order that all "contraband" (slaves) should be left behind, as troops moved out for battle. However, the Twenty-Second Volunteer Infantry failed to comply, picking up more slaves in the process. Thus, Utley found himself doing battle with his own side as he offered the male ex-slaves protection and working positions within the regiment. The "Abolition Regiment" nickname was born. Citizens of Kentucky complained bitterly about the regiment that seemed to be siphoning away their slaves.

Then came the twist. At first, all fugitives had been males. But then, a female slave found her way to the Twenty-Second encampment just north of Lexington, Kentucky. She had recently been sold to a new master for the princely sum of $1,700, and this owner planned to use the eighteen-year-old in his brothel in Lexington. Realizing that her presence in camp might require too much restraint for the all-male regiment, Colonel Utley asked for volunteers to escort her to the Grand Central Station of the Underground Railroad, the home of Levi Coffin, a Quaker abolitionist in Cincinnati, some one hundred miles away.

History has proclaimed Coffin as the unofficial president of the Underground Railroad, a complex system of roads throughout the country with a primary nexus at his home, where several thousand slaves eventually sought safe passage.

Two men volunteered to make the trip—Quartermaster Jesse L. Berch and Pvt. Frank Rockwell of Company C. The inherent danger came not only from the slave owner who would scour the camp in search of his escaped "property" but from Union troops outside the Abolition Regiment. At this point in the Civil War, the Union's written policy was clear-cut—Union commanders were not to receive or protect fugitive slaves who sought refuge. Some slaves were sent back, while other Union commanders allowed masters to come and retrieve them. In the words of Levi Coffin, "This policy was very repugnant to some true-hearted Northerners who had all their lives sympathized with the slaves and hated the bondage that held them in thralldom; and they scorned the half measures dictated by policy."

Berch and Rockwell made the trip in a sutler's wagon, starting out in the middle of the night with the slave girl hiding in the back, disguised as a male soldier. Driving all night and the next day, they reached Coffin's home safely. Berch telegraphed friends in Racine, willing to take the girl farther north. It was shortly after their arrival in Cincinnati that the threesome, understanding the bold-spirited nature of their journey, sealed their destiny at a daguerreotype gallery owned and operated by an African-American photographer, J. P. Ball.

Levi Coffin kept detailed diaries, called *Reminiscences,* and he described the entourage's arrival in Cincinnati this way:

> They came immediately to my house, and were ushered into the sitting-room, accompanied by their charge, who presented the appearance of a mulatto soldier boy. As there was other company present, they called me to one side and related their story. The "soldier boy" was given into my wife's care, and was conducted up-stairs to her room. Next morning he came down transformed into a young lady of modest manners and pleasing appearance, who won the interest of all by her intelligence and amiable character. The party remained a day or two, to recover from the fatigue of their journey, and during the interval visited a daguerrean gallery, where they had their pictures taken, the lady sitting, the soldiers standing, one on either side, with their revolvers drawn, showing their readiness thus to protect her, even at the cost of their own lives. Not content with escorting her to a free State, these brave young men telegraphed to Racine, Wisconsin, and made arrangements for their friends there to receive her, and I took her one evening in my carriage to the depot, accompanied by her protectors, and put her on board the train with a through ticket for Racine, via Chicago . . . as the train moved off they lifted their hats to her, and she waved her handkerchief in good-by. They afterward remarked to me, that it seemed one of the happiest moments of their lives when they saw her safely on her way to a place beyond the reach of her pursuers. They had done a noble unselfish deed, and were rewarded by that approval of conscience which contains the most unalloyed joy of life.
>
> After their return to camp, I received the following letter from one of them:
> IN CAMP, NEAR NICHOLASVILLE, KENTUCKY, November 17, 1862
> Friend L. Coffin: As the Lord prospered us on our mission to the land of freedom, so has He prospered us in our return to our regiment. At five o'clock on Friday evening, after a ride of three days, we arrived at our camp near Nicholasville; and you would have rejoiced to hear the loud cheering and hearty welcome that greeted us on our arrival. Our long delay had occasioned many fears as to our welfare; but when they saw us approach, the burden of their anxiety was gone, and they welcomed us by one hearty outburst of cheers. The colonel was full of delight, and when he heard of the Friend L. Coffin, who had so warmly welcomed us to the land of freedom, he showered a thousand blessings on your head. The way was opened, and we were directed to you by an unseen but ever-present Hand. The Lord was truly with us upon that journey.
> Your humble friend, Jesse L. Berch

Levi Coffin continued: "The name of the other soldier was Frank M. Rockwell. Both were young men of true principles and high character, and, as representatives of the solid worth of Wisconsin's noble sons, were men that their State could regard with pride."

Ten years later, Levi Coffin wrote, "I received a letter from Jesse L. Berch, a few months ago, making inquiries in regard to a book which he had heard I published. When I replied, stating that my book was not yet published, I asked for news of the slave girl whom he had aided to rescue. He responded, giving information of her safe arrival in Racine, and of her residence there for a few months, concluding by saying, 'Afterward, she married a young barber and moved into Illinois, and I have never been able to ascertain her whereabouts since I came from the army, though Mr. Rockwell and myself have tried repeatedly. . . . '"

While the date for the flight to Cincinnati is listed in the *Wisconsin Magazine of History* as "early November," likely based on the letter above from Jesse Berch, the back of the historic photo is marked September 16-22, 1862. Incidentally, the names of both men are written on the back of the photo, along with their ranks, and *both* men are noted as being "on the left." This originally caused some confusion at the photograph's home base, the Library of Congress Collection, but identities were corrected at my request based on a separate photograph of Jesse Berch from the Marc and Beth Storch Collection that had been used in the Wisconsin magazine.

Still, some remain confused about the bizarre picture. Without the details to accompany the photograph, the men appear to be slave trackers, as the makers of the PBS documentary had assumed. The photo is now making its way online and into other books, often untitled and misleading.

One of the remaining questions, still unanswered, is the fate of the escaped slave girl escorted by Berch and Rockwell. The 2002-3 edition of the *Wisconsin Magazine of History* ran a one-page companion story to "Wisconsin's Abolition Regiment," this second piece titled, "Missing for 140 Years." Wisconsin Historical Society archivist Dee Grimsrud went to extraordinary lengths to learn of the young girl's fate, but without success. She searched Underground Railroad participants in Racine, marriage records (not required until 1907), and the 1861 Racine City Directory, looking for barbers and cross-referencing marriage records, all efforts greatly limited by not knowing this young woman's name. If your family includes a female ancestor who was escorted by Union soldiers

Left to right: Sgt. Jesse L. Berch, regimental quartermaster; unidentified teenage slave, self-liberated; and Pvt. Frank M. Rockwell, regimental postmaster. Photograph taken in Cincinnati, 1862, at J. P. Ball's Photographic Gallery after completion of their 100-mile journey that provided protective escort of the former slave along the Underground Railroad. The unfortunate angle of Jesse's gun has prompted this photograph to be used incorrectly in the public domain as an example of slave trackers. (Courtesy of Bill Gladstone Collection at U.S. Army Military History Institute and Library of Congress)

as a self-liberated slave along the Underground Railroad to Cincinnati, please contact me via this book's website. By now, this ancestor would have at least three or four "greats" in her relationship to living progeny.

On March 25, 1863, the Abolition Regiment was defeated at Brentwood, Tennessee, and the slaves who had joined them were "removed from the camp," lost to history. The victorious Confederate commander, known to assassinate prisoners, was none other than Gen. Nathan Bedford Forrest. This raises the possibility that the ancestors of George Carter and Albert Junior in Marlow, Oklahoma met each other as enemies on the battlefield in 1863, sixty years before Albert's murder for hiring and harboring a black man.

The Abolition Regiment was later paroled (traded for Confederate prisoners). Internal dissent on the Union side was intense, with Utley being charged with incompetence in the defeat. This prompted a lifetime feud with Colonel Bloodgood, who had assumed command during the disaster.

The Abolition Regiment enjoyed later victories as part of General Sherman's March to the Sea, and the men of the regiment were among the first to enter Atlanta. Finally, the regiment marched to Washington, D.C. in May 1865 and paraded down Pennsylvania Avenue in the grand review of Sherman's army before being mustered out of service and sent back to Wisconsin.

★★★

Albert Berch, Sr., was not born until four years after his father's daring feat, yet it is presumed that he heard of it many times growing up. "Orphaned" at twenty-two, he left for San Diego, where he took up a new life as a rancher. However, Aunt Helen and Uncle O. J. could serve as a safety net should things go awry, at least while the couple was wintering in Los Angeles. For Albert, the birth of a son was followed by the death of his wife, and for the next two decades, the details for both Senior and Junior remain hazy, though clearing now to a degree.

That said, a fair presumption would allow that Albert Junior heard the tale of his grandfather's famous exploit, as had been the case for Albert Senior. Then, with the adornments that so often accompany such accounts, it is not too much of a leap to assume the story achieved legendary status in the family lore, providing an interesting parallel. Albert Junior's knowledge of his unknown grandfather was distilled to a single heroic act, the same that occurred for me and my sisters with our grandfather.

Given Aunt Helen's intensity in everything she did, it is easy to imagine her working to instill Jesse's act of heroism in little Albert Junior while he ate Sunday dinner at her home, on break from his nearby lodgings at the orphanage. With Aunt Helen realizing already that Albert Senior was a weak and troubled man, she likely intensified her drill to explain noble roots to the younger Berch, and how his grandfather—"may he rest in peace"—had saved a young slave girl from a life of sheer misery. Although I am taking license here, the odds are strong that Aunt Helen immortalized her brother-in-law in his one great deed, just as she had described her sister, Marian, in a letter to Lula, as the "saintliest woman I have ever known."

When Albert Junior ran away from home after the eighth grade, we do not know if it was from his father, stepmother, or both. Nevertheless, he landed in the Kansas State Reformatory, with no intent to reform. His recalcitrance led him to graduate not out of prison but further inside, as he was transferred from reformatory to penitentiary, then deeper still into the coal mines.

What happened? What transformation took place in prison that allowed him to waltz into Oklahoma with a new identity and the ability to live a life so spotless that even highly motivated defense attorneys could find nothing with which to slander him at the murder trials?

Whatever caused Albert Weldon Berch to turn his life around, there is one specter that can haunt a former trespasser or debtor—the ghost of redemption. Even if no one in Oklahoma knew of Albert's past life, he did. And even when the need for redemption is driven internally, it's still a powerful force that can result in overcompensation. So now, let me propose that Albert Berch felt a "duty" to bring rural Oklahoma into the twentieth century, by intentionally breaking the color barrier in Marlow.

Just as his grandfather had written himself into the history books with a solitary deed, so would Albert Junior, and he would do it with an act juxtaposed to his grandfather's rescue of a slave. Instead of traveling 100 miles to Cincinnati, he would travel 10 miles to Duncan and transport a black man to Marlow, in an act that would make Aunt Helen proud, as well as Jesse, looking from above. A single act, redemption, purpose, legacy: all of these can be dangerous words at times.

There are other points of conjecture. Did Albert Berch boast in Marlow that his grandfather had once fought for the Union against Gen. Nathan

Bedford Forrest, the eventual first Grand Wizard of the Ku Klux Klan? Did he mention that he had lived in a Catholic orphanage, leading to the erroneous assumption (even for his surviving daughter) that he was a Catholic? Did he let Aunt Helen know about the sundown laws and the signs posted at Marlow's perimeter? Was Helen appalled? Did she encourage Albert to "be noble, just like your grandfather would have been"? Was Albert Berch on a mission, or was he simply picking a fight? As I discovered in his prison records, he was no stranger to a fight.

In considering the possible role of Aunt Helen, recall that the second version of the KKK was not just a Southern phenomenon. It was nationwide, involving an estimated 20 percent of the adult male population in the early 1920s. In states where race was not the primary issue, the KKK's focus was on "true Americanism" and whichever target carried the greatest threat. In North Dakota, the threat was primarily Catholicism.

Catholics were seen as "invading" school systems, as well as local and state governments, with their pope functioning, in effect, as a king. For some Klan members, this went beyond the pope serving as a misguided light on spiritual matters to a papist conspiracy to overthrow the U.S. government and turn over complete control to Rome.

The hotbed for the North Dakota Klan seems to have been in Grand Forks, located just eighty miles directly north of Fargo on U.S. 81. The thoroughfare serves as a ribbon to this story, where a journey south on U.S. 81 from Fargo will eventually take a traveler through the heart of El Reno, Marlow, and Duncan, Oklahoma.

F. Halsey Ambrose, a Presbyterian minister in North Dakota, took up the charge of white Protestant Americanism. In 1918 Grand Forks, his anti-Catholic sermons garnered him fame, mushrooming church attendance, and finally, the position of Exalted Cyclops of the Ku Klux Klan for the "realm" of North Dakota.

In Fargo, the Klan once drew a crowd of 8,000 spectators as 800 white-robed marchers and horseback riders paraded through town. They chose a route where they could file past St. Mary's Cathedral, where O. J. DeLendrecie. had helped lay the cornerstone. A statewide rally for "true Americanism" on July 4, 1924, drew hundreds of Klansmen from Fargo and Grand Forks, and the Imperial Wizard made a guest appearance to the crowd of 5,000.

Helen and O. J. DeLendrecie had, by this time, retired to their home in Los Angeles, but they had to be getting a sense of Klan antics from friends and family in North Dakota. In another odd parallel, the North

Dakota legislature introduced a bill in 1922 to outlaw the wearing of a mask or regalia that concealed the identity of the wearer, much in the same vein as Oklahoma's State Question 123. In North Dakota, both houses of the legislature approved the bill, and Gov. R. A. Nestos signed it into law. In doing so, he bestowed upon himself the wrath of the Klan, similar to what Oklahoma's governor Jack Walton had endured by proposing similar legislation.

Given Aunt Helen's activist influence on so many members of this family, it is not difficult to think that, in her correspondence with Albert, she might have addressed the problem of the Klan and the law that had been passed in North Dakota the year before. Albert might have seen an opportunity for redemption in the eyes of Aunt Helen, not to mention his own and those of society.

The similar timing of Albert's decisions to hire Robert Johnigan and to circulate the petition for State Question 123 suggests the two efforts were linked. Lula never described any such forethought. In her account, Johnigan's hiring was based on a specific need. Nevertheless, we have Aunt Helen, whose reach is so powerful that, from Los Angeles, she christens my newborn mother as "Almarian," tying together the name of her grandnephew and her sister, almost as if the baby's mother, a tough woman in her own right, didn't have a say. So, I can almost hear Aunt Helen giving directives to Albert Berch regarding his social obligation to fight the Klan as a newly molded "leading citizen" in Marlow, Oklahoma.

Although intriguing, this theory can be set aside, as Aunt Helen is not a requisite figure for the story to unfold in Marlow as it did. In fact, she might not have been a catalyst at all. Albert Berch had wasted his youth in spectacular style yet was somehow able to reinvent himself (with or without Helen's spiritualism), thrive in his business, and raise a family in Marlow without a blemish. Part of this success had to be a commitment for redemption, but as the redemptive man discovers so often, it's not enough to pay the debt. In contrast to giving gold coins away as the convenient metaphor for life's great secret, the currency of redemption often works differently. For every penny of altruism given away in the name of restitution, the giver might think he owes even more.

Albert Weldon Berch had grown up under a heavenly cloud of heroism, a legendary Berch grandfather who'd made his mark with a single act. Over sixty years later, Albert realized he was living within a zeitgeist foreign to his own disposition on matters of race. Whether or not his liberal bent was forged by the story of Jesse's famous trek, Aunt Helen's influence, or his interracial experience as a prisoner in the coal mines, he had a destiny to fulfill. But sometimes, destiny needs a nudge. Albert would recreate the act of Jesse, ushering a "crippled negro" out of the quasi-slavery of segregation and into the twentieth century.

The great mystery of this story is not so much whether there was a "mastermind," or if the KKK issued an edict to be enacted by a mob of unwitting young men. Instead, the mystery has always been: why? Why did Albert Berch go against such a strong societal mandate, putting himself and his family in such clear jeopardy? Reassurance from the town leaders may have fooled a hayseed, but Berch had lived a thousand lives already, wallowing among life's lowliest scoundrels. Surely, he was savvy enough to know that a man can easily talk out of both sides of his mouth, spinning public approval from one corner and private disapproval from the other. Was the hubris of the redemptive life so powerful that he forgot everything he learned during those years of wanderlust?

While State Question 123 might have been the straw that broke Albert's back, I believe that the hiring of Robert Johnigan was a primary act of civil disobedience, conceived as a reenactment of his famous grandfather's heroic journey. These two acts by the two Berch men were morally correct but specifically condemned by societal statutes. Jesse violated the written law of the Union, and while Albert was said to have violated an unwritten law, there is nothing "unwritten" about sundown signs at the outskirts of town.

Jesse Berch understood the magnitude of his epic journey before he ever left the Union camp in Kentucky. The threesome's trip to the daguerreotype studio in Cincinnati to memorialize the heroics says it all. Although I believe that Albert Berch was equally proud of his stance, any attempt of mine to dissect his underlying motives decades later is doomed to fall short. Yet, my contention is that both acts were noble in the eyes of the would-be heroes.

Unfortunately, Albert underestimated the forces lined up against him and, in the process, dragged another innocent man, Robert Johnigan, into whatever complexities were at work in the Berch brain. While the dark of night facilitated Jesse's journey, that same sundown spelled doom for Berch and Johnigan. And while the unnamed girl was spared a slave's life in a brothel, in contrast, six decades later, Robert Johnigan's last agonizing words pleaded with God for understanding as to why this had happened to him, a black man who had spent his entire life trying to do good while tiptoeing to avoid the ire of the white man.

27

A Second Act Revealed—135 Years After the First

J. G. Stuttz was a well-known actor in the Midwest who owned several theatrical touring companies after the Civil War. As a Hollywood script today might dictate, he fell in love with one of his leading ladies and they married on April 26, 1869. The *Chicago Tribune* reported that the new wife embarked on her theatrical career with "little to aid but courage, ambition and undiscovered talent." Wherever their troupe performed, the reviews for Helen Stuttz were glowing, often outshining her husband's.

The husband-wife production company took on various shapes, but an early ensemble included twenty-five members and was known as the Olympic Theatre Company, which toured mostly in Ohio and surrounding states for five seasons, eight months out of the year. In the summers, the Stuttz couple would rest in Racine, where J. G. had discovered his talented wife-to-be.

In 1872, Mrs. Stuttz hired her twenty-one-year-old brother Edward as business and theatrical manager of the group, by then known as the Old Reliable Theatre Company. Edward billed his sister as "The Great Classic Actress" and "The Brilliant and Accomplished Actress." Tours extended to the Southern states, playing to overflowing crowds and enthusiastic critics. Hyperbole in the newspapers was the standard of the day, and reviewers did not hold back in their predictable exaggerations, good or bad. For Mrs. Stuttz, it was all good. Reviewers stumbled over each other with their praise, striving awkwardly to find new ways to say, "There wasn't a dry eye in the house."

For example, after Mrs. Stuttz's portrayal of Maud Livingstone in *Heart Hungry* on September 2, 1873, in Reading, Pennsylvania, the drama critic for the *Reading Daily Eagle* wrote that the play appears "like a masterpiece original creation with this very extraordinary young woman . . . what great perfection melo-dramatic art can be brought and presented by one who is yet comparatively strange to the dramatic world. . . . " The reviewer continued, "She was most magnificent . . . in such scenes as appealing to her husband not to leave her or cast her off, her acting was grand in every particular . . . one of the very finest emotional representations ever presented in this city. . . . Her acting was superbly grand, and when the descending curtain closed the story of the evening, the audience put away their handkerchiefs and left convinced that they had seen one of the most meritorious interpretations ever presented in Reading."

The *Daily State Journal* in Richmond, Virginia reviewed the new play *Fanchon, the Cricket,* based on a George Sand novel, as performed by the Old Reliable Theatre Company. Primary kudos went to Helen. "In the character of the cricket, especially, [Mrs. Stuttz] displayed talent of the highest order, and fully established her claim as a worthy rival of the celebrated Maggie Mitchell," wrote the critic, comparing her to the actress who had made the role famous.

The company was renamed the Helen d'Este (pronounced *des-tay*) Dramatic Combination in 1873, based on the stage name of Mrs. Stuttz, and they toured Ohio, Indiana, Kentucky, and Virginia. The next season, the troupe performed in Tennessee, Alabama, and Georgia. Then, they made the big announcement—in an ad in the *New York Clipper*, the entertainment newspaper, the couple publicized their upcoming "tour of England, France, Spain, Austria, and Denmark."

But something went awry, and it likely relates to romance. The European tour never materialized. By 1876, tension between the Stuttzes grew to the point that J. G. formed his own company and hired a new leading lady, whom he would later marry.

Helen d'Este took over the original troupe but ran into financial trouble in 1878. Aware that burlesque was gaining popularity and profits, she dove into that medium, only to be arrested in New Orleans for a performance that was described as "indecent and demoralizing." The charges were dropped only after she agreed to discontinue her act. In addition, the charges of "improper exhibition by Parisian blondes" were inaccurate, as the girls were neither Parisian nor blonde. Mrs. Stuttz finally disbanded her company in 1879 after its last show in Winona, Mississippi.

Meanwhile, in Yazoo City, Mississippi, sixty miles southwest of Winona, a modestly successful merchant, perhaps a Stage Door Johnny who had seen Helen d'Este perform, struck up a whirlwind romance with the actress. Although the merchant was far from rich at that point, he impressed the actress with his dreams of traveling north to a rapidly growing town in northern Dakota Territory—Fargo, where he hoped to secure a fortune.

O. J. DeLendrecie and his actress-lover, Josephine Helen Basye Stuttz, traveled north to Milwaukee. There she finalized her divorce from J. G. on September 1, then married O. J. one week later.

Curt Eriksmoen is a writer who contributes to North Dakota newspapers, largely about interesting people who have lived in that state, packaging his columns in book form as *Did You Know That . . . ?* His online article for the *Bismarck Tribune* in 2014 is where I discovered the stunning backstory for our Aunt Helen.

Eriksmoen points out, "This was the time when Victorian morality began to sweep across American society in what Edith Wharton aptly called 'The Age of Innocence.' Her popular novel clearly illustrated that divorced women were shunned by high society."

But divorce wasn't the only baggage Helen carried into Fargo. Eriksmoen draws from Jan MacKell's book, *Brothels, Bordellos, and Bad Girls,* centered on the same time period, where the author noted that "socializing with actresses was frowned upon in decent society." Actresses were, almost by definition, women with loose moral values. The twice-wed Helen DeLendrecie had two strikes against her as a divorced actress, not to mention her arrest in New Orleans.

Yet, she was thrust into the limelight by O. J.'s rapid success and wealth in Fargo, and no one ever knew that she "didn't belong" in high society. Even more remarkable is the fact that she rose to such heights within that society, where she would have likely been shunned had the truth been known. Think now of her mesmerizing oratory before the North Dakota legislature, where the vote to legalize the practice of osteopathy was 24-7. If ever a second act was pulled off flawlessly, Helen d'Este did it. No one in Fargo knew of her origins—that is, for the first 135 years. As Curt Eriksmoen wrote in his 2014 article, "Considering everything that she accomplished over the 35 years she lived in Fargo, many may argue that it was a secret worth keeping."

So how did Eriksmoen uncover the secret, so long after the fact?

It was a book in progress. Not this book, which was already looking for a publishing home when the secret was revealed. It was a second book idea being researched by Greg Nesteroff, a newspaper reporter in Nelson,

British Columbia, who was planning to write the story of a colorful character with a lost history, the actor J. G. Stuttz. Although the saga of the second Mrs. Stuttz was well documented, including her death in a fire caused by a bad mix of flammable grease paint and theater lights, Nesteroff could not find out what happened to the first wife. Working only with her stage name, Helen d'Este, he hit a dead end.

Like train tracks being laid from one coast headed east, and similar tracks being laid from the other coast headed west, the Golden Spike at Promontory Summit was the Eriksmoen article in the *Bismarck Tribune*. I found it searching for Helen in one direction, while Greg Nesteroff found it working in the other direction. We both landed in Bismarck. Nesteroff confided in Eriksmoen that he was looking for Helen d'Este, and he suspected that she and Josephine Helen DeLendrecie were one and the same. They exchanged notes, and yes, it was true. The actor, J. G. Stuttz, performing in Wisconsin in the late 1860s, had likely spotted Helen onstage in a local production in Racine and had whisked her away with promises of fame and fortune.

I had made the mistake of assuming the easiest geography possible—that O. J. dropped down from Canada into North Dakota to start his department store, while Helen drifted over from Racine to Fargo to buy things there. It sounded easy but was incorrect.

O. J. was born in Montreal, where he was educated through college and became a teacher. After two years in that profession, he immigrated to the U.S., spent some time in New York, then made the improbable move to Yazoo City, Mississippi, where he would meet the regionally famous actress, Helen d'Este. Importantly, O. J. and Helen traveled north and entered the bustling town of Fargo *together as a married couple,* where they set up shop, literally, as the Chicago Dry Goods Store. No questions were asked, at least not for the first 135 years.

The geography was far from the "shortest distance between two points." For a Canadian to meet a Wisconsin native in Yazoo City, Mississippi defies all logic, but it speaks to yet another skeleton that has tumbled out of Johnson's Hotel—and another character in this story who reinvented themselves through a tour-de-force performance. And there wasn't a dry eye in the house.

Perhaps it makes more sense now why quick-change artist Aunt Helen never gave up on her wayward grandnephew, Albert Weldon Berch, a man who experienced a transformation of his own when he crossed the border from Kansas to Oklahoma.

O. J. and Helen DeLendrecie in front of their Los Angeles home, November 1922. Helen is holding her great-grandniece, Almarian Berch, age nine months.

Buried in what was then known as Hollywood Memorial Park Cemetery, Aunt Helen, formerly the actress Helen d'Este, lies eternally amidst the greatest movie stars of the era, including her neighbor Rudolph Valentino. To visit her grave and that of husband O. J., travel to the southeast corner of the grounds, where you will find the Hollywood Cathedral Mausoleum, a site reserved for Catholics, rich, famous, or both.

28

The Butterfly Effect or Cascade?

At the beginning of this book, I wrote that the cascade of events following the murders would make up the bulk of the story. It never occurred to me that I would discover forces at play long before the murders. The farther one moves away from December 17, 1923, in either direction, the events become less and less chained to the murders. Therefore, it is necessary to invoke the "butterfly effect."

Alluded to earlier, the butterfly effect has been mined by science-fiction authors, Hollywood screenwriters, and anyone else who likes to dabble in time travel. By going back in time and altering the tiniest of events, present or future outcomes are drastically changed. The term "butterfly effect" is drawn from chaos theory dealing with complex systems, the first experimenter having been a meteorologist who, in 1960, was using a primitive computer model to predict the weather. The phrase caught on in 1972 when he presented his paper entitled, "Predictability: Does the Flap of a Butterfly's Wings in Brazil Set Off a Tornado in Texas?" Importantly, the butterfly effect is not describing causation. The butterfly flapping its wings in Brazil does not *cause* the Texas tornado. It merely alters conditions ever so slightly within a complex system with countless moving parts, such that the minor tweak yields unpredictably powerful events downwind. Prior to the vivid butterfly descriptor, only the ten-dollar word "concatenation" sufficed.

Contrast this to the domino theory, which deals with direct causation. When I began working on this story, I focused on the "cascade," my tag for the domino theory. Albert dies, Lula struggles, Aunt Helen pays, Almarian learns, the next generation does this or that . . . one domino after another. Yet, the more I learned about the murders and the people behind them, the less confident I felt in discussing dominos.

Late in life, Lula wanted to know why. Why did all this happen? She boxed her memories, and while issuing those haunting words that life had been a "great disappointment," Lula also pointed to the fact that—well—at least her daughter had married an MD. And their children, her grandchildren, were turning out okay, with the oldest daughter becoming a medical technologist, the son becoming an MD who would join his father in practice (half-correct), and another daughter choosing the arts, starting with theater design in Chicago, later commercial lighting in Los Angeles. Lula was fine with these career choices but refrained from expressing her displeasure that we all left Oklahoma—that is, until the youngest grandchild announced her plans to move to Chicago. My sister Dawn recalls a singular moment of outrage from Lula after that announcement, when our grandmother said to her with total disgust, "I can make a living here. Why can't you?"

In all the writings of despair by Lula, I came across this phrase only once: "I guess it was finally worth it." She never voiced pride or joy in her grandchildren, at least not to us directly. She lived alone, quietly underlining our names in red as they appeared in the newspaper. Her magnum opus had been Almarian.

Although chaos theory might not fit family memoirs as well as weather forecasting, I consider the two vignettes that follow more butterfly than domino.

Of her many activities, Almarian probably would have listed her years of service to the Girl Scouts as her favorite. Even though she was an unflagging optimist born of a woman who was an equally dedicated pessimist, I believe that her childhood was tough, especially when her friends dropped out of boarding school, and Almarian needed more from Lula than Lula was able to give. Although never given the opportunity to become a Scout herself, Almarian devoted many years to being a troop leader, mostly to one group of girls that included my sister Susan, shepherding this group all the way through their school years.

Always one to reach for the stars, or at least Mexico, Almarian believed that the girls should earn money and take a trip to Our Cabaña World Centre in Cuernavaca, the centerpiece for the World Association of Girl Guides and Girl Scouts. Our Cabaña had opened in 1957, and the El Reno troop began hosting fundraising events for several years before Almarian organized a bus tour in the summer of 1962. Extra seats were sold to El Reno citizens who journeyed to Taxco and Acapulco while the Girl Scouts split off in Cuernavaca. A few bratty younger brothers and their friends went along for the ride as well.

In April 2012, nearly all of the "girls" of this Girl Scout troop, now

mostly grandmothers and scattered across the country, returned to
El Reno to celebrate the fiftieth anniversary of this unique trip. The
organizers chose to dedicate the Friday luncheon, held at Redlands
Community College in El Reno (where Almarian had, incidentally,
taught creative writing), to the memory of Almarian, who had died
the year before. I was invited, both as her son and as one of the bratty
younger brothers on the bus.

At the luncheon, the former Girl Scouts each spoke about what
Almarian had meant to them. I had no idea. I had been oblivious to her
impact on these women. One after another, they described with heartfelt
passion how Almarian had been a "second mother" to them all. Then, as
Girl Scouts are prone to do, they broke into song—"make new friends,
but keep the old; one is silver and the other gold"—sung in rounds. I had
not heard the tune in fifty years, but I remembered it well. It reminded
me that Almarian lived those lyrics. She tried to keep in touch with
everyone whose life had affected hers in any way, all while amassing new
friends along the way.

I was halfway through my research for this book on the day of the
reunion, and as the Girl Scouts continued their song, I had to consider
how the Lula-Almarian relationship had been carved out of tragedy at
Johnson's Hotel. A peculiar mother-daughter fissure had formed, yet it
rarely quaked, the only devastating upheaval being the real-estate crisis
chronicled earlier. To help assure that young girls had access to wise
counsel from a role model, Almarian made the Girl Scouts her passion.

One other train of thought persisted throughout the singing of "Make
New Friends"—that is, where I had been one year earlier, same day, same
hour. I had no intention of mentioning it to the group, or even as a
reminder to my sister Susan, as I was already gulping away my emotions.
Then she announced it anyway: "I think everyone should know that
Mother died one year ago today."

On April 26, 2011, I drove to El Reno, nervous that Almarian was
not answering her telephone, especially given her odd call to me early
that morning. She knew that both her household alarm and her panic
button would prompt third-party phone calls to me. This was a common
occurrence in her final years, often due to an accidental tumble in spite
of all possible precautions. Usually, however, it was a false alarm.

She insisted on living at her home until the end. Early that morning,
around 3:00, she called to tell me not to worry—that, in fact, I should
ignore the phone call I would be getting from the paramedics shortly.

She stated she was okay, and she sounded perfectly lucid. Her voice was calm: no big deal. But in fact, the aneurysm had burst. Whether or not she was confused, or wanted to make sure she was not going to be a bother, it was as though she wanted me to have a good night's rest in spite of the circumstances of her dying.

I found her in bed, and she had probably died shortly after the phone call to me early that morning. She was in the same room, same bed, where our father had died a decade earlier, prompting me to quip in her obituary that they had shared the same portal to heaven.

When Susan announced the first anniversary of Almarian's death that day, a collective gasp swept the audience, with one Scout commenting that this was "not a coincidence." Whether it be a butterfly, domino, or more divine cascade, the reader can decide.

This brings me to my second butterfly vignette. As I wrote this manuscript, one nagging thought kept coming back time and again. I was leaving out one member of our immediate family. Then, when I discovered Aunt Helen's unique bout with breast cancer, and the bizarre "melting away" of her second cancer, I felt the call to add the final member of our household.

So, at this late hour, let me introduce Mildred, starting with the facts gleaned from her obituary. Mildred B. Fowler Russworm was born June 3, 1905, in Indian Territory. She died February 19, 1996, in El Reno, Oklahoma. She married Jack Brown in 1923, and both her children from that union, Gwen and Jimmie, died of cancer, as did her husband. She was predeceased by her second husband, Flynn Russworm, and step-daughter, Verdell Russworm. Mildred sang in the choir of Mt. Moriah Baptist and was a member of the Missionary Society. She was buried in El Reno.

Absent from her obituary was another husband, Homer Harris, squeezed in between Jack and Flynn, and my sister Dawn recalls Mildred describing him as the "love of her life." Another point missing from the obituary—Mildred's grandmother had been born a slave.

Mildred was our maid or, as she would have been called one generation prior, our daytime "mammy." At least, that's how it all started in 1955 when Almarian hired her on a friend's recommendation. By the time she joined us, Mildred was already a Russworm, and the children from her first marriage were not yet dead of their cancers. Flynn was alive and well. Mildred was rotund and jovial, though not in the stereotypical Hattie McDaniel sense. Mildred was serene, wise, and savvy, with large eyes that often spoke her piece without words.

My sister Dawn sobbed uncontrollably as a little girl upon learning that Mildred was not a blood relative to our family. Technically "one-fourth Indian," Mildred was culturally African-American all the way, and as the years went on, she became Almarian's tour guide through black history and racial inequality.

Sure, when Almarian hired Mildred, it was within the confines of "hired help," with all its racial overtones and undercurrent. Almarian had been about the same age as the sixteen-year-old Scarlett O'Hara in the first pages of *Gone with the Wind* when the blockbuster novel was published in 1936, and it was a clear influence. Thus, Almarian accepted some aspects of the New South ideology that was subsequently challenged by historians. At the same time, as a teenager, she surely bought into the oath of "as God is my witness, I'll never be hungry again," as she watched her mother downscale year after year. But the relationship between Almarian and Mildred would evolve dramatically over the course of many years, in no way resembling that of Scarlett and Mammy.

In the El Reno excavation, I located some reel-to-reel audiotapes Almarian made in the 1950s, using her suitcase-sized recorder, a new technology that she was proud to have introduced to the town. In listening to the tapes, I was caught off-guard by an enthusiastic Almarian, who urges her new employee, Mildred, to "say a few words." Mildred replies in her slow, syrupy voice, "My name is Mildred Russworm. I work for Mrs. Hollingsworth, and I really should be ironing."

That's the way it started, but that's not the way it ended. Just as Almarian had been a second mother to so many, Mildred became our second mother, raising us in the foundations of good living, beginning in grade school and on through the quagmire of high school. Cynics, and I often include myself in that group, will point out that this relationship is stereotypical and still contains elements that some would call soft racism. But while the employer-employee line may be impossible to dissolve, we came as close as anything I know to forging a genuine familial bond with Mildred, distinct from what one saw in the popular book and movie *The Help*.

Did we eat together? Yes, as time went on. Did she sit in the same circle with the family and exchange Christmas presents? Yes. Did she scold us children? Yes. Did we openly say, "I love you"? Yes.

And when she became housebound due to her weight and crippling arthritis in her knees, we visited her at her home, whenever we "kids" were in El Reno to see our parents. In spite of her weight, she lived a long life, maintaining an undying faith in God in spite of personal tragedies that included the loss of her two children as young adults. Once we kids grew up, Mildred made no secret of the fact that she saw the three of us as her natural children.

Because my second-story bedroom in El Reno was located over the kitchen, I had the unique experience of waking each morning not only to the smell of bacon but also the sound of a crystal-clear soprano singing spirituals. And growing up, we thought the yummy pancake recipe was Mildred's, only to find out much later the true origin—the café at Johnson's Hotel.

One day, the sound that came through the ceiling from the kitchen was not the beautiful soprano but the wailing lamentations of a woman whose healthy husband, a construction foreman, had dropped dead on the job. Flynn was still a young man when he died. Jimmie, Mildred's son, had died in his thirties of lung cancer, and daughter Gwen succumbed as a young woman to breast cancer.

Mildred "worked for" Almarian for over thirty years, and during that time, the relationship changed from employer-employee to that of peers, two women struggling together to make sense of their lives. They were both empty-nesters for different reasons—Mildred's children were dead while Almarian's were gone, all three of us living in California at the time. And as Mildred's weight and disability grew, she was no longer able to do the laundry downstairs in the basement, the cleaning upstairs, nor much of the cooking. For the final ten years of their relationship, I believe that Almarian paid Mildred to sit and chat over coffee.

In the late 1980s, I returned to academics in Oklahoma, where I limited my surgical practice to breast cancer. A visit to El Reno always meant a visit to Mildred's house as well, but on one occasion, my mother made sure I was headed that direction: "Mildred has something wrong with her breast." By this time, Mildred was confined to her home, nearly bedbound and no longer "working for Mrs. Hollingsworth."

When I entered Mildred's bedroom, she had a sheepish look that said, "I know you're going to tell me I should have done something earlier." Mildred lifted her immense breast out of the elastic band of her nightgown, and the jarring sight told me it was Stage III breast cancer, at least. Stage III indicates locally advanced disease, while Stage IV denotes metastatic disease.

The skin was discolored and firm, with ten to twelve "growths" shaped like cauliflower heads, each on the verge of breaking through the stretched and shiny skin that still covered them. Shortly, her breast would be a cluster of ulcerations. My mind raced through the different ways she could be managed, but with Mildred in her mid-eighties, she had already resigned herself to the inevitable and did not plan to leave her bedroom, much less submit to any therapy. In fact, I would not even be able to perform a diagnostic biopsy. I would have to treat her breast cancer on the assumption that it was cancer, as was done in the 1800s, the very act that I mocked in chapter 26 when Aunt Helen went to visit the founder of osteopathy.

In my opinion, Mildred had only one chance at improvement. Maybe it would buy a little bit of time. Maybe it would even keep her breast from ulcerating. It was the drug tamoxifen.

Originally called an "antiestrogen," the drug is more complicated than that, having both estrogenic and antiestrogenic effects, depending on what part of the body one is talking about. For many malignant breast tumors, it is antiestrogenic and, thus, therapeutic. Even though other drugs are available today, tamoxifen was the primary option at the time and had not been studied as a single form of treatment.

I'm old enough to remember what surgeons did for women who had locally advanced breast cancer or metastatic disease prior to tamoxifen—surgical removal of the adrenal glands and sometimes the ovaries if the patients were premenopausal. Later, this approach was eclipsed by the remarkable surgical "advance" of removing the master gland, the pituitary, in order to knock out all hormones in one fell swoop. Because the pituitary hangs down from the brain like a piñata, the gland can be whacked away through a sinus at the base of the nose, far easier than abdominal surgery, though quite disruptive to the overall endocrine system. So, as much as tamoxifen is maligned today for its side effects, in relative terms, it was a miracle born in the 1970s.

I wrote a prescription for Mildred to take tamoxifen ("off label"), handing it to a friend who assured me she would get the order filled. I wasn't sure Mildred would take the drug. She had made her peace with the Lord decades earlier, and who was I to interfere with that pact?

A few months later, while I visited my parents in El Reno, Almarian made sure I was planning to drop by Mildred's before returning to Oklahoma City. "She has something to show you."

It was a dark and stormy night. I'm not kidding. And as I entered Mildred's home, greeted by the blast-furnace effect from her preferred air temperature of eighty-five to ninety degrees in the winter, I was surprised to see a crowd of her friends from church lined up in the hallway leading to her bedroom. As I walked through the gauntlet, humble heads nodded to me without formal introduction, and I heard the whispers of hyperbole that "big-city docs" sometimes receive: "He's one of the best in the world, you know, and Mildred raised him, she did."

In her room in her usual pose of equanimity, Mildred hid a faint smile. This time, when she pulled her breast out from the stretchy neckline of her gown, it was normal. Again, I'm not kidding. The cauliflower protuberances were gone; the skin was the same color as everywhere else; the hardness was gone. There were no lumps. The breast was completely normal.

I fumbled for words because I knew this was not a miracle in the strictest sense, but I also knew that Mildred was absolutely convinced that it was. Although I had never seen results this dramatic at that point in my career, published case reports had indicated that it was possible if advanced tumors were highly sensitive to antiestrogen therapy.

I contemplated the power of this triphenylethylene derivative and how it had blocked circulating estrogens from entering the malignant cells, causing cellular apoptosis and so forth. I don't recall at what point my thoughts converted to words that sounded absolutely foolish in light of the miracle that had just occurred in the minds of Mildred and the church members assembled at her house.

Mildred smiled without speaking, using only her eyes to communicate. She lowered her chin and left her gaze riveted on me, in a manner she might have used in gentle reprimand many years ago. I shut my mouth. Here's my translation of those eyes: "Oh, Alan, you will never see the miracles of God unless you acknowledge them for what they are. Yes, He used your hands and your mind, but it's a miracle all the same. So don't stand there and tell me all that fancy stuff about the science of it all."

The cancer did not come back, at least not in the breast. We don't know what was going on in the rest of her body, but Mildred never developed symptoms of metastatic disease. She died peacefully in her sleep several years later, apparently cancer free.

At her funeral, the church was packed with friends, even though she

The Hollingsworth "kids" with Mildred Russworm at her home in El Reno, Oklahoma in 1989. Left to right: Alan, Susan, and Dawn surround Mildred. The portrait on the wall behind the group is Mildred's daughter, Gwen, who died of breast cancer as a young woman.

had lived to age ninety. Somewhat to my surprise, when the eulogies began, Almarian rose as one of the few whites in attendance and approached the podium. She introduced herself to a curious audience, many of whom probably had little idea who was preparing to speak. She said, "My name is Almarian Hollingsworth, and—and I guess I'd have to say that Mildred Russworm was my best friend."

29

Deconstructing Johnson's Hotel

And now, I will share the secret formula "from the recipe file of Almarian Hollingsworth."

HOT CAKES

1½ cups flour
2 heaping tsp. baking powder
¼ tsp. salt
3 tbsp. sugar
Mix and add: 1 cup milk. Beat until smooth.
Add: 2 beaten eggs
Add: 5 tbsp. softened bacon grease

Spoon onto hot greased griddle, tested with water drops (if drops dance, griddle is right temp.), or about 380 degrees on automatic griddle. If batter is too thin add small amount of flour. If batter is too thick add another egg.

(This recipe was originally used at the Hotel Johnson coffee shop, where I was born. Mother got the recipe and passed it on to me.)

In the parentheses of the recipe, "Mother" is Lula. And note that it is five *tablespoons* of bacon grease, not teaspoons, a point of contention each year as the smell of bacon grease permeates every fiber of our home, and my wife questions whether or not something in the recipe was lost in translation.

This recipe reflects my profound level of ignorance about the Marlow shootout until after my mother's death. I marvel that I could have been so comfortable knowing only a pinch of the Berch saga, a mere dollop about Johnson's Hotel, reduced to this simple card that held the key to tasty pancakes and nothing else, not bothering to ask more questions.

As it turned out, there were many more secret ingredients to this story than the bacon grease.

Just as the discovery of Albert Berch's clothes and personal items added flesh to his skeleton, so it was with the rediscovery of Johnson's Hotel. The afternoon of Almarian's interment marked only my second trip to the hotel, this time with the whole family. Perhaps it was my vulnerable nerve endings this second time around that brought the hotel to life, its walls inhaling and exhaling, its lobby floor confessing that it had once cradled a pool of blood, its ceiling of pressed tin overseeing it all. Nevertheless, the hotel and its past were thrust once again into the present.

With my second visit to the hotel, on the day we buried Almarian, we had the advantage of recently discovered photographs that helped resuscitate the dying edifice. After the Berch marriage and before the Berch murder, a handful of family photographs had been taken from the hotel's sidewalk along Main Street in front of a large window with *Café* painted on the plate glass. With various combinations of Berch family members, the common denominator of the day was showing off the new baby, Almarian. Our single photograph of Dr. Albert Berch was taken in front of the café sign as well, the brim of his hat blackening his face—a handy symbol, as it turned out.

In 2011, the interior had been so partitioned by drywall that the only recognizable feature from our 1920 photograph was the pressed-tin ceiling. The stairway I thought I remembered from my 1970s visit, where Albert Berch fell near its bottom steps, was no longer evident. Presumably it was destroyed or covered in the makeovers of the building for various purposes, ranging from a gymnastic center to a site for A.A. meetings. The exterior had changed too, largely due to decking that had been attached to the second floor.

As I began to research this story, in my subsequent trips to Marlow, I would stop by the hotel, by that time abandoned completely, to rummage around for any clue that would allow me to reconstruct the very different lobby that I had seen in the 1970s. Thoughts of buying and renovating the building would fly through my head, but nothing much to spur me in this direction, given that the hotel was so far gone from its heyday. And renovate for what: a museum, or a pancake house?

Then, several months after Almarian's interment, I received a newspaper clipping out of the *Marlow Review*, mailed to me in Oklahoma City by one of my patients, who is a longtime resident of Marlow. It was the story of the double murder in 1923 at Johnson's Hotel, with more coverage of the events than the newspaper had carried at the time, so said the reporter who had been surprised at the paucity of information in his own archives. The article, of course, made no mention of the twenty-month-old who had been at the scene, nor that the toddler-witness, eighty-eight years later, had recently been laid to rest in the Marlow cemetery along with Albert and Lula, nor that the progeny of Albert Berch had been poking around the hotel for the past few months. The author of the story had no idea of these things. The reason that the article divulged the history of the 1923 murders was because the landmark hotel had been condemned by the city of Marlow and was scheduled for demolition in thirty days.

What an odd rush of emotions followed. It was as though one's new best friend had just been diagnosed with terminal cancer. Johnson's Hotel had sprung to life only to die after its final gasp of air. What my family and I couldn't see from the front, where we had entered, was that the interior of the building had completely collapsed, and it was now considered a safety hazard.

I scrambled to learn all I could about Marlow's intent for downtown improvements and the requirements for a national historic landmark. Then, I took my ideas ranging from museum to pancake house more seriously. Magical thinking infected my analytic mind when I discussed a price for the hotel with the current owner, only to learn that the 2011 purchase price was the same price my grandmother had sought after the murders. It was as though she were selling the building directly to me thirty years after her death, nearly ninety years after Albert's death.

I even served as my own armchair psychologist, asking myself if a restoration of the hotel was merely a sublimated attempt to hang on to my mother, who had slipped six feet below. But it was more than that. I felt a bond with Albert Berch, the seed planted in my youth, then blooming only months before the scheduled demolition.

In the end, my sisters and I decided that the building should serve as a symbol for the entire saga and be allowed to go peacefully. My younger sister, Dawn, said, "Spend time on the book rather than spending money on the hotel. The hotel won't last no matter what you do, but words are eternal."

During the demolition, I made several trips to the site, taking pictures, retrieving a few souvenir bricks and a square of the pressed-tin ceiling. As boarded windows were uncovered and drywall partitions brought down, I was able to enter the room where my mother was born and to walk upstairs for the first time ever, viewing those rooms still standing. And at the site of the café, the original tile floor was uncovered, as seen in our one interior photo, the same surface upon which some of the bystanders in the lobby crawled on hands and knees when the gunfire began in 1923.

On my final visit to the hotel, its casket was opened for final viewing. With drywall stripped away, I saw the lobby as I had seen it in the 1970s. There, once again, was the stairway that emptied into the lobby near the writing room, the site of the murders. The thick plaster that covered the walls, partially torn away, was coated on one surface with perhaps a dozen layers of paint, seen end on as tree rings, some of which could certainly be attributed to Lula. Behind the plaster was solid brick, construction meant to last. I couldn't resist tearing away chunks of the inch-thick plaster that covered the brick, looking for a stray bullet that might have lodged there eighty-eight years earlier. Of course, there was nothing but more brick.

Then, I left the hotel for good. I traveled to the Berch family plot in the cemetery, steps away from the Garvin family, and with some Kincannons resting in between. My sisters were right—it was time to put an end to the killing of Albert Berch. After my siblings and I join our ancestors, albeit in different graveyards, the Berch DNA in this limb of the family tree will have come to an end. Although all three of us are part of loving families, we have no direct offspring. This makes Dawn's admonition to deal in the currency of words, not bricks, that much more apropos.

My initial idea was to end the story with some original thoughts about evil. The problem, of course, is that there are no original thoughts about evil. During the writing of this story, so many hate crimes based on race were covered in the news that it seemed pointless to state the obvious. It has been said a thousand ways for thousands of years—humanity is joined at the hip to inhumanity.

Another idea for ending the book was to draw on the platitude, "That which does not kill us makes us stronger," although coining this particular phrase didn't do Nietzsche much good. Furthermore, "that," in fact, killed Albert Berch and Robert Johnigan, making it hard for them to learn from their experience. Of course, we could apply "that" to Lula, but she did not grow stronger either. In the end, life beat her to a pulp. Repeated trauma often does quite the opposite of making us stronger. It can turn us into pancake batter.

"Second chances" was another theme to consider, from my early mention of the surviving Marlow brothers, or a car thief named Wiley Post, all the way to Albert Berch and Aunt Helen. Yet, this concept is so closely aligned to Nietzsche's bromide that I couldn't make it work for Albert Berch, whose second chance was cut brutally short.

Or I could resort to using a child's eye to end the story, a simplicity that cuts through the Gordian knot. My step-grandson is intrigued by history (and superheroes). At age eight, he took the Wisconsin magazine story of Jesse Berch to school while his class was studying the Underground Railroad. For this show-and-tell, I had labeled Jesse as his great-great-great-great-step-grandfather, a hero in the annals of abolition. I then told him the tale of Albert Berch and Robert Johnigan, explaining that I was writing the story of my grandfather. I believed that he was trying to be the same hero that his grandfather Jesse had been; but instead, Albert had been murdered, along with the porter. My grandson didn't miss a beat: "Then your grandfather is up in heaven right now, looking down, telling you to finish the book so that he can be a hero, too."

For a different finale, I tried to imagine what zipped through Albert Berch's mind from the moment the bullet hit him in the chest until he died several minutes later, his head resting in Lula's lap. If an entire life flashes before one's eyes in the moments before death, then Albert Berch saw misfortune and misadventure from day one–a dead mother, a scheming father, an orphanage, a boarding school, living the life of a vagabond and miscreant that landed him in the reformatory, then to the penitentiary and hell bound to the coal mines. Or perhaps a thought like this flared prior to the snuffing out of his life: "After going through all that heartache and wretchedness, I cleaned up my act, I did everything right, I turned my life around completely, I have a wife and a new baby— why? Why now?"

Redemption was cut down in its prime by someone's reprisal. That one-two punch robbed Albert Berch of his purpose. I have to wonder, though, if out of the corner of his eye, as his vision dimmed, Albert looked over at the bawling toddler Almarian and thought, "Maybe not me, but her."

In many ways, for the porter Robert Johnigan, the injustice was worse. His mutterings prior to death, as logged by Lula, asked the tough question as well—"Why? Why? I did nothing wrong." For Robert, it was not a story of redemption cut down by reprisal; it was hatred unleashed from its compartment.

In the end, I was most drawn to the idea of characters whose lives are defined by a single act. The vast majority of us count on a lifetime balance where we hope the good outweighs the bad, leaving a net positive memory for two or three generations before we are forgotten. But some individuals have the luxury of a single act of benevolence (or alternatively, evil) from which their lives are tallied and remembered. Be it Paul Revere's ride, or Doug Flutie's Hail Mary pass, the single-act scenario is intriguing.

Yet, for Albert Berch, his single act in the defense of Robert Johnigan was erased from history, an error that is perhaps corrected now. After all, his grandfather had succeeded with a single act. Notably, in tracing the life of Jesse Berch *after* the Civil War, I can find nothing more than clerical positions and an early death. Yet, Jesse's heroic effort, recounted in Levi Coffin's memoirs and the newly resurrected photograph of the odd threesome in Cincinnati, reveals the lasting effect of the singular, ascendant act.

The author (wearing bowtie and suspenders) holds court at Sunday dinner at Arrie and Lula's house in Oklahoma City (circa 1954). Clockwise from lower left: matriarch Arrie Combs, "Aunt Jessie" (Lula's youngest sister), Almarian Berch Hollingsworth, Alan Berch Hollingsworth, "Uncle Barrett and Aunt Nettie" (parents of Brig. Gen. Glenn Collins, MD; Nettie was one of Lula's younger sisters), Susan Hollingsworth, and in profile closest to the camera is Lula (Lucinda Jane Combs Garvin Berch Reynolds).

I believe that Albert Weldon Berch sought to secure his redemption with a single noble act, be it at a conscious level or not. Just as I heard the story of my grandfather growing up, Albert must have experienced the same. Nobody told me my grandfather's act was noble; the story simply *felt* noble. The saga of Jesse Berch must have had a similar influence on grandson Albert, even though Jesse was long dead before Albert was born. The parallel between their two deeds is too striking to ignore.

The discovery of my grandfather's "missing years" led to the deconstruction of the mythology surrounding Albert Berch, sending the story in a different direction. Yet, in the end, I admired even more his years in Marlow and his final act, realizing what he had overcome. Instead of the "stranger who came to town," as was my original premise, I was left with a flawed human who managed to turn his life around against all odds. What did he gain, other than a bullet in the chest? For what it's worth, he gained the respect of his unborn grandchildren.

I placed the murders of Albert Berch and Robert Johnigan in the opening paragraphs of this book, instead of at the end. So now, in closing, I will start at the beginning.

On a September day in 1862, the Twenty-Second Infantry from Wisconsin was camped near Lexington, Kentucky, prior to engagement with Confederate troops. When Col. William L. Utley called for volunteers to provide safe escort of a runaway slave girl to the Underground Railroad, the epic nature of the journey struck a chord with many of the soldiers. Their minds raced through various scenarios in order to decide, "Do I lift my hand or not?" A Union soldier from a different regiment could catch the volunteers violating the Fugitive Slave Law, while slave trackers or the slave owner could kill them for aiding a runaway slave. The volunteers' act could result in hollow death or heroic legacy.

And then, the willing right arm of Regimental Quartermaster Jesse Berch, shaking imperceptibly with both eagerness and fear, rose toward the sky. Jesse knew himself to be a man ready to make his mark through a single, towering act. The air that surrounded his trembling hand stirred imperceptibly on this calm autumn day, causing no more turbulence than the wings of a butterfly.

Acknowledgments

For allowing me to empty the closets of Johnson's Hotel, thanks go to Debbe Ridley, executive director of the Marlow Chamber of Commerce, as well as Marlow residents D. B. Green, Janet Loveless, and Dr. Jack Gregston. I also appreciate the staff at the Oklahoma History Center for their assistance, starting with my remedial training in microfilm. My search for original photographs led me to the *Marlow Review* on several occasions, with a willing staff always helpful. This newspaper was a key source for information leading up to the murders. Though my scrutiny of several hundred issues of the *Marlow Review* was actually accomplished via microfilm at the Oklahoma History Center, a special nod to that newspaper is in order, given the shocking murders of the Hruby family, its publishers, in October 2014, shortly after I completed the first draft of this book. The unnerving impact of such a tragedy on an entire citizenry cannot be overstated.

I thank the staff at the Closed Records Unit, Department of Corrections, State of Oklahoma, for performing a manual search for long-forgotten prison records. And thanks go to Lin Fredericksen and LuAnn Harris in the Archives Division of the Kansas Historical Society for their manual search through archived records that overcame a misfiling. This seemingly small gesture solved the longstanding mystery of Albert Berch.

Bill Fliss, archivist at Marquette University-Raynor Memorial Libraries, inadvertently added great depth to my story through his work on Wisconsin's Abolition Regiment, published in the *Wisconsin Magazine of History,* plus his discovery of the bizarre gun-to-the-head photograph. In the same vein, archivist Dee Grimsrud, while working for the Wisconsin Historical Society, gave 110 percent in her unsuccessful (so far) efforts to learn the identity of the self-liberated slave whose rescue set the stage for this story. And thanks to Beth and Marc Storch for sharing the only known solo portrait of Jesse Berch from their Civil War collection.

Although she came up empty-handed, Deborah Bruce, JD, executive director of the Oklahoma State Board of Osteopathic Medicine, still provided a key "pertinent negative" in searching medical licensure records in early Oklahoma. Thanks also to the helpful staffs at the Stephens County Genealogical Society, Stephens County Courthouse, and Marlow town museum. And thanks to Pee Wee Cary, former director of the Stephens County Historical Museum who recalled a framed photograph being used for decoration that proved to be a snapshot of the all-star cast of this saga. Later in the research process, Cova Williams, executive director of the museum, helped with the same photograph and the publication rights.

Angela Drabek, at Oklahoma Web Design & Hosting, was responsible not only for the website that accompanies this book but also much of the photography of brittle newspapers and artifacts that appear online and in print. It was a complex task involving over 150 pictures, and I'm very grateful for Angela's help.

Of course, the story would have faltered without the discovery of the original trial transcripts by Oklahoma Supreme Court Justice Yvonne Kauger, with assistance from Derek Smalling. Many thanks, too, for the manuscript critique and the foreword written by Justice Kauger.

For their work researching Helen and O. J. DeLendrecie, where the crossroads of their inquiry uncovered a long-held secret, I thank Curt Eriksmoen, the North Dakota writer, and Greg Nesteroff, journalist from Nelson, British Columbia. Both were simply doing their jobs when they inadvertently wandered into this story.

A nod must go to Frank Harrison, who has, with unflagging persistence since 1992, insisted that I write this book. And for critiquing the original manuscript line by line, thanks go to my two sisters, Susan Hollingsworth Aggarwal and Dawn Hollingsworth. They helped fit together the pieces of the puzzle while cross-checking our collective memories. I offer special thanks to my wife, Barbara, who graciously accepted the timeout from life I needed to research and write this story, and to other family members and friends who indulged me with polite patience while listening to revelations that meant little out of context.

As a step-grandfather with strong focus on our grandchildren, honed in light of the fact that my grandfathers and great-grandfathers were all deceased prior to my memory, I am grateful for the promise of tomorrow manifest in Shawn and Clara (children of Ryan and Susannah Bebee) as well as Luke, Patrick, and Charlotte (children of Jeff and Emily Belisle).

It was the oldest grandchild, Shawn at age eight, who took an interest in this story and recommended that I cast Albert Berch as a hero (albeit short of a superhero).

I would be remiss if I failed to mention my other sounding board, my barber and friend, Doyle Crim. I have slipped his name into prior works of fiction, but he would otherwise be absent here. Doyle's interest in this story is due, in no small part, to the fact that the title character was once a barber.

And finally, thanks to Pelican Publishing Company and Editor in Chief Nina Kooij for putting into print a story that our mother, Almarian, wanted to know and tell for nearly all of her eighty-nine years, as did Lula.

Index

Enid, Oklahoma, 227
Eriksmoen, Curt, 271-72
Exalted Cyclops, 73, 93, 231

Fallin, Mary, 232
Fanchon, the Cricket, 270
Fargo, North Dakota, 18, 56-57,
  60-61, 137-38, 166, 168, 181,
  223, 244, 252, 254, 256, 258,
  271-72
Farmer-Labor Reconstruction
  League, 77, 83
*Feminine Touch: Women in
  Osteopathic Medicine,* 253
First Presbyterian Church of El
  Reno, 154
First United Methodist Church,
  Marlow, 88-89, 212, 219, 232-
  34, 237
Fliss, William, 259
Forrest, Nathan Bedford, 67, 71,
  221, 264
Ft. Worth, Texas, 238
Foster-Harris, 56
Freud, Sigmund, 248
Fugitive Slave Law, 289

Gandy, Elza, 32, 35-36, 39-40,
  85-87, 97-102, 107-18, 121-22,
  134, 152, 156, 161, 163-64,
  201-2, 204, 211-12, 214, 216,
  218-19, 227
Gandy, Gladys, 218-19, 227
Gandy, Hazel, 212
Gandy, H. R., 32, 85, 107, 134,
  164, 202, 206, 212, 218-20, 227,
  229-30, 236
Gandy, Leila, 218-19, 227
Garvin, Della, 54

Garvin, G. T., 54-55
Garvin, Glenn, 48, 53-54, 177
Garvin, Guy, 27, 48, 50-51, 54-55,
  148, 177, 237
Garvin, James Robert, Sr., 54
Garvin, Nancy, 54-55
Garvin, Roy, 54
Garvin, Walter, 48, 50, 53-54, 67,
  177, 217
Garvin County, 48
Gillmore, Quincy, 260
Girl Scouts, 154, 275-77
Gone with the Wind, 278
Gore, Thomas, 79
Grand Dragon, 73, 80, 115, 234
Grand Wizard, 67, 221
Granite, Oklahoma, 216, 227
Great Depression, 140
Great War, 66
Green, Mrs. John, 101
Gregston, Jack L., 152
Griffin, D. W., 95
Griffith, D. W., 68
Grimsrud, Dee, 262
Guthrie, Oklahoma, 142

Halliburton, 210
Halliburton, Erle P., 140
Halsted, William Stewart, 254-55
Harding, Warren G., 65, 74
Harris, Homer, 277
Helen d'Este Dramatic
  Combination, 270
Herrin, Steve, 78
Hickock, Richard, 247
Hobart, Oklahoma, 212, 218
Holdenville, Oklahoma, 130-31,
  222
Holder, Otis, 86